Taking the stress out of teaching

DEDICATION

To Patricia C. Bernard, whose continuous and loving support enabled this project to be completed.

Also by Michael Bernard
Clinical Applications of Rational-Emotive Therapy (New York: Plenum Press, 1985) with Albert Ellis.
Inside Rational-Emotive Therapy: A Critical Analysis of the Theory and Practice of Albert Ellis (New York: Academic Press, 1989) with Ray DiGiuseppe.
Rational-Emotive Approaches to the Problems of Childhood (New York: Plenum Press, 1983) with Albert Ellis.
Rational-Emotive Therapy with Children and Adolescents (New York: Wiley, 1984) with Marie Joyce.
Reading Rescue A Parents' Guide to Improving Their Child's Reading (Melbourne: Australian Council for Educational Research, 1989, 2nd edition) with Susan Gillet.
Staying Rational in an Irrational World (Melbourne: McCulloch, 1986).
You Can Do It! What Every Student (and Parent) Should Know About Success in School and Life (Melbourne: Collins Dove, 1987) with Darko Hajzler.
You Can Do It! Video Program (Melbourne: Seven Dimensions, 1990) with Eve Ash.

Taking the stress out of teaching

Michael E. Bernard, Ph.D.,
Reader and psychologist, School of Education,
University of Melbourne

COLLINS DOVE
Melbourne Australia

Published by Collins Dove
A division of HarperCollins*Publishers* (Australia) Pty Ltd
22–24 Joseph Street
North Blackburn, Victoria 3130

First published 1990
Reprinted 1991
Designed by John Canty
Cover designed and illustrated by John Canty

Typeset in Garamond by SRM Production Services
Printed in Australia by Griffin Press

The National Library of Australia
Cataloguing-in-Publication Data:

Bernard, Michael E. (Michael Edwin), 1950–
  Taking the stress out of teaching.

  Includes index.
  ISBN 0 85924 918 2.

  1. Teachers—Job stress—Prevention.
  Title.

371.10019

CONTENTS

PREFACE

Teaching today is harder than it's ever been. The pressures for change from without and the resultant demand for change from within make teaching in the 1990s a very stressful occupation. In many schools, student behaviour continues to deteriorate. Teachers are blamed for not coming up with the goods, but are offered little support and a great deal of criticism. More and more time is being demanded of them. Their achievements remain largely unacknowledged both monetarily or professionally.

Under these circumstances, teaching is not only a challenging job but holds the possibility of significant job stress for the unprepared. This book is a guide for the individual who wishes to continue to stay in teaching, but who wants to take the stress out of daily work life. The techniques and skills outlined here will make teaching less stressful.

The greatest amount of emphasis is placed on what teachers can do on their own to take the stress out of teaching, presenting the latest set of stress management skills as applied to the school and the classroom. The importance of the social-peer system of teachers is also recognised and learning how to use social support at times when stress becomes distress advocated. Finally, the book looks at how the school organisation can change in order to reduce the stress-creating conditions which lead to teacher stress in the first place.

I have worked as a psychologist in schools for many years as well as having taught teachers within the School of

Education at the University of Melbourne, Australia. I have also worked with groups of teachers who have retired from teaching because of teacher stress and who wish to return. Most of the material in this book I have used with teachers; it has been refined in the light of experience and feedback received from individual teachers receiving counselling for stress, from my in-service work and from my teaching.

I started off in the early 1980s believing the 'right' mental attitude is the key to stress management — especially as there are so many objectively stressful aspects to teaching which the individual teacher cannot change. Today I still believe that by destressing your attitudes you can reduce overall teacher stress and increase job satisfaction. However I now firmly believe there are also many ways in which schools are organised and administrated that can and should be modified in order to take the stress out of teaching. As well, I am a much stronger believer in the importance of teachers supporting each other in peer support groups. These groups can help staff further professional development, gain acknowledgement for professional achievements and exert greater influence over factors within a school contributing to poor conditions and ineffectiveness.

It is impossible for any one professional to be an expert on all the different stress management procedures. There are too many. In attempting to cover the most popular and effective I have relied on a number of different sources I would like to acknowledge.

Yvonne Willoch, member of the Victorian Department of Education's Workcare Unit, provided me with her time and generously shared with me her experience in running programs in schools designed to reduce stress. She provided me with access to material which she and her colleague, Karen Stammers, developed designed to lower teacher stress from an organisational point of view. The material in this guide on decision making, feedback, the 'Whole School Approach to Staff Development', personal sources of self-esteem, and peer support has been distilled from discussions with Yve and from her innovative work.

I would like to acknowledge a report, *Teacher Stress in Victoria*, written by the Applied Psychology Research Group at the University of Melbourne for the Office of

Schools Administration in 1989. This report provided interesting research data on the nature of factors associated with teacher stress which helped me in the refinement of my teacher stress model in Chapter 1.

William Rogers, an innovator in design of discipline policy and classroom management procedures, was kind in allowing excerpts from his writing to be included in Chapter 10 on classroom management.

Material on self-esteem developed by the late Ian Adams, consultant to the Victorian Ministry of Education, is gratefully acknowledged.

Professor Hedley Beare and Peter Gill, members of the School of Education, University of Melbourne, provided ideas and resources for the development of material in this book.

Elisabeth Lundahl-Hegedus was extremely helpful in putting together the list of recommended readings which appear at the end of each chapter. All of the books and audio- and video-cassettes listed are available in Australia.

Dr Bob Montgomery's books, *You and Stress* (with Lynette Evans) and *Working Together*, inspired ideas in this book on lifestyle enhancement, assertiveness, communication skills and collaborative decision making.

The *Relaxation and Stress Reduction Workbook* by Martha Davis, Elisabeth Robbins Eshelman and Matthew McKay provided an invaluable resource for the material on relaxation and meditation.

Anne Sarros' excellent dissertation on teacher support and teacher burnout provided many useful ideas presented in my chapter on social support.

Garry Eastman, managing director of Collins Dove, is to be a acknowledged for persisting in his desire to see this book see the light of day. I am grateful to Michael Conn, Victorian Department of Education, for the time he made available for discussion and feedback on the first two chapters.

Thanks are due to Albert Ellis, founder of rational-emotive therapy, for his seminal ideas on the role of attitudes in emotional stress and for his powerful techniques of cognitive restructuring and stress reduction.

This book can be read in a number of ways. For those

teachers seeking immediate relief, I refer you to the material which appears in the following few pages. You can choose to read any chapter without having read preceding ones. (The exception to this is Chapter 3 on personal responsibility, which should be read before Chapters 4 and 5.) If you are not someone who likes to read books from cover to cover, I suggest looking over the table of contents for material which might be of interest and use.

I have included in each chapter a number of distractors which serve to break the tedium of continuous text. The quotes selected summarise some of the important ideas in each chapter. Concluding most chapters is a section called 'Actions Speak Louder Than Words' — material designed to encourage you to put into practice some of the ideas contained in each chapter. I have also written short vignettes in each chapter about the lives of three teachers: Bill Witherspoon, Mary Brunette and Alyce Greenway. The material is meant to be slightly humorous and informative and is not intended to trivialise nor ridicule.

There is a great deal of information in this book. Hopefully, you will find at least one idea and skill which can help you take the stress out of your teaching. Teachers are a most important resource. You are the caretakers of our children and the future. If this book can help take some of the stress out of teaching and replace it with satisfaction and fulfillment, then I feel my efforts in writing it will be well rewarded.

Michael E. Bernard
Melbourne, March 1990

'INSTANT' RELIEF!

If you are experiencing a lot of stress at the moment, I know that you are not particularly interested in reading thirteen chapters to find a solution. If you are experiencing feelings of extreme exhaustion, anxiety, anger, depression or possibly feeling nothing at all about your teaching work, the following techniques can help bring immediate relief. They have each worked for different teachers I have known. Read through the list and pick the one(s) which you predict will work for you. Keep trying different ones until one works.

Rag doll This technique has been described by Dr Audrey Livingstone Booth, director of the Stress Foundation in England. It is designed to shut off your stress response completely. The directions are as follows. 'Sit in an armless chair. Do ten deep, slow breaths and with every outgoing breath breathe out quite forcefully, deflating like a balloon, and begin to flop forward at the head and neck. Gradually flop further forward with each breath out, letting the shoulders and arms fall further forward until you are hanging limply from the waist like a rag doll. Hang there for a moment or two and then come up very, very slowly. Rest your head back on the chair and breath slowly, gently and easily with your hands resting limply and lightly on your lap. Sit quite like this for as long as you can manage. When you are ready to move again, take a deep, forceful energising breath.'

Support Find some time to talk with someone whom you trust and who knows you, cares about you and who, if possible, appreciates your work achievements. Don't feel guilty about taking up their time. Tell them honestly how you feel and describe the specific things at work which are getting to you.

Replay of past teaching achievements Find some time to be alone. Think back to those times when you felt good about your work and about things that had gone well for you. Remember any specific positive comments other teachers, students, parents and the principal may have made in recognising what you did. Replay each scene, slowly savouring the positive feelings you experienced at the time.

Take a warm, slow bath Soaking in a warm bath with bath salts or scented lotions can afford great relief of physical tension. If you bathe for approximately for thirty minutes and then go straight to bed and relax for another thirty minutes, you'll have a potent anti-stress remedy.

Listen to music Listening to music for an hour or more can be very relaxing. You might want to take a music break during morning recess or while grading papers. Lying down listening to your favourite piece of classical music can also slow your system right down.

Exercise There are two forms of exercise which can relieve your stress. If you have been exercising regularly, then I suggest a vigorous period of no less than twenty minutes where you jog, swim, play squash, etc. Alternatively, if you are not a regular exerciser, go on a long walk at a steady pace, stopping every so often to catch your breath.

Time management If you are stressed because you've got too much to do and you haven't been getting everything done, write down on a sheet of paper everything you want to get done over the next week. Place a '3' next to the things you have to get done, a '2' next to the important but not essential activities, and a '1' next to the ones which would be nice to accomplish but are not essential. On a separate sheet of paper titled 'What I Will Get Done Tomorrow', list all the activities that have a '3' beside them which you have to get done tomorrow. Schedule '2' activities if time permits. Forget about the '1' activities. Cross activities off your list once completed.

Time out If you are feeling overwhelmed, schedule time alone when you leave school. If you have a family or are in a relationship, tell your loved ones that you need time out. Tell them that your request has nothing to do with them and that you need time for refueling. Then take at least one hour to be by yourself in your garden, walking through the neighbourhood or in the city. If you can organise it, going away overnight can do the world of good.

Time with friends When people get very stressed, they sometimes forget about their friends. Your friends can help distract you from your work. There is nothing like a good laugh to ease your tension. Call them up and either invite yourself over or invite them over.

Catastrophe scale Think about the one thing at work which really seems to be causing your stress, like a student or class misbehaving, your principal hassling you, too many meetings to attend, etc. On a scale of 1 to 100 where 100 is the worst thing which could be happening to you, fifty is medium bad, and ten is a little bad, how bad is it that this thing has happened or will be happening tomorrow? (Remember the scale only goes to 100.) Rate how bad the problem is on this scale (mentally record or write down a number).

0	10	50	90	100
Not bad	A little bad	Medium bad	Very bad	The worst

Now turn the page.

Catastrophe Scale

```
       World war; death of a
┬100   loved one; life-threatening
│      illness;permanent paralysis
│
├90    You have a serious car
│      accident; house burns
│      down; family member very
│      ill; you are fired from job;
│      you break your leg; house
│      burgled
│
│
│      You break an antique
├50    vase; you have a fight with
│      a friend
│
│
│
│
│
│
│
│
├10    You have a flat tyre
│
┴0
```

The above is a list of catastrophes rated by severity. While you might not agree with all the ratings, I think you'll agree with the ones listed above and just below ninety. Using this objective scale, where would you now rate the problem at work which seems to cause you so much stress? Place crosses on the scale where you generally place it and where you now rate it. A scale such as this enables people to see how under stress they blow the stressful event out of proportion and make it worse than it is. If you did, join the club. It's human nature. One key solution to stress management is keeping things in perspective.

CHAPTER 1
WHAT IS TEACHER STRESS?

'Stress is the speedometer of life...sum of all the wear caused by any kind of vital reaction throughout the body at one time.'
Hans Selye, Stress Without Distress, 1976.

If you have experienced a fair amount of stress as a teacher, then you may well find yourself questioning the wisdom of your occupational choice at best, or nearing burnout at worst. You will, no doubt, know that you are not alone. Recent surveys into teacher stress world-wide found only a relatively small percentage of teachers *unaffected* by stress. At any one time, between 20 and 25 per cent of teachers indicate they find teaching either very or extremely stressful while another 50 per cent or so find teaching moderately stressful. Recent research also indicates that teaching is one of the most stressful professions.

It is quite possible that at this very moment you are not experiencing a great deal of stress related to your teaching. This may be the case for a variety of reasons. Stress can be thought of as an ocean tide — it is not always experienced at the same level in the same way. We know that teacher stress ebbs and flows. Sometimes it is apparently calm while at other times during the school year it crashes up against you.

Now, while you might find some solace in knowing that you are not alone in finding teaching stressful, such an awareness is definitely not enough in most cases to help alleviate your stress. (We know that misery loves company!) Knowing there are large numbers of teachers who experience stress might, however, help relieve some of your worries about your own sanity. The fact that there are so many very stressed teachers suggests there is something about the current conditions of teaching which places all teachers 'at risk' for stress.

WHY IS TEACHING A STRESSFUL PROFESSION?

Depending on who you speak to, you will receive different reasons for why teaching ranks as one of the most stressful professions along with medicine, the law, the public service, the police and air traffic control.

It is generally recognised that a higher incidence of stress-related illnesses can be found among people whose jobs require them to bear a large amount of responsibility for the welfare of others. Many teachers make a big commitment to the students they teach and this can include strong emotional ties. They have to deal with a wide range of students' educational and human needs. They are expected to put in a large number of hours giving of themselves to others and have to perform a wide variety of activities unrelated to their job description, including ministering to the emotional and family problems of students. Generally speaking, teaching is a helping profession where there are too many students to serve with too few attendant resources.

Research over the past decade into the causes of teacher stress have located four main sources. *State departments boards of education*, which exercise a fair amount of influence over policy formulation including promotion policy and salary, have recently imposed onto schools a large number of changes introduced rapidly which many teachers perceive as being very stressful. Your *school's organisation*, including the style of leadership of administrators, purpose and clarity of the mission of your school, staff relations and workload, also exerts an influence on the stress levels of teachers. The *classroom* epitomised by poorly disciplined and unmotivated students also represents a major source of teacher stress. The *individual teacher*, including attitudes towards self, others, and work tasks as well as needs for recognition, also can be seen to having a bearing on the stressors encountered on the job.

From my own research and personal experience in working with many stressed teachers in Australia and the United States, I have concluded that teaching is experienced as stressful because when you teach in front of a class, your ego is constantly exposed and on the line. By that I mean, if you are like most teachers, you have entered teaching with high professional aspirations for success. Unfortunately, because of events frequently beyond your control (e.g., students with special disabilities; conduct-disordered students; large class sizes) you have to deal with the fact that you will not always be as successful as you would like. Students will not perform up to their potential. Classroom noise levels may well reach Caruso's upper octave range. Try as you might, you will probably never quite achieve what you had hoped for in teaching.

Moreover, you are in a job where many other people are in a position to judge your ability on a fairly regular basis. Teaching is a very public activity. Your students evaluate you constantly. Your colleagues and superiors frequently observe how well you are doing. And, come report time, parents have a basis for rating your competence. I have found that two very great sources of stress in the teaching profession are when you do not live up to your own expectations and when you do not get the support or recognition from others (and when this manifests in implicit criticism and personality clashes). Why should these two sources create so much stress? Because, human nature being what it is, we frequently take lack of achievement and criticism personally. More on this later.

Another main reason I have found teaching to be so stressful is that at certain times of the school year a great deal of work is demanded of you and you frequently have too much work to do and not enough time to do it. This is especially the case if you have heavy administrative responsibilities. And if you also carry a large amount of domestic responsibilities, including looking after your children, you are at even greater risk. Even if you are not a senior administrator and do not have children, the periods surrounding end of term have been found to be enormously stressful. This book will show how to manage yourself during these times so that they are not such a strain.

WHY IS TEACHING TODAY SO STRESSFUL?

Without going into a detailed account of the complex reasons why the stresses placed on you are greater than ever, the following factors seem to be making teaching more stressful and have been reported as affecting teachers' morale and sense of job satisfaction.

Breakdown of discipline

There appears to be universal agreement that students these days are less self-disciplined and, in many cases, less respectful of you simply because you are a teacher. These students, who frequently demonstrate similar patterns of undisciplined behaviour at home, place large demands on your time and energy in establishing a teaching environment where learning can take place. The communication of knowledge and skills from you to your students is challenging enough on its own: even the simplest teaching activity may become extremely stressful when it is combined with having to maintain classroom discipline.

It is also the case in some urban schools that teachers can be exposed to the threat of physical harassment and violence in the classroom in addition to being subjected to verbal abuse and continuous threats to their authority. Now I am not saying that all urban classrooms are threatening places to teach. Many schools and school districts within urban settings have succeeded in building good teacher-student communication and have established the classroom as a positive setting to learn. However, there are classrooms where teachers are placed under a great deal of strain by their students who have values which are not those of the mainstream educational system and whose behaviour reflects this incompatibility.

Schools vary a great deal in the degree to which they have responded to the increase in discipline problems and, in particular, in whether they have formulated a discipline policy and set of procedures which the individual teacher can rely on when confronted with a difficult student.

Media criticism

Within recent times the teaching profession has been subjected to a great deal of public scrutiny and, in certain quarters, a great deal of unfavourable press coverage. Teachers have been scapegoated as being primarily responsible for the fall in educational standards and the lack of achievement and motivation of students. This 'teacher bashing' has resulted in some teachers being unwilling to admit their real profession at social gatherings for fear of having to defend themselves.

Change

All sectors and levels of public and private education are currently experiencing change being imposed from without and responded to from within. The rigorous 'cost-benefit' analysis to which politicians are subjecting the educational system means that economic resources are becoming scarcer. As a consequence, departments of education in the various states have resorted to amalgamation as one of the main solutions to the perceived inefficiencies of schools. With amalgamation and subsequent threats to job security, many teachers are being faced for the first time with uncertainties about their future and with changing and ill-defined job requirements coming from outside. These factors, combined with the lack of any control over decisions which affect their job definition, have made teaching more stressful for many teachers.

Another aspect of change is the lower priority education seems to have in governmental planning. In the early 1980s, both state and federal governments increased the amount spent on school improvement, teachers' salaries, etc. Schools and teachers benefited from the increased governmental support both practically and in terms of professional self-esteem. Today, with education at all levels undergoing cuts and with governments shifting their emphasis to schools having to demonstrate educational accountability, professional prestige has been significantly dampened.

New assessment procedures and curriculum innovations

Innovations both in the assessment and curriculum areas abound. Many different methods are being introduced for the individualising of teaching including those to do with assessing student progress. Moreover, there are an endless number of new curriculum programs and subjects all competing for inclusion into the curriculum. The amount of effort required to keep abreast of changes in the assessment and curriculum areas is greater than ever before.

Integration

There continues to be an increasing trend internationally to integrate students of all exceptionalities into 'normal' or 'regular' classrooms. Many teachers find themselves for the first time expected to be able to cater for students with emotional, behavioural and learning handicaps along with other developmental and learning disabilities. While some teachers have been provided with adequate support in the form of special service personnel, others are not so fortunate.

Increased parental and community expectations

There is little question that over the past two decades parents have become increasingly outspoken in their demands for better educational opportunities for their children. Communities are expecting teachers to be much more accountable not only for the quality of the teaching they provide but also for insuring the overall emotional and social welfare of children. Teachers are increasingly being expected to be all things to all students. In some instances, parent-teacher interviews have become battlegrounds where parents air their frustrations about the lack of progress on the part of their child and the teacher has to justify his or her efforts on the child's behalf.

Increased workload pressures

One of the greatest stressors on teachers today is having too much work to do and not enough time to do it. This is especially so during certain times of the year, particularly right before and during exams. Teachers who carry major homemaking and childminding responsibilities as well are especially at risk of stress-related difficulties at peak work periods during the year.

Lack of influence over decision making

Educational districts, individual schools and school administrators vary a great deal in terms of how much individual teachers are involved in decisions which affect their teaching. Some schools have very good communication channels between teachers and administrators where information is freely and openly exchanged and teachers have a significant say in decisions about what they teach and how they go about it. A significant number of teachers are employed at schools where they are omitted from the decision-making process and are treated in a cavalier fashion by administrators. Not surprisingly, teachers can find teaching within this type of school environment extremely frustrating.

Inadequate salary

It is only recently that the salaries of teachers have begun to be attractive and competitive with other comparable professions. Base salaries for beginning teachers and senior teachers at the top end of the salary scale continue, though, to be relatively low. Many schools have lost some of their better teachers — especially those with a computer or mathematics background — to industry, which is willing to pay a more competitive salary.

In order for you to be at your very best as a teacher, it is vital for you to be aware that stress can both help you maintain peak performance as well as negatively influence your teaching effectiveness. It is vital, therefore, that you not only be aware of some of the main techniques for managing stress but also of the most common symptoms of stress. Let us start, then, with a brief discussion of what teacher stress is, its cause and effects, before we provide you with ways of detecting your stress levels.

STRESS VERSUS DISTRESS

In beginning to provide a way of understanding what teacher stress is, I believe it is important to start with a key concept discovered by the founding father in the area of stress inquiry and research, Hans Selye. Dr Selye, a world-renowned biological scientist, made the point that stress is not something which can be avoided and, moreover, is not something you would wish to avoid. In the face of *both* positive and negative teaching demands and threats your body experiences an increase in physiological activity (which Selye refers to as 'stress') which provides the fuel to your physical and intellectual machinery to enable you to deal with the many and varied demands you encounter on a daily basis. However, when the outside demands reach extremely high levels of intensity — which can vary along a continuum from over-stimulation to complete boredom — stress can become distress and damage to your physiological system can occur.

Simply stated, Selye has shown that stress can either be life sustaining, beneficial and enjoyable ('positive stress') or detrimental and life destroying ('negative stress' or 'distress'). What this book is about is providing you with an understanding of teacher stress as well as with skills so that you can manage and enjoy it as well as preventing it from becoming distress. We are not concerned with trying to do away with stress altogether.

'Complete freedom from stress is death.'

Hans Selye

WHAT IS TEACHER STRESS?

There are many different ways that people have defined teacher stress and there are an equally large number of explanations offered as to the reasons why teachers experience stress. Some have tended to hold the educational bureaucracy and the organisation of a school as responsible for stress in teachers. Others have looked for the cause of stress within the individual 'stressed' teacher. Yet another group of researchers in the area has been concerned with examining the physiological and psychological reactions of the individual teacher to stress. The meaning of the word 'stress' can become confused because you do not know if people are talking about stress as something within the educational environment, something within the teacher, or as a physiological or psychological stress reaction.

The position taken in this book is that *stress is a process*. Teacher stress is a byproduct between you and your outside world. To describe this transaction it will be necessary to examine important aspects of your outside world, important aspects of yourself, and the way you react physiologically, psychologically and behaviourally as a consequence of your world impacting on you.

Definition of teacher stress

Simply stated, *teacher stress is the way you as a teacher react and adapt to demands and threats you encounter in teaching*.

In this simple definition, demands refer to those many and varied activities which you are required to perform on a daily basis while threats refer to the actions of others which can harm you either physically, physiologically or, more commonly, psychologically. As you can see from the model of teaching stress following, whether you experience stress or distress will depend on both what your outside world is like both in and outside of school as well as the type of person you are.

It is more than likely that you will be experiencing a great deal of stress if you have many general life stressors outside of teaching. These can include personal stresses (e.g., financial, relationships problems, health concerns); environmental stresses (e.g., noise, pollution, traffic); your department of education or school council initiating a great deal of change which affects what you do as a teacher; your school's organisation characterised by poor leadership, morale, communication and consultation between administration and staff; poor staff relationships and significant time/ workload pressures; where you have a large number of undisciplined and unmotivated students in the classes you teach; and if there is little peer and administrative support available.

Your stress level will also be influenced by different aspects including your attitudes towards yourself, others at school, the school organisation and the department and/or school council, your coping skill repetoire (e.g., assertiveness, time management) and your lifestyle (e.g., exercise, diet, recreation).

Your physiological and psychological stress reactions which result from the combined interaction between you and your outside world determine in the short run whether your behavioural reactions successfully manage the outside stressors or whether you tend to mismanage the outside stressor through self-defeating behaviours such as avoidance or aggression. Adaptive behaviour will neutralise, modify or remove the demand or threat, thereby reducing the stress, while unadaptive behaviour prolongs and often intensifies the stress. Over the long haul, your typical physiological and psychological reaction to demands and threats will determine your state of physical and mental health including—in extreme cases—burnout and breakdown.

Model of Teacher Stress

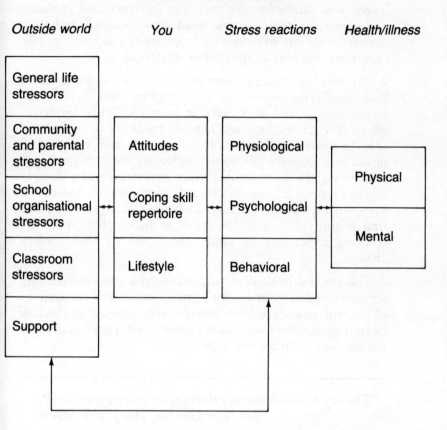

Outside world	*You*	*Stress reactions*	*Health/illness*
General life stressors			
Community and parental stressors	Attitudes	Physiological	Physical
School organisational stressors	Coping skill repertoire	Psychological	
Classroom stressors	Lifestyle	Behavioral	Mental
Support			

There are several assumptions which underly this model which are worth noting.

1 Stress is a product by of your outside world and yourself. Distress is most likely to occur when your outside world is lousy and your inside world is functioning poorly. Put another way, to understand your stress it is important to identify not only those stressors in your teaching (and outside world) which are obnoxious, threatening and demanding but also to identify those aspects of your internal functioning which are contributing to your stress. While your current lifestyle and coping skill repertoire are both

11

seen as important parts of you which influence your stress levels, *your attitudes, the way you interpret and evaluate and, generally, the way you think about yourself and your outside world has an extremely large bearing on whether you experience teaching as stressful or distressful.*

2 The effective management of your stress depends upon both modifying aspects of your teaching and outside environment as well as aspects of yourself. While improvements in your teaching and outside world are to be encouraged (organisational factors for stress reduction are covered in the last chapter) this book emphasises more those things which you can do to modify your own stress when changes in your school are not immediately forthcoming. Moreover, my own experience has been that when changes take place first within you, it is far easier to make changes in the teaching conditions of your school and to effect policy change.

3 The amount of control you believe you can exercise over stressors within your teaching environment and the amount of control you are able to exercise over yourself in the face of outside stressors you cannot control will greatly influence the amount of stress you experience.

'The key to surviving and thriving on success is **control***'.*
Dr Peter Hanson, **The Joy of Stress.**

---

4 It is becoming increasingly clear from research into the nature of stress that *daily, repetitive hassles* are one of the main sources of stress. While not wishing to discount other factors, it is apparent that certain types of stress reactions, including fatigue and feelings of being overwhelmed, are due to all the many different and taxing daily chores you have to perform both inside and outside of school.

'[It is the] insidious day-to-day sources of stress with their cumulative effect, and not the less frequent intense

> *sources of stress, which teachers are most concerned with.'*
> *Chris Kyriacou, international expert on teacher stress.*

Let's look briefly at the different parts of the teacher stress model.

Your outside world

The model lists five aspects of your outside world which influence your stress about teaching.

1 *General life stressors* Much research, including my own, and much experience shows that the stress you experience outside of teaching can contribute to teacher stress. The more stress you bring with you to your work, the less your tolerance will be to cope with organisational and classroom stressors. Common general life stressors include death of a love one, divorce, serious illness in a member of your family, relationship breakdown, financial problems, personal injury or illness, increase in family arguments, pregnancy, birth of a child and change in your residence, to name some of the major ones.

Research conducted in the late 1960s shows that there is a strong relationship between the number of these negative events in your life and stress-related illness. If you have a number of these events occurring in your life it might well be the case that you are finding teaching more stressful than it would be otherwise. You will be able to use many of the stress management techniques described in this book to combat the added stress you are under.

2 *Community and parental* Included in this category is negative media coverage as well as parental criticisms. As well, the extent to which parents share common goals of your school and encourage by their actions the goals you have for their children will also moderate stress.

3 *Department of Education/school council policy* When changes are imposed on a school from without, then the

potential for teacher stress increases. Whether change is imposed by the Department of Education, school council or some other body, the research clearly indicates that when the rate of change imposed on a school is too great, teachers (and principals) will demonstrate increased job stress and dissatisfaction. In particular, the amount or quantity of change imposed as well as the degree of uncertainty and ambiguity of the goals of the changes will aggravate or add to pre-existing levels of job stress.

Other ways in which forces outside of your school can influence your stress is in the extent to which they have formulated and communicated a clear and strong discipline policy, the ways in which teachers are recognised and promoted, the amount of support provided (aids, specialist, welfare) and class size.

4 *Organisational stressors* There are a number of areas within your school which can add to your stress level. 'Organisational climate' refers to how well you relate to your colleagues and people in authority, the type of leadership/managerial style exhibited by people in senior positions (e.g., 'difficult' versus 'easy' personality; 'democractic', 'authoritarian' and 'laissez faire' management styles) as well as the degree of enthusiasm and commitment you and your colleagues have to achieve the goals of the school. 'Time/workload' pressures refer to the amount of work which is allocated to you compared with the amount of time you have available at school and at home to satisfy all the demands. Schools which have good staff-staff and staff-administrator relationships, where the staff have confidence in its leadership and are committed to its policy, and where time/workload pressures are seen as fair and equitable, are likely to have low overall levels of teacher stress all other things being equal.

5 *Classroom stressors* What goes on in your classroom will have a direct bearing on your stress. Poorly behaved students, unmotivated students and students who vary greatly in skills and abilities are some of the sources of within classroom stress. Other factors include having too many students in your class, overcrowding, lack of teaching resources, extremes of temperature, and noise.

Summary of beginning teachers' sources of stress
Handling problems of pupil control and discipline; adjusting to deficiencies in school equipment, physical conditions and materials; adjusting to teaching assignment; adjusting to needs, interests, and abilities of pupils; motivating pupil interest and response; contractual stipulations; orientation to school system; faculty relations; grading papers; arguing over test answers; restlessness of students; attending college and doing student teaching at the same time; introducing new ideas to stimulate discussion; cheating by students; relations with parents; methods of evaluating teaching; knowing enough to teach units; personality conflicts with supervising teachers; difficult relations with students; concerns with self; method about providing feedback about teaching; viewing teaching performance on videotape.

Summary of experienced teachers' reported sources of stress
Classroom interruptions (bulletins, announcements, special events); individualizing instruction; promotion standards; clerical activities; size of individual class; type of pupil; inadequate school facilities; extracurricular responsibilities; instructional planning; inadequate salary; incompatible relationship with supervisor; assignment of paraprofessional duties; discipline problems; obtaining funds for purchasing extra classroom aids; finding time for creative teaching; ability to understand pupils' capacities; specifying objectives for them; assessing their gains; determining pupils' difficulties.
                    Report by Coates and Thoresen, 1976.

6 *Support* Some types of social support can be of tremendous value in helping you to minimise the effects of stress. One of the best types of support you can receive is when an administrator or principal offers you some words of praise for your overall performance when you are at a low point, feeling very despondent about and frustrated with your teaching.

Another type of support which helps to minimise your stress is offered through peer support. An example of a peer support scheme which has helped to reduce stress in inexperienced teachers involves new teachers meeting once or twice a week to discuss classroom management and other problems they are experiencing during their first year of teaching. With specialists invited in from time to time to offer advice, this peer support program helps younger teachers develop coping and practical skills for managing classroom disruptions and thereby reduces one main source of teaching stress.

If your school provides the opportunity for you to 'affiliate' with other teachers and, in particular, where groups are formed on the basis of common interest and problem solving, your ability to take control of stress, receive acknowledgment and influence school policy will help moderate your stress.

Ineffectual social support takes the form of someone constantly complaining about his or her problems to anyone who will listen. Such whining or complaining frequently makes the stress worse by reinforcing the whiner's sense of injustice and self-pity.

An example

Bill Witherspoon, thirty-seven years of age, is an eighth-grade science teacher.

Bill is running a little late for school when he gets held up in traffic. Taking back roads, he manages to get to school with two minutes to spare. He runs to his office to collect his books. As he is about to sprint off to class, he is stopped by Mrs Pain who wants to find out what work young Johnny Pain should be doing while at home with the mumps. Arriving in class five minutes late, he finds his middle school coordinator, Mr Gunn, standing in front of his class with a big glare on his face. 'And another thing', the coordinator is bellowing, 'the way you are dressed is a disgrace. Your shirts are tucked out, your hair is not combed... This whole class is to clean up the yard at recess time—ah, here comes Mr Punctual—I mean, Mr Waithers.'

'Actually, it's Witherspoon.'

By this time, Bill is feeling a mixture of nausea and extreme anger at both himself, Mrs Pain, the coordinator, his students, their parents, etc. He feels pain starting to stretch across his chest. As he turns to his class to begin the lesson, he can see by the great sea of hostile faces that they have not appreciated him being late and having to endure the coordinator's morning greeting. As the class progresses, Bill finds himself more and more frustrated and feeling unable to cope. He discovers that the laboratory assistant has failed to set up all the necessary equipment for the experiment he had planned for the class. The noise level in his class keeps growing louder all the time and at the back of his mind he keeps expecting the coordinator to walk by his room any minute.

As his class draws to a close, he thinks of the five remaining periods of teaching he has for the day, of having to supervise recess clean up, of the two interviews he has scheduled with parents after school, of the mid-year exam he has to finish for tomorrow afternoon's science meeting, of having to cook dinner tonight and bathe his two young toddlers (it was Bill's rostered night for childminding). As he grabs his books, making sure not to be late for Period 2, he wonders how he is possibly going to bear the rest of the day.

In this example, you can readily see the different demands and threats in Bill's environment. The demands include having to make up time on his way to school, spend time with Mrs Pain, teach a class with insufficient equipment, supervise cleanup, attend meetings after school, prepare an exam and look after his children. The threats are not so much physical as psychological ones aimed at his professional competence and self-esteem. The psychological threats include Mr Gunn's disapproval of his being late, the unruliness of his class, indicating possible deficiencies in his classroom management skills, and not getting his exam written on time at a suitably acceptable standard, suggesting lack of professional competence. Together these demands and threats, which as a group we shall refer to as stressors, have the potential for creating within Bill an extremely high level of distress.

You can well imagine how Bill's stress level might have been negatively affected by additional outside factors such as a new child in the family, mortgage problems, and inter-personal domestic hassles.

Let's now see how your inside world can influence your stress level.

Inside factors which can cause stress

There is little question that teachers vary considerably in their capacity to manage stress and ward off distress. Put another way, some of your colleagues (including yourself!) are impressive in their ability to handle certain stressors and in managing their reactions to threats and demands. It is now possible to profile some of the things inside of you which help innoculate you against the destructive aspects of stress. Just as with outside stressors, some of these things you have the ability to change and improve. I cover these only factors briefly now, as they will be expanded on in later sections.

1 *Attitudes* My own research into the variety of causes of teacher stress has shown quite clearly that your attitude to what goes on in your classroom, towards your colleagues, school administration and change as well as your attitudes to major life events and to outside stressors at home will have a decisive effect on your stress level, no matter how bad the outside situation is. Bill's attitudes towards himself in the face of his difficult circumstances will determine whether his inevitable stress converts into unhealthy distress. The control of Bill's stress level potentially resides in the extent to which he gets down on himself and condemns himself as reflected in 'I should have handled this situation better; I can't stand the co-ordinator's poor opinion of me; I'm a real failure'.

2 *Coping skill repertoire* When you come face to face with one or more stressors, your estimation of the likelihood that

you can manage the stressors will influence your stress reaction. It is therefore not surprising that the skills you have on hand will determine your estimation of your coping and whether you cope or you don't. For example, if Bill had assertion skills to be able to ward off Mrs Pain and deal with his coordinator, then not only would he have been less likely to have interpreted his situation as stressful, he would also have been more likely to have successfully managed both difficult situations, thereby removing the stressors. Unfortunately, Bill did not feel comfortable and confident in asserting himself. Other important skills for managing teacher stress will be discussed later on including time management and classroom discipline.

3. *Lifestyle* Your lifestyle plays an important part in your ability to manage stress for all sorts of reasons. By lifestyle, I refer to *recreation, exercise* and *diet*. If you do not take time out to rest and relax, if you are out of shape and if your diet is poor, then you will be much more vulnerable to outside stressors. You will experience distress sooner than if you have a good lifestyle. You will be less able to think your way through and around stressful situations and, as a consequence, your behaviour will be less efficient in modifying the situation. Your recovery time from a stress-related problem will be longer and you will be more vulnerable to further stress attacks.

STRESS REACTIONS

Over the years, researchers have studied how demands and threats in the environment which call for a response or adaptation result in both physiological and psychological reactions. We have learned that physiological and psychological processes work together in reacting to demands and threats in the outside world. Let's first examine how your body reacts to stressors.

Physiological stress reactions

Two main physiological systems are responsible for your

stress reactions. There is the *sympathetic nervous system*, that part of your autonomic nervous system responsible for arousing ourselves initially for 'flight' or 'fight'. There are also the *endocrine glands* which help support the arousal efforts of your sympathetic nervous system and which carry out the important function of supplying you with the energy needed for action. The main endocrine glands involved in your physiological stress reactions are the adrenal glands, located near your kidneys.

Imagine the ancient ancestor of our eighth-grade teacher, Bill Witherspoon. Caveman Harry (Witherspoon) was designed especially well to ward off the dangers of his day be they human or animal. You'll see what I mean from the following example.

One night as Harry is preparing to go the bed he hears a loud crash outside his cave. Inside Harry, his body is instantaneously preparing for either 'flight' or 'fight'. As he searches around in the darkness for his spear, Harry's sympathetic nervous system begins readying him to defend against the external threat. His heartrate increases along with his blood pressure, allowing for additional blood to be circulated to his brain and muscles and away from his skin, digestive and sexual organs. His muscles automatically tighten for potential action. As he begins scrambling around the cave and getting over-heated he sweats heavily to dissipate his increasing body heat. At the same time, his eyesight becomes more sensitive, enabling him to realise that he has left his trusty spear outside.

As he creeps outside to have a look for his spear and what is responsible for the loud crash, his airways expand, allowing more oxygen to be delivered throughout the body. At the same time, his adrenal glands are madly pumping out hormones. Increased adrenalin is helping to release his body's main energy supply, glucose, from his muscles and liver. Combined with oxygen, Harry's body is beginning to produce extra energy.

As time passes Harry's fat tissues release fatty acids, which involve additional glucose production. As he hears another sound which he identifies as a footstep (increased hearing acuity) and is still unable to locate his spear, his body throws more chemicals into his system. Glucocorticoids help transform amino-acids from his muscles, skin and bones into more glucose and energy. Lactic acid, another source of sugar, is released.

As Harry rolls a boulder away from his path as he searches for his foe and spear, the boulder rolls back down Harry's path and crashes into his left knee. Fortunately for poor Harry, the increased cortisone in his system works automatically to reduce his pain and lessen the inflammation at the crash side. Unfortunately for Harry, not only is his trusty spear crushed by the rolling boulder, but his muffled scream is heard by Harriet, a tribesperson from a nearby village, who pounces on Harry and claims him for her own!

Now this is a silly example, but it does, hopefully, illustrate the nature of the physiological system which we have inherited from our ancestors. Years ago it served a very functional purpose; preparing us to expend energy, if necessary, to fight or flee from an external, frequently physical, threat.

In twentieth-century modern-day society, and, in particular, in our schools, there are no dangerous dinosaurs and cavepeople out to do us in (or are there?). We have the same stress-arousal physiological system designed for 'flight' or 'fight' with no real outside physical threats (except in extreme circumstances) and, moreover, given our basically sedentary existences, we do not tend to work off the increases in body chemicals throughout our system by vigorous exercise.

Hans Selye has identified a three-stage physiological response system to threats and demands which he termed the 'general adaptation syndrome' (GAS). It is called a *general* syndrome because his research has shown that your body responds in a similar way to all demands and threats regardless of the specific identity of the stressor. Your body 'turns on' when your brain interprets a situation as threatening regardless of whether you are faced with a wild animal or a wild student.

Bill Witherspoon experienced the identical physiological arousal on his way to work as he confronted in turn Mrs Pain, Mr Gunn and his eighth-grade class as did his ancient forebear, Harry Witherspoon, when he was faced with the unknown, his inability to find his spear, getting knocked down by a boulder, and being taken captive by Harriet!

Indeed, even in the face of pleasant stimulation, when you feel excited and curious, your body reacts in precisely the same way as it does when faced with noxious stimuli. The three stages reveal when you are most vulnerable to stress-related physical symptoms and problems.

During the *alarm reaction* (stage 1), the hypothalamus, that portion of your brain responsible both for much of your emotion and motivation as well as for activating your central nervous system and endocrine system, receives a signal from your brain's cortex that a situation is physically demanding or psychologically threatening. Your sympathetic nervous system reacts rapidly to the threat or demand by sharpening the alertness of your body to 'flight' or 'fight' in the form of changes to your senses (hearing, vision), heart rate, respiratory and digestive systems and increased muscle tension.

In order to maintain your body's alertness and preparedness, your sympathetic nervous system also directly stimulates your *adrenal medulla*, the interior part of the adrenal gland which produces *adrenaline*, a hormone responsible for mobilising extra energy in the form of glucose. Adrenaline provides you with a burst of energy but this response tends to be rather short-lived.

The other part of the adrenal gland involved in the stress respone is the *adrenal cortex* located on the exterior part of your adrenal gland. The adrenal cortex is also activated by your hypothalmus but through a different route. The hypothalmus activates the *pituitary gland*, located within the deep recesses of your brain, which sends many hormones throughout your body. For example, the pituitary gland stimulates the *thyroid gland* which raises your level of metabolic functioning at times of stress. The pituitary also produces a hormone called ACTH (adrenocorticotrophic hormone) which in turn stimulates the adrenal cortex to produce a wide range of chemicals. Selye believed that ACTH was the most important hormone for studying your physiological stress reaction. The adrenal cortex produces *cortisol* or *cortisone* which helps your body in the short term to ward off pain and the invasion of foreign substances. (In the long term, elevated cortisone levels reduce your body's resistance to cancer, infection and illness.) *Mineralcorticoids* also produced by the adrenal cortex influences the mineral balance of your body and, in particular, converting food into energy.

If you have been unable to neutralise or remove the outside stressor, the general adaptation syndrome will advance to *resistance* (stage 2). During this phase, the alarm bells of the initial stage have ceased ringing and your body runs at a higher rate in an effort to cope with the stressor. In particular, your endocrine system supplies increased minerals and chemical hormones needed to maintain the extra energy and effort. Until fairly recently we dealt with (or they dealt with us) outside stressors relatively quickly. We didn't spend a great deal of time in the resistance stage and we generally resolved the outside stressors with some sort of strong active and physical response.

When you are able to successfully deal with the outside stress, your physiological systems begin shutting down as your body returns to a previous level of rest and equilibrium. Your parasympathetic nervous system takes over from the sympathetic system and helps restore your organs and yourself to a relatively stress-free state.

Unfortunately, in our twentieth-century society, and especially in the teaching environment, the outside stressors are seldom dealt with quickly. Some of your stressors (e.g., poorly disciplined students) may well be with you forever. Moreover, the way you now handle stressors is more in a 'passive' than 'active' mode, making it more difficult for you to rid yourself of the negative effects of the chemicals which you haved poured into your system to deal with a demand or threat. The repeated and prolonged exposure to stressors and your inability to recover sufficiently between episodes leads us to the most damaging of Selye's stages of stress.

Exhaustion (stage 3) occurs when you have been unable to deal with the stressors in your world and you do not have the energy to put into resisting any longer. It is during stage 3 that you are most vulnerable to stress-related physical and mental illnesses. While your body's chemical-hormonal and central nervous system response to an outside stressor is seen as being very necessary and useful, the prolonged 'turn on' of your system without your system being able to restore itself is when all the damage occurs.

In a nutshell, your communication system is telling you

23

you are still in danger, but your arousal and energy-producing physiological system is on empty. And worse still, you have a much reduced immunity system. Your bodily organs are at risk of injury due, in part, to elevated cortisone levels, and you are extremely vulnerable to the invasion of noxious foreign substances which bring with them illness and disease. At worst, if you do not respond to your body's signals which suggest that you are physiologically spent, physical (and nervous) breakdown may be imminent. At best, you will begin to manifest a variety of physical and psychological stress-related symptoms.

In a study of burned-out teachers in 1982, Belcastro reported the following somatic symptoms commonly found in people with high levels of stress: abdominal pain, difficulty in breathing, eczema, hives, tinnitus, occupational injuries, bowel difficulties, and tearfulness. Several illness and chronic conditions also have been related to teacher stress including high blood pressure, kidney or bladder trouble, arthritis, lung or breathing problems, gall bladder disorders, cardiovascular disorders, insomnia, gastritis, stomach ulcers, anaemia, asthma and colitis. In Chapter 2 you will have an opportunity to assess your own particular physical stress reactions.

Some negative side-effects of common physiological stress reactions

1 *Release of cortisone from adrenal glands; continuous elevation lowers body's capacity to resist infection and illness; immune system breakdown; gastric and duodenal ulcer susceptibility dues to stomach's inability to break down its own acids.*
2 *Increase in thyroid hormone in bloodstream resulting in increased metabolism, lowering of heat tolerance, nervousness, sleep difficulties and tiredness.*
3 *Release of endorphines from the hypothalmus which helps to reduce pain; prolonged release leads to reduced levels of endomorphs resulting in migraines, arthritic pain and bodily aches.*

4 *Shutting down of digestive tract which can result in nausea, diarrhoea, cramping and general discomfort.*
5 *Decrease in sex hormone production; loss of interest.*
6 *Release of sugar into bloodstream with an increase in insulin levels to metabolize; elevated blood sugar levels.*
7 *Cholesterol increase in blood mainly from liver.*
8 *Accelerated heart beat; increase in blood flow to lungs and muscles; high blood pressure.*
9 *Thickening of blood to help deliver oxygen throughout the body and to ward off infection; increase risk of heart attack and related problems.*
10 *Increase in sense acuity (e.g., pupils dilate, hearing acute); prolonged stress leads to errors in body's detection-sense system.*

Dr Peter Hanson, The Joy of Stress.

Psychological stress reactions

'Psychological stress' most commonly refers to your emotional reactions to the outside stressors you encounter; in particular, your feelings of *anxiety* (and panic), *anger* (and rage), and *depression*. Included within emotional reactions are feelings of apathy and alienation, feeling out of control, emotional exhaustion, lack of self-confidence, excessive guilt and moodiness.

'Psychological stress reactions' may also include disturbances in your ability to think clearly. You may lose concentration easily, fail to remember important details, be mentally confused and indecisive, and lose your capacity to solve problems easily.

Indeed, as will be discussed in detail later on, human beings have a tendency—especially when confronted with psychological stressors which threaten our ego—to be irrational in our thinking. We are apt to magnify events out of proportion, selectively focus on the negative aspects of the situation, make predictions and draw conclusions in the absence of hard or contradictory evidence, and irrationally evaluate the significance of certain stressful events in ways that create more intense and negative emotional reactions than the situation warrants. In addition, teachers under extreme stress may develop negative and cynical attitudes towards students, other school staff and parents.

You have probably found that when you feel extremely stressed about a person or event in your life that it is very difficult to think objectively about the situation and figure out the best thing to do to manage the outside threat or demand. The early part of this book is directed at teaching you emotional 'survival' or self-management skills so that you become less emotionally stressed about an aspect or aspects of your teaching and are able to think more constructively about the problems around you.

Bill Witherspoon experienced a full range of psychological reactions to the events which he encountered on his way to teach his science class.

'I feel absolutely furious with my coordinator for embarrassing me in front of my class. He should know better! What an ass! Showing up for my next class is a big worry. What if my students behave badly? And worse, what if my coordinator finds out! This is really awful! I wasn't so hopeless, I would be better organised and have a stronger approach in my discipline. I should know better. I'm really a born loser! Teaching is too hard for me... I'd be in better off shining shoes.'

It is not uncommon for a stressed teacher to experience a range of different emotional reactions. Here, Bill is angry with his coordinator (and himself), worried about what the future might bring, overly frustrated with the demands of teaching and, all around, down on himself. In his state of emotional turmoil, is it any wonder that he is worried about how he is going to cope the next time? One of the goals of this book is to show you methods for reducing extremely intense emotional stress reactions so that you can be in better charge of yourself and your teaching situation.

Studies which have examined the effects of teacher anxiety on students have found that high anxiety teachers have more disruptive students than low anxiety teachers. These students have also been found to have low achievement. There is a positive relationship between teacher anxiety and student anxiety.

Behavioral stress reactions

Certain teaching stressors can have a detrimental effect on your behavior. For example, research shows that teachers who experience high anxiety suffer a deterioration in teaching performance. High teacher anxiety has been found to be related to low verbal support of students, hostile speech and behavior, low teacher warmth in relating to students, ineffective use of rewards and punishment, and dogmatic and authoritarian behavior. Other behavioral consequences of teacher stress include absenteeism, tardiness, turnover and use of alcohol and drugs.

When confronted with stressors people typically react with one of two behaviours: 'direct action' and 'inactive' methods. Direct action methods involve you in actively doing something to modify the stressors or in dealing with your own emotional stress reaction. An example of direct action methods would be using one of your coping skills (e.g., assertion, classroom management) to modify the stressor. Direct action methods for coping with excess emotional stress reactions when you haven't been able to neutralise the outside stressor include seeking support, relaxation, exercise, and modifying your attitude towards the stressor.

Inactive methods involve you doing very little to take control of the situation or your emotional reactions. Commonly, you might simply ignore the situation and resort to alcohol or food to combat bad feelings. Research is pretty clear in pointing to direct action as the method which can minimise the effects of the stressor as well as helping you maintain good physical and mental health.

Your behavioural stress reactions can also be differentiated in terms of whether you tend to employ aggressive, submissive or assertive behaviours. Once again it is possible to identify assertive behaviour as an interpersonal style which will minimise the effects of stress.

Burnout

A condition resulting from high and sustained levels of stress has been referred to by Freudenberger in 1974 as *burnout*. Burnout has been applied to persons working in the helping professions and is described as emotional and mental exhaustion caused by excessive emotional and psychological demands.

'Burnout involves a change in attitudes and behaviour in response to a demanding, frustrating, unrewarding work experience...a form of adaptation to stress.'
C. Cherniss, **Professional Burnout in Human Service Organizations.**

Basically, burnout refers to a combination of negative symptoms resulting from job stress. Terms used to describe the condition include irritability, fatigue, emotional exhaustion, detachment, apathy, cynicism, rigidity, loss of idealism, loss of sympathy, loss of trust, loss of commitment, and negative self-evaluations. Maslach and Jackson, who developed the Maslach Burnout Inventory, identified three components of burnout: *emotional and physical exhaustion* brought about by the high psychological demands placed on human service providers; *depersonalisation* which they characterise as cynicism towards clients brought about by poor working conditions; and *low personal accomplishment* which encompasses negative self-evaluations with regard to the work with clients.

Burnout is not something you either have or do not have. Rather, it can be represented on a continuum of intensity ranging from mild to severe burnout. Given the high and constant level of arousal required to perform throughout each day teachers are especially vulnerable to burnout. While teacher stress and teacher burnout are not synonymous, recent research has found that teachers who experienced teacher stress also reported greater burnout.

MY OWN RESEARCH

Over the past five years I have been involved in researching teacher stress. In particular, I have tried to identify those outside environmental factors and factors within teachers which are most closely associated with teacher stress. Let me briefly summarise the results of three of these studies.

1987 study

The first study I conducted was designed to examine the relationship between teacher stress and teacher attitudes. I developed the Teacher Irrational Belief Scale which measured the extent to which teachers a) put themselves down (self-depreciation) when in their judgement they didn't perform up to their own or others' professional standards; b) held authoritarian attitudes towards classroom discipline and student behaviour; c) held unrealistic expectations concerning the ways in which school organisations operate in terms of consultation and communication; d) held attitudes associated with low tolerance of work frustrations. This scale appears in Chapter 2. I was also interested in determining which teaching stressors teachers found most stressful. Some 792 male and female teachers from a wide variety of Victorian primary and secondary, state, denominational, non-denominational and technical schools filled out questionnaires.

The teaching stressors which this sample of teachers found stressful, in order of most to least stressful, were: time and workload pressures; classroom management pressures; student learning/emotional problems; problems with school administration.

I also found a moderately strong relationship between teacher attitude and teacher stress. The greater the extent to which teachers put themselves down, were authoritarian, unrealistic in their expectations of the ways school operate, and had relatively low tolerance for the frustrations of work, the greater their teacher stress.

1988 study

I conducted a two-phase study in 1988. Phase 1 examined the relative importance of teacher attitudes and coping skills (classroom discipline, time management, relaxation, communication, assertion, emotional control, overall teaching) in teacher stress. Phase 2 compared the attitudes and coping skills of a group of twenty-six teachers who had retired from teaching because of teacher stress with the attitudes and coping skills of a representative group of teachers.

The results of the first phase of the study, which involved 140 male and female teachers across the full spectrum of Victorian schools, are as follows. In terms of work problems found stressful, the order from most to least stressful of problems was: time and workload pressures; classroom management problems; lack of student motivation/interest; problems with school administration; poor student academic performance; helping students with special needs; changes.

Both teacher attitudes and coping skills correlated with teacher stress. Of particular interest was the finding that teacher attitudes were more closely associated with teacher stress than were coping skills.

In the second phase of the 1988 study, teachers who had recently retired from teaching rated themselves lower than teachers in general on the following coping skills (in order of greatest difference): emotional control, relaxation, assertion, time management and communication. No differences were found in self-rated coping skills between the two groups of teachers on overall teaching skills and classroom discipline skills. On the Teacher Irrational Belief Scale, the group of highly stressed retired teachers more strongly endorsed self-downing and low frustration tolerance attitudes than the sample of regular teachers. Attitudes towards classroom control and to school organisations did not differ.

The results of the 1987 and 1988 studies suggested to me that it was possible to identify some key attitudes which seem to be present in very stressed teachers and which were not held as strongly by non-stressed teachers. In particular, the tendency to depreciate oneself and to be less tolerant of work frustrations was significant. Given that these attitudes are known to be associated with emotional distress, it was not surprising that the group of highly stressed teachers also lacked emotional control and relaxation skills. Self-downing and low frustration tolerance attitudes appeared to be those aspects of teacher attitudes which turned teacher stress into distress. Authoritarian attitudes and unrealistic attitudes towards the ways in which school organisations operate were associated with stress but they did not separate those teachers who retired from teaching because of stress from those who were stressed but were still teaching.

These results also suggested to me that teacher stress programs which are designed to help the individual cope with stress had better place as much emphasis if not more on attitude change and emotional control techniques as on coping skills such as time management and communication skills. This book is organised to take into account these findings.

1989 study

In a study I undertook of over 400 teachers in Victoria and Western Australia, I broadened my scope to examine the range of factors in the environment (general life stress, school organisational stressors, classroom stressors, social support) and within the individual teacher (attitudes, lifestyle, coping skills) which my own and others' research had found to be associated with teacher stress. I was particularly interested in seeing if I could determine whether it was outside factors or inside factors or a combination which were most closely associated with teacher stress. The results from male and female primary and secondary teachers in a range of schools who completed a 110-item questionnaire are as follows.

In terms of this sample of teachers, 26 per cent reported to be 'very' or 'extremely' stressed, 32 per cent reported being 'somewhat' stressed, and 42 per cent reported being either 'a little' or 'not at all' stressed.

Eight of the problems they found most stressful from a list of over thirty stressors were: inadequate salary; disruptive classroom behaviour; school workload pressures; media/community criticism; policy changes; extremes of temperature in classroom; workload pressures outside of school; financial problems.

In terms of the factors associated with teacher stress, the results showed a combination of outside and inside factors were associated with teacher stress. In terms of outside factors, organisational stressors and classroom stressors were associated with teacher stress. General life stressors and social support were not. In terms of inside factors, teacher attitudes were also associated with teacher stress. Lifestyle was not. The relationship of coping skills was somewhat inconclusive, being associated with one measure of teacher stress and not another.

I also examined factors associated with teachers' self-ratings of 'general life stress'. Outside and inside factors associated with life stress in order of importance were: total number of organisational stressors, teacher attitudes, total number of outside stressors, total number of classroom stressors and lifestyle. Support and coping skills were not found to be at all associated with general life stress.

The results of the 1989 study along with the previous two confirmed the validity of the transactional model of teacher stress I proposed earlier. In a nutshell, the greater number of teaching stressors the greater the teacher stress. The problems teachers viewed as most stressful are consistent with my earlier studies; namely, time-workload pressures, classroom discipline and policy changes. As well, the attitudes which teachers hold about themselves, students, their work and their organisation also mediate stress. While I have placed great emphasis in this guide on what individuals can do to modify their own stress as well as on how they can profit from others' support, I am aware that improvement in the ways schools are administered and organised are also likely to lead to a drop in teacher stress. For example, schools which have undertaken to develop well-articulated and implemented discipline plans report lower teacher stress levels. The last chapter considers ways in which the organisation affects teacher stress and offers suggestions as to how it can modify the way it operates in order to reduce teacher stress.

My own and other recent research has failed to find the presumed link between social support and coping skills and teacher stress. As almost all research in the area of teacher stress is based on self-report data, and as measuring instruments abound with the problem of whether they are validly measuring what they purport to be measuring, I continue to believe that these two factors are involved in teacher stress. It is up to researchers to find the right methods for accurately measuring the effects of support and coping.

STRESS MANAGEMENT

Over the past two decades, mental health practitioners have developed and adapted a large variety of techniques, which if employed effectively can reduce your stress. The techniques vary in terms of whether they are designed to affect physiological stress (e.g., relaxation, exercise), psychological stress, (e.g., rational thinking skills, attitude change) or behavioural reactions (e.g., assertiveness, classroom management techniques).

In my 1989 study described above, I asked teachers to indicate their knowledge of common stress management techniques, how frequently they used these techniques and their relative effectiveness. In order from greatest to least knowledge, teachers rated the different stress management techniques as follows: diet/nutrition; classroom discipline; exercise; rational thinking; time management; assertion; relaxation.

Teachers were then asked to indicate how often they used common stress management techniques. The results for frequency of use from most to least often are as follows: classroom discipline; diet/nutrition; rational thinking; time management; exercise; assertion; relaxation; meditation.

When teachers were asked to indicate the effectiveness of common stress management techniques the following results from most to least effective were obtained: classroom discipline; diet/ nutrition; exercise; rational thinking; time management; assertion; relaxation; meditation.

These results suggest that the more popular and effective stress management techniques for teachers are classroom management skills followed by good diet, exercise and rational thinking. Assertion and time management are somewhat down the list with relaxation and meditation the least preferred and effective methods.

I also asked teachers informally to write down those things they do which are helpful in coping with stress. Their answers can be loosely grouped in five categories.

Lifestyle

'Relax with a cup of tea.'
'Listen to music.'
'Do something totally different, e.g., play sports, cards.'
'Spending time away from home.'
'Gardening.'
'Courses in personal interests.'
'Shopping for clothes.'
'Painting.'
'Hobbies.'

'Recreation and relaxation: music, art, paint and draw.'
'Being by myself.'
'Playing sport.'
'Attempt not to take work home with me.'
'Go for long walks.'
'Take time out for myself.'
'Have complete quiet times, e.g., reading, games and music.'
'Yoga.'
'Working with animals.'

Coping skills

'Try new discipline techniques.'
'Firmness in class.'
'Setting short-term goals.'
'Avoiding negative people.'
'Advance planning.'

'Writing down priorities— sorting things out on paper.'
'Writing lists and crossing off what I've done.'
'Being time efficient.'
'Speak my mind.'

Support

'Support from your colleagues.'
'Talk to my spouse.'
'Talk to friends.'

'Use of educational psychologist for assistance.'
'Simply talking about the

'Help from staff.'

thing which is stressful helps.'

Attitude

'Positive outlook on life.'

'Self-talk; in my mind talk myself through a stressful situation.'

'Believing in myself.'

'Being positive.'

'Positive self-image.'

Palliative

'A few beers.'

'Distract myself from the situation.'

'Sex.'

'Take Panadol.'

'Doing nothing.'

It is clear that individual teachers vary enormously on their preferred mode of dealing with stress and which one works the best. For example, I know a number of teachers who find relaxation extremely effective. Others find a more active approach such as playing sport stress relieving. The key for you is to keep an open mind until you find out what works best for you. And to start the process of being actively involved in the management of stress.

Your own motivation is vital in determining the extent to which you can modify teacher stress. This is because it is only when you use a particular stress management technique effectively that it begins to work and to use it effectively requires practice and effort.

Regardless of how onerous your teaching circumstances, to harness and control teacher stress you have to have the motivation to take charge and approach the task whole-heartedly. If you find yourself still blaming and condemning your school and class for your stress and only 'lightly' learn the techniques presented in this and other stress management books, your chance of making your work better will be greatly reduced. *The procedures reviewed in this book need to be practised until they become habits.*

Now you have a clearer understanding of what comprises teacher stress. Before turning to ways of reducing it, let's assess how stressed you are and identify some of the factors within your teaching which you find demanding.

RECOMMENDED READING

Jacqueline M. Atkinson, *Coping with Stress at Work* (Wellingborough: Northhamptonshire, Thorsons, 1988).

Audrey Livingstone Booth, *Stressmanship* (London: Severn House, 1985).

Audrey Livingstone Booth, *Less Stress More Success* (London: Severn House, 1988).

Edward A. Charlesworth and Ronald G. Nathan, *Stress Management* (New York: Ballantine Books, 1985).

Vernon Coleman, *Overcoming Stress* (London: Sheldon Press, 1988).

Cary Cooper, Rachel Cooper and Lynn Eaker, *Living with Stress* (London: Penguin, 1988).

Donald E. Demaray, *Watch Out for Burnout* (Grand Rapids: Michigan, Baker Borke House, 1983).

Michael Epstein and Sue Hosking, *Living with Stress Breakdown* (Melbourne: Matchbooks, 1989).

David Fontana, *Managing Stress* (London: Routledge, 1989).

Jeffrey W. Forman with Dave Myers, *The Personal Stress Reduction Program* (Englewood Cliffs: New Jersey, Prentice-Hall, 1987).

Meyer Friedman and Ray Rosenman, *Type A Behavior and Your Heart* (New York: Alfred A. Knopf, 1974).

C. Michele Haney and Edmond W. Boerisch, Jr., *Stressmap: Finding Your Pressure Points* (San Luis Obispo: Impact Publishers, 1987).

Peter Hanson, *The Joy of Stress* (London: Pan Books, 1987).

Alix Kirsta, *The Book of Stress Survival: How to Relax and Live Positively* (London: Gaia, 1986).

Samuel H. Klarreich, *The Stress Solution* (London: Cedar, 1989).

Edwin Knight, *Living with Stress* (Australia: Edward Arnold, 1987).

Joe Macdonald Wallace, *Stress: A Practical Guide to Coping* (Marborough, Wiltshire: The Crowood Press, 1988).

Ainslie Meares, *Life Without Stress* (Richmond, Vic.: Greenhouse, 1987).

John Message, *Dealing with Stress* (Sydney: Arrow, 1989).

Bob Montgomery, *Coping with Stress* (Carlton, Vic.: Pitman, 1982).

Bob Montgomery and Lynette Evans, *You and Stress* (Melb.: Nelson, 1984; Melb.: Penguin, 1989).

Avala Pines and Elliot Aronson, *Career Burnout: Causes and Cures* (New York: The Free Press, 1989).

Beverley Potter, *Beating Job Burnout* (Berkeley, CA: Ronin, 1985).

Ken Powell, *Stress in Your Life* (Wellingborough, Thorsons, 1988).

Hans Selye, *Stress Without Distress* (New York: Signet, 1975).

Hans Selye, *The Stress of Life* (New York: McGraw-Hill, 1978).

Harry Stanton, *The Stress Factor* (Sydney: Fontana, 1983).

Peter Tyer, *How to Cope with Stress* (London: Sheldon Press, 1980).
Robert L. Veninga and James Spradley, *The Work Stress Connection: How to Cope with Job Burnout* (New York: Ballantine Books, 1981).
William Wilkie, *Understanding Stress Breakdown* (Richmond Vic.: Greenhouse, 1985).

CHAPTER 2
SELF-ASSESSMENT OF TEACHER STRESS

'The first and most important step in managing stress and its harmful effects is recognising that it exists and that the individual is fully capable of managing it.'
Sheldon Greenberg,
Stress and the Teaching Profession, 1984.

It is not always easy to know when you are actually experiencing stress. One of the reasons is that the signs and symptoms are often, especially in their milder forms, subtle. The everyday strain experienced as a result of teaching is something you most probably accept as normal. Sometimes it is only when you reach the more advanced stages of stress, such as is commonly experienced towards the end of a teaching term, that you may notice you are not feeling your normal (strained) self.

Stress is also hard to detect because your body and mind can absorb and sustain a lot of stress without you being consciously aware of it. You might be able to work for extended hours during the day, on weekends, for weeks on end without being aware of how stressed you are. It is only when you start yelling at your loved ones or drinking excessively to reduce your discomforts that stress is apparent. And drinking and its after-effects can distract you from the signs that you are under stress. Furthermore, many of your physiological reactions to stress are not detectable. It is, for example, impossible to notice directly your elevated cortisone levels. You may, however, become aware of the effects of sustained high levels of cortisone and the weakening of your immunity system as you experience colds, infections and allergy reactions.

Another reason stress is sometimes hard to detect is that you may not label physical, psychological and behavioural manifestations of stress, such as exhaustion, anxiety or aggression, as such. You might think of yourself, 'Gee, I feel crummy...have a sore throat...feel rundown...I need a break', but not draw the conclusion that you are experiencing excess stress or distress. I'm not saying that all unhealthy bodily and psychological reactions are related to stress. You can strain your back while gardening and experience the 'blues' because of events which have nothing to do with teaching. However, research and experience clearly shows that ill health and injury are far more likely to occur when you are under sustained and negative job demands and threats.

One final point about the difficulty in evaluating your degree of stress. People experience stress in different ways. In thinking about your stress own reactions and manifestations, consider your dominant 'stress zone'. Sometimes called your 'weak link', it appears that each of us has a psychological and physical area which seems to bear the brunt of stress. It is the area which seems to 'break down' soonest when under extreme stress. Some of the major physical systems which respond differently to stress in different people include the cardiovascular system (heartrate, headaches), respiratory system (breathing), gastrointestinal (stomach) and immune system (allergy, lowered immunity). Similarly, everyone's psychological reactions to stress are different. While some experience depression, others find themselves getting quite angry. It is impossible to provide a small, concise list of the 'definitive' stress symptoms. They vary enormously in number and kind.

It's pretty clear that the beginning point to taking charge of your stress is to become aware of your typical stress reactions and the stress factors in your life as well as things about yourself which contribute to your stress. The model of teacher stress presented earlier will guide your self-evaluation process.

SELF-EXAMINATION OF STRESS REACTIONS

Let's begin by having a look at the ways in which you react to demands and threats at work. As indicated in the model of teacher stress, it is possible to separate three interrelated yet distinct types of stress reaction: physiological (physical), psychological and behavioural.

Common physical stress reactions

Clues to when you are physiologically stressed and the degree of stress you are experiencing are your physical symptoms. See the lists below for the symptoms you most commonly experience and also try to identify the system (or systems) which seem to be your weak link.

Cardiovascular

heart pounding	erratic heart beat
cold, sweaty hands	headaches (throbbing pain)
high blood pressure	dizziness
heart racing	palpitations

Respiratory

rapid erratic or shallow breathing	shortness of breath
	asthma attack
difficulty in breathing because of poor breath control	

Gastrointestinal

upset stomach, nausea, vomitting, cramps	constipation
	diarrhoea
sharp abdominal pains	

Muscular

headaches (steady pain)	nervous tics
back, neck, shoulder, chest pains	frowning
	stuttering
arthritis	grinding, clenching teeth

muscular tremors, hand shaking	jaw pain finger or foot tapping

Skin

acne	dandruff
perspiration	excessive dryness skin/hair

Immunity

allergy flare-up	skin rash
catching colds	low grade infections
general, lowered immunity	hives
catching the flu	

Metabolic

increased appetite	thoughts racing
increased craving for tobacco or sweats	difficulty sleeping
feeling of increased anxiety or nervousness	

Endocrine

diabetes	menstrual problems
thyroid difficulties	arthritic pain

Recognising your physical symptoms on these lists and other lists will better prepare you to detect the early warning signs and take some disaster prevention action. For example, I noticed on the way to the bank that I was frowning as I tend to do when I'm thinking about what I'm about to write. I massaged my temples, stopped frowning, took a few slow, deep breaths and felt better.

An additional awareness worth gaining is to monitor how often you experience stress reactions relative to other people. If you experience stress symptoms more often than others, it can be said you are under more stress than others. By completing the inventory below, you will get a sense of whether your experience of common physical stress re-actions is average, above average, or below average relative to teachers in general.

Inventory of Common Physical Stress Reactions

Directions: Indicate *how often* you have experienced the following symptoms over the past teaching year.

	Not at all	A little	Some-times	Very often	Extremely often
1 Arriving at school physically exhausted	1	2	3	4	5
2 Arriving at school with a physical ailment (cold, sore throat, allergy flare up)	1	2	3	4	5
3 Arriving at school with muscular-skeletal pain (backache, neck or shoulder)	1	2	3	4	5
4 Having trouble sleeping at night	1	2	3	4	5
5 Having a headache sometime during the day	1	2	3	4	5
				Total score	_____

Now compare your scores on individual symptoms and your total score to see how the frequency of your stress reactions compares with the general population of teachers.

	Average score
1 Physically exhausted	2.41
2 Physical ailment	2.58
3 Muscular-skeletal problems	2.15
4 Trouble sleeping	2.32
5 Headaches	2.18
Total symptom score	11.64

If your scores are higher than the average range on one or more symptoms or for the total list of symptoms, then the frequency of your physical stress reactions is higher than it is for the general population of teachers.

Common psychological stress reactions

Along with physical stress symptoms, you will also experience psychological stress symptoms when confronting stressors both inside and outside of teaching. As indicated earlier, psychological symptoms are your feelings about what's going on in your life. Additionally, your cognitive (mental) activity and thought processes can be negatively influenced when the stressors in your life are many and especially when they have endured for some time. Have a look at the list of psychological symptoms below and see if you can recognise those which you experience when under extreme stress.

Emotional symptoms of stress

extreme anxiety or panic lasting more than a few days

explosive anger in response to minor irritations

feelings of doubt, poor confidence, insecurity, and depression

feeling not able to cope

not feeling in control

frequent or prolonged feelings of boredom

feeling desperate

feeling tired, listless and emotionally exhausted

Cognitive symptoms of stress

poor memory and forgetfulness

poor concentration

poor problem-solving ability

indecisiveness

mental confusion

irrational thinking

negative self-image

racing thoughts

difficulty falling and staying asleep

Emotional and cognitive stress reactions go hand in hand. The more upset you get, the more your thinking goes down the drain—and the more likely your behaviour will suffer. Remember Bill Witherspoon? The more he found himself getting upset with his predicament the less he was able to focus on his disruptive class and think of ways to gain control over his class. The result? He virtually gave up trying.

This time, complete the Inventory of Common Emotional Stress Reactions to see how your emotional reactions to stress compare with others.

Inventory of Common Emotional Stress Reactions

Directions: Indicate *how often* you have experienced the following stress symptoms over the past teaching year.

	Not at all	A little	Some-times	Very often	Extremely often
1 Arriving at school with the feeling that things are out of control	1	2	3	4	5
2 Arriving at school with extreme feeling of anxiety	1	2	3	4	5
3 Arriving at school with extreme feelings of anger	1	2	3	4	5
4 Arriving at school feeling depressed	1	2	3	4	5
5 Feeling emotionally drained from your work	1	2	3	4	5

Total score _____

Once again, you can compare the frequency of your common emotional stress reactions with the frequency of the general population of teachers.

	Average score
1 Feeling out of control	1.79
2 Feelings of extreme anxiety	1.96
3 Extreme feelings of anger	1.66

4 Feeling depressed	2.19
5 Feeling emotionally drained	2.82
Total stress score	10.42

This book will offer you some extremely effective techniques for managing emotional stress.

Common behavioural stress reactions

Now let's have a look at a few common behavioural patterns we observe in people under stress. See if you can recognise your typical pattern of reacting when you get towards the end of your stress tether.

rushed speech
withdrawal, non-assertion
yelling
throwing things
hitting someone
overactivity
procrastination
sleeping more than usual
increase in alcohol or drug
  consumption

lack of drive
disorganisation and
  untidiness
poor use of discipline
  techniques
authoritarian approach to
  students
little encouragement to
  students
absenteeism
tardiness

This list of behavioural stress reactions is somewhat short. The reason is because the variety of specific behavioural stress reactions are literally endless. For example, Bill spent ten minutes saying nothing to his class, hoping they would quiet down, and then two minutes lecturing and threatening them. During his one free period of the day, rather than finish the mid-year science exam he read the sporting pages of the newspaper and ate two chocolate bars. You will have an opportunity later on to do a more thorough self-examination of your behavioural approach when you are under stress.

Hopefully you will now have a clearer idea about your own typical stress reactions and how they compare with those of teachers in general. If you know that you have been or are under a great deal of stress and your scores on the above inventories fail to show that you fall in the above average range, remember that each individual experiences stress in a unique way. For example, your experience of teacher stress may be characterised by your simply not caring, rather than by specific emotional or physical symptoms. The following two sections may hold further insights for you into the nature of your teacher stress.

SELF-EXAMINATION OF TEACHER STRESS

Many of the general symptoms of stress just discussed can arise both from stressors at work, such as demands in teaching, and in the rest of your life. The experience of the emotional exhaustion of caring for children at home or anxiety about meeting monthly mortgage repayments is similar to emotional stress reactions encountered when handling a group of students in the classroom or when your students' end-of-term results are not what you expected. This section and the next examine events you may find particularly stressful at work. They will enable you to identify some of the demands and threats which perhaps contribute to your being dissatisfied or distressed with your work. You will also be able to compare your level of stress in response to events at work with the stress levels of teachers in general.

The quickest way to assess your degree of stress and how it compares is simply to answer the following question.

'Over the past teaching year, how stressful have you found teaching?'

1	2	3	4	5
Not at all stresstul	A little stressful	Somewhat stressful	Very stressful	Extremely stressful

Over the past three years, I have posed this question in written form to over 2000 teachers. Approximately 20–25 per cent indicate they find teaching very to extremely stressful, around 33 per cent indicate they find teaching somewhat stressful while 45 per cent indicate they are not at all or a little stressed. But although this simple question may indicate how stressful you find teaching relative to other teachers, it doesn't provide you with any real insight into what is it about teaching that you find particularly stressful.

Your teacher stress profile

The model of teacher stress presented earlier suggested a number of different stressors in the educational environment which contribute to teacher stress including: policies and actions of the Department of Education; workload pressures; administrative leadership; work relationships; classroom stressors; community attitudes; availability and quality of support. The inventories which follow will help you identify clearly the particular stressors at work which you find stressful, the degree of stress you experience and how your stress level compares with other teachers.

Inventory of Teaching Stressors

Directions: The following areas of teaching are recognised as being potentially stressful. Please indicate by circling the right number *how often* these events problems have occurred during the past or present teaching year and *how stressful* you have found them.

To indicate *how often* the stressors occur: circle 1 for 'not at all'; circle 2 for 'a little'; circle 3 for 'sometimes'; circle 4 for 'very often'; circle 5 for 'extremely often'.

To indicate *how stressful* you have found the stressors: circle 1 for 'not at all stressful'; circle 2 for 'a little'; circle 3 for 'somewhat'; circle 4 for 'very'; circle 5 for 'extremely stressful'.

How often   How stressful?
Never . . . extremely often   Not at all . . . extremely

How often	*Ministry of Education stressors*	*How stressful*
1 2 3 4 5	1 Ministry policy changes	1 2 3 4 5
	2 Teachers expected to implement policies to	

47

How often						How stressful				
1	2	3	4	5	ministry	1	2	3	4	5
					3 Teachers unable to change the direction of					
1	2	3	4	5	policies	1	2	3	4	5
					4 Large amount and high rate of change expected					
1	2	3	4	5	of teachers and schools	1	2	3	4	5
1	2	3	4	5	5 Inadequate salary	1	2	3	4	5

Total frequency of stressors score _____
(*Average score: 15.70*)

Total stress score _____
(*Average score: 14.64*)

How often					*Workload stressors*	*How stressful*				
					6 Role overload (teacher, committee work,					
1	2	3	4	5	administration)	1	2	3	4	5
					7 Demands on time before, during and after school to					
1	2	3	4	5	attend meetings	1	2	3	4	5
					8 Too many things to do (records, interviews,					
1	2	3	4	5	preparation)	1	2	3	4	5
					9 Work tasks interfering					
1	2	3	4	5	with personal time	1	2	3	4	5
					10 Little or no relief time					
1	2	3	4	5	from daily teaching	1	2	3	4	5

Total frequency of stressors score _____
(*Average score: 14.77*)

Total stress score _____
(*Average score: 13.82*)

How often					*Administrative leadership stressors*	*How stressful*				
					11 School organisation acts in a conservative, inflexible and authoritarian way in					
1	2	3	4	5	response to new ideas	1	2	3	4	5
					12 Times when the morale of					
1	2	3	4	5	the school appears low	1	2	3	4	5
					13 Lack of opportunity for staff participation in					
1	2	3	4	5	school decision making	1	2	3	4	5

14 Poor communication be-
tween administration and
1 2 3 4 5   staff   1 2 3 4 5
15 Internal demands of your
school with little bearing
on your teaching
1 2 3 4 5   1 2 3 4 5
Total frequency of stressors   Total stress score _____
score _____   (*Average score: 11.74*)
(*Average score: 12.11*)

How often   *Work relationship*   *How stressful*
     stressors
16 Poor relationships with
colleagues (negativity,
1 2 3 4 5   criticism)   1 2 3 4 5
17 Relationship problems
with superiors
(personality clashes,
1 2 3 4 5   criticism)   1 2 3 4 5
18 Colleagues who act in
1 2 3 4 5   very unprofessional ways   1 2 3 4 5
19 'Cliquishness' among
1 2 3 4 5   colleagues   1 2 3 4 5
20 Lack of support from
1 2 3 4 5   colleagues   1 2 3 4 5
Total frequency of stressors   Total stress score _____
score _____   (*Average score: 10.93*)
(*Average score: 10.84*)

How often   *Classroom stressors*   *How stressful*
21 Disruptive classroom
1 2 3 4 5   behaviour   1 2 3 4 5
22 Poor facilities in
1 2 3 4 5   classroom   1 2 3 4 5
23 Unable to meet the needs
of an atypical child (non-
English speaking,
learning disabled, lower
1 2 3 4 5   ability)   1 2 3 4 5
1 2 3 4 5   24 Extremes of temperature   1 2 3 4 5

	25	Large number of students	
1 2 3 4 5		in your class	1 2 3 4 5

Total frequency of stressors
score _____
(*Average score: 13.71*)

Total stress score _____
(*Average score: 13.26*)

How often		*Community stressors*	*How stressful*
	26	Criticism of the teaching	
1 2 3 4 5		profession by the media	1 2 3 4 5
	27	Members of the community being unsympathetic to	
1 2 3 4 5		teachers	1 2 3 4 5
	28	A clash between values held by teachers and those held by parents or members of the	
1 2 3 4 5		community	1 2 3 4 5
	29	Parents who show little interest in the education	
1 2 3 4 5		of their child	1 2 3 4 5
	30	Parents who are too involved with the education	
1 2 3 4 5		of their child	1 2 3 4 5

Total frequency of stressors
score _____
(*Average score: 10.70*)

Total stress score _____
(*Average score: 10.54*)

It can be quite useful for you to compare both the total frequency of stressors and the amount of stress for the different categories of stressors you experience at school. You will be able to see which of the categories of stressors occur most frequently and which you find most stressful. On the graph on the following pages , enter the 'how often' and 'how stressful' total scores for each of the six categories of stressors. An example of Bill Witherspoon's Profile of Teaching Stressors is presented initially.

Bill Witherspoon's Profile of Teaching Stressors

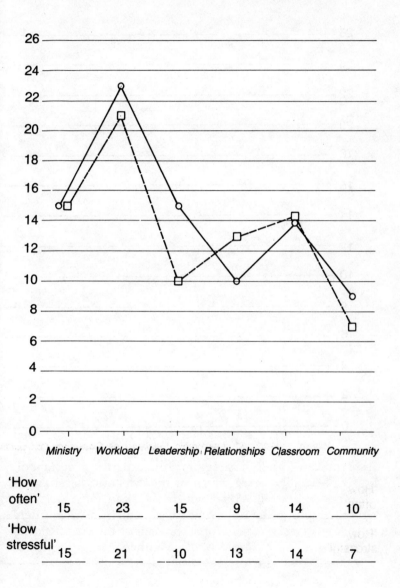

	Ministry	Workload	Leadership	Relationships	Classroom	Community
'How often'	15	23	15	9	14	10
'How stressful'	15	21	10	13	14	7

Your Profile of Teaching Stressors

	Ministry	Workload	Leadership	Relationships	Classroom	Community
'How often'						
'How stressful'						

Support

There is little question that when you have specific problems at work, such as not knowing the best way to handle a poorly behaving student or when you are feeling rather emotionally whacked, effective support can be a lifesaver. We know that schools whose senior administrators' management styles are supportive seem to be able to reduce significantly the stress of individual teachers. Conversely, non-supportive administrators can significantly add to your stress. Support from colleagues, students and your significant other can do much to dampen down your stress.

You might be interested in knowing how the amount and quality of support in your life compares with those of your fellow teachers. The following brief inventory will help shed some light on your support system.

Teacher Support Inventory

Directions: In question 1 below, you will be asked to answer *how often* you have supportive discussions and *how useful* you find them. In question 2, simply indicate *how often* certain people recognise the value of your work.

1 When things go wrong with you at school, *how often* have you discussed these issues with the following people over the past teaching year and *how useful* have you found the discussions?

How often		*How useful*
1 2 3 4 5	Principal	1 2 3 4 5
(*Average: 1.93*)		(*Average: 3.20*)
1 2 3 4 5	Colleagues	1 2 3 4 5
(*Average: 3.53*)		(*Average: 3.63*)
1 2 3 4 5	Social partner	1 2 3 4 5
(*Average: 3.39*)		(*Average: 3.43*)
Total frequency of		Total usefulness of discussions ____
Supportive discussions ____		(*Average: 10.26*)
(*Average: 8.85*)		

2 *How often* have the following people recognised your teaching and work effort as being useful or worthwhile over the past teaching year?

How often	Principal
1 2 3 4 5	
(*Average: 2.50*)	Students
1 2 3 4 5	
(*Average: 2.93*)	Colleagues
1 2 3 4 5	
(*Average: 2.94*)	

Total frequency of recognition ____
(*Average score: 8.37*)

More will be said on the type of support which can help reduce stress and the type which will not.

SELF-EXAMINATION OF YOUR INSIDE WORLD

A point made earlier is an important one to repeat. Human beings are not like blades of grass which sway and bend in proportion to the direction and amount of wind blowing. Each of us can make a difference in determining how 'stressed out' we are in response to stressors at work and in life. You have a choice about how much effort you will expend on *yourself* in order to minimise the negative effects of stress. Let's briefly examine the three different aspects which are involved in stress and which, if they are burdening you, you can do something about.

Attitudes

My research clearly shows that your attitudes towards yourself and your workload are closely linked with stress. Moreover, irrational attitudes are linked to poor coping skills and lifestyle as well as to limited knowledge, use and ineffectiveness of common stress management procedures. The inventory following will give you a quick 'check up from the neck up' on your teaching attitudes.

Teacher Irrational Belief Scale

Directions: Indicate the extent to which you agree or disagree with the following statements. Circle 1 for 'strongly disagree' (SD); Circle 2 for 'disagree' (D); Circle 3 for 'not sure' (NS); Circle 4 for 'agree' (A); Circle 5 for 'strongly agree' (SA)

Self-downing attitudes

	SD	D	NS	A	SA
1 I think I'm really inadequate when I don't get the approval or respect for what I do	1	2	3	4	5
2 The prospect of teaching a class I don't have good control over is more than I can take	1	2	3	4	5
3 I think I'm a failure when I haven't 'got through' to a student or class	1	2	3	4	5
4 I really should be able to solve all my students' problems perfectly	1	2	3	4	5
5 I should be able to succeed at all the important things I do at school	1	2	3	4	5
6 To make mistakes or perform poorly as a teacher is for me one of the worst things in the world	1	2	3	4	5
7 I feel totally hopeless when I don't get all my work done on time	1	2	3	4	5
8 I can't stand being criticised or thought badly of when I haven't finished something or done it properly	1	2	3	4	5

Total score _____

(*Average: 25*)

If your total score is above twenty-five, you are definitely at risk for excessive stress when you are confronted with lack of success, disapproval, criticism or lack of recognition.

Low frustration tolerance attitudes	SD	D	NS	A	SA
9 I find it too hard to balance my home and work demands	1	2	3	4	5
10 I shouldn't have to work so hard	1	2	3	4	5
11 Schools are really lousy places because they give teachers too much work and not enough time to do it	1	2	3	4	5
12 It's really bad to have to put in so many hours both inside and outside the classroom	1	2	3	4	5

Total score _____
(*Average: 11*)

Those teachers who cope best with too much work and not enough time to do it have a high tolerance of frustration. They seem to be able to put up with high levels of tension and discomfort associated with work overload. Other teachers find not being able to finish all that they set out to do unbearable, even when they know it is not humanly possible to get everything done on time and in the way that they think things should be done.

Attitudes to school organisation					
	SD	D	NS	A	SA
13 One of the things I find totally bad is the lack of communication between teachers and central administration	1	2	3	4	5
14 Teachers should be consulted about decisions	1	2	3	4	5
15 Schools really should attend more to teachers' problems and it is totally unfair when they don't	1	2	3	4	5
16 Without good teacher-administrator communication and support, schools are the very worst places to work	1	2	3	4	5
17 I can't stand it when I am not consulted about a decision which affects my teaching	1	2	3	4	5

Total score _____
(*Average: 18*)

If your score is higher than twenty-one, then there is a good chance that you will find stressors relating to policies and actions of the Ministry of Education as well as your own school organisation particularly stressful.

Authoritarian attitudes towards students

	SD	D	NS	A	SA
18 As a teacher, I should have the power to be able to make my students do what I want	1	2	3	4	5
19 Students should always be respectful, considerate and behave well	1	2	3	4	5
20 Students who constantly mis-behave are horrible and should be severely punished	1	2	3	4	5
21 I can't stand it when students misbehave	1	2	3	4	5
22 It's really awful to have to teach in a class where there are so many problems	1	2	3	4	5

Total score _____
(*Average: 14*)

If you score above fourteen and especially if you score higher than twenty, you will be 'at risk' for stress associated with poorly behaved students. You'll experience either extreme anger when they disrupt your class, high anxiety — especially if you scored above average in 'self-downing' — or both.

Ways of modifying stress-creating attitudes will be illustrated in Chapters 4 and 5. Specifically, you will see how reformulated attitudes can reduce the intensity of troubling emotional stress reactions.

Coping skills

Good coping skills can help to neutralise or manage stressors you encounter inside and outside the classroom. The inventory below will help you compare the strength of your different coping skills which are seen as important in managing teacher stress. You can compare your self-ratings with those of teachers in the general population.

Teacher Coping Skill Inventory

Directions: Indicate *how competent* you have been in using the following skills in your teaching over the past year. Circle 1 for 'poor'; Circle 2 for 'fair'; Circle 3 for 'good'; Circle 4 for 'very good'; Circle 5 for 'excellent'.

	P	F	G	VG	E
1 Classroom discipline skills	1	2	3	4	5
(*Average: 3.41*)					
2 Time management skills	1	2	3	4	5
(*Average: 3.18*)					
3 Relaxation skills	1	2	3	4	5
(*Average: 2.79*)					
4 Communication skills	1	2	3	4	5
(*Average : 3.36*)					
5 Assertion skills	1	2	3	4	5
(*Average: 3.19*)					
6 Emotional control skills	1	2	3	4	5
(*Average: 3.15*)					
7 Overall teaching skills	1	2	3	4	5
(*Average: 3.46*)					

Total coping skill score _____
(*Average total coping skill score: 22.51*)

This book will provide illustrations of how to use many of the above coping skills effectively.

Lifestyle

The third important aspect which has been shown time and again to be significant is lifestyle. You've probably heard ad nauseum that good recreational habits as well as exercise and diet can help innoculate you against stress. The research into stress is consistent on this point. Take the brief inventory below to see how your lifestyle compares with others.

There is no way of determining whether the 'average' lifestyle is sufficient to ward off the detrimental effects of stress. It may well be that you need an 'excellent' lifestyle for it to act as a buffer to stress.

Lifestyle Inventory

Directions: Rate the quality of the following areas of your life over the past teaching year (1 = poor, 2 = fair, 3 = good, 4 = very good, 5 = excellent).

	P	F	G	VG	E
1 Recreation	1	2	3	4	5
(*Average: 3.12*)					
2 Exercise	1	2	3	4	5
(*Average: 2.71*)					
3 Diet	1	2	3	4	5
(*Average: 3.16*)					
Total lifestyle score _____					
(*Average: 8.99*)					

GENERAL LIFE STRESS

The stress you experience as a teacher is not isolated from the stress you might bring to teaching from other areas of your life. My own research shows the correlation of teaching stress with general life stress apart from teaching to be fairly high (.65). If you are stressed from events outside your teaching, such as when you have relationship or financial hassles, it is much harder to cope with the stressors of teaching. The inventory following will enable you to examine stresses outside of teaching.

Inventory of General Life Stressors

Directions: The following areas of life are recognised as being potentially stressful. Please indicate by circling the right number *how often* these events or problems have occurred during the past or present teaching year and *how stressful* you found them. (Circle 1 if the question doesn't apply to you.)

To indicate *how often* the stressors occurred, circle 1 for 'never', circle 2 for 'a little', circle 3 for 'sometimes', circle 4 for 'very often', circle 5 for 'extremely often'.

To indicate *how stressful* you have found them, circle 1 for 'not at all', circle 2 for 'a little', circle 3 for 'somewhat', circle 4 for 'very', circle 5 for 'extremely stressful'.

How often		*How stressful*
1 2 3 4 5	1 Time-workload pressures outside of school (home, community demands)	1 2 3 4 5
1 2 3 4 5	2 Relationship problems with significant other	1 2 3 4 5
1 2 3 4 5	3 Problems with your children (educational, behavioural, emotional, vocational)	1 2 3 4 5
1 2 3 4 5	4 Wider family problems (conflicts, criticism, intrusion)	1 2 3 4 5
1 2 3 4 5	5 Further study	1 2 3 4 5
1 2 3 4 5	6 Financial problems	1 2 3 4 5
1 2 3 4 5	7 Health problems in your family	1 2 3 4 5
1 2 3 4 5	8 Inadequate salary	1 2 3 4 5
1 2 3 4 5	9 Heavy traffic on way to work	1 2 3 4 5

Total frequency of life stressors ＿＿＿＿   Total life stress ＿＿＿＿
(*Average: 18.94*)   (*Average: 18.48*)

Many of the techniques and ideas provided in this book which are geared to managing teacher stress can also be adapted to help manage your more general life stressors. There is no doubt that alleviating the stress from outside events will help you to respond in a positive way to your work.

ACTIONS SPEAK LOUDER THAN WORDS

If you are someone who likes to write things down, you might find this summary section a useful way of highlighting some of the major things you learned from your self-examination. Please add things to the summary which did not appear in previous sections but which now occur to you.

Stress reactions

My common physical stress reactions are:

1 _____ 2 _____

3 _____ 4 _____

My common psychological stress reactions are:

1 _____ 2 _____

3 _____ 4 _____

My common behavioural stress reactions are:

1 _____ 2 _____

3 _____ 4 _____

Work stressors

The things at work I find most stressful are:

1 _____ 2 _____

3 _____ 4 _____

5 _____ 6 _____

Support

The people who are not providing me with support and could be are:

1 _____ 2 _____

Inside world

My stress-creating attitudes areas are:

1 _____ 2 _____

3 _____ 4 _____

My weaker coping skills are:

1 _____ 2 _____

My stronger coping skills are:

1 _____ 2 _____

General life stressors

1 _____ 2 _____

RECOMMENDED READING

Martin Cole and Stephen Walker, Editors, *Teaching and Stress* (London:
Open University Press, 1989).
Sheldon F. Greenberg, *Stress and the Teaching Profession* (Paul H. Brooks
Publishing, 1984).
Rosemary Otto, *Teachers Under Stress* (Melbourne: Hill of Content,
1986).

CHAPTER 3
PERSONAL RESPONSIBILITY

'It is the act of an ill-instructed man to blame others for his own bad condition; it is the act of one who has begun to be instructed to lay blame on himself; and of one whose instruction is completed neither to blame another, nor himself.'
                    Epictetus, philosopher, second century A.D.

One of the most important questions to ask yourself in order to maximise your management of teacher stress is: 'Is there anything I can do to take control of this stressful situation?'. The most common response to this sort of question focuses on changing what it is that is helping to create the stress.

My own experience suggests that an equally important area to consider is your own emotional stress reactions. The answer to the question of what to control when stressed becomes 'I can take control of my own emotional stress reactions'. You see, when you gain control over your emotional reactions to stress then not only do the demands of work not appear so stressful but you are in a far better position to use your direct action coping skills to change the situation.

Seeing aspects of yourself which you can change in the face of a stressful event can be described as taking 'personal responsibility'. This means that when you are feeling down, anxious or furious about what's been happening at school as well as physically wornout, you look within yourself to determine whether there are things you can do to manage your psychological and physical stress reaction better. The three areas of personal resources which this book promotes as offering you relief from stress are attitude change, coping skill enhancement, and improved lifestyle. Let's examine more closely this pivotal concept of personal responsibility.

TAKING CHARGE OF STRESS

Mary charged into Bill's office breathing fire.

'I've had it up to my eyeballs with teaching. The kids in my class are real rude, snot-nose drop kicks. They make me so furious. You should have seen what your mate Mike Bloggs did today. He painted "Bill Witherspoon is an old duck" across the whiteboard. Can you believe it! And what's worse, on the classroom door he sprayed in bright pink "Mary is hairy"!! And to top the day off, I've just got a memo from the principal saying I've got to start to re-write my art curriculum to make it consistent with the new departmental guidelines. He hasn't even read my current curriculum to know if it needs to be revised at all. Where's the aspirin? I've got a splitting headache.'

Bill had little energy to be of any support to Mary. 'Calm down or you'll cork it before you're thirty-five,' replied Bill weakly. 'Let me tell you what sort of a day I've had.'

After hearing Bill's long list of hassles, Mary became even more indignant. 'This school stinks! They should be more considerate and consult with us, not just inform us of decisions. I'm off to the principal's office to give him a piece of my mind.'

'Hey, stop! The only thing you'll accomplish in your current frame of mind is getting the principal totally "anti-you". Here, have one of these', offering Mary his last Snickers chocolate. 'You don't know how lucky you are, I just saved your life.'

In the illustration above, Mary's thought is focused on changing Mike Bloggs' behaviour as well as getting her principal to change his style of making and communicating decisions. And if Mary can get Mike and her principal to change their behaviour, her stress will be lessened. As discussed earlier, direct action coping skills which focus on managing your work situation better are definite answers to the question above how to go about taking control of stress at work.

If somehow she can learn not to get so furious when she is confronted with rude student behaviour and an inconsiderate bureaucracy then not only will these events appear to her to be less stressful but her ability to change her students' and principal's behaviour will improve.

A point which can be debated is whether your response of stress is caused by stress stimuli in your teaching environment. You've heard, no doubt, of stimulus-response learning. Something happens to you which causes you to react in a certain way. While I think that this simple stimulus-response model is adequate to describe why pigeons peck for pellets and mice run down mazes for cheese, it does not appear to me to hold much value in explaining stress reactions in human beings. As you'll see in a minute, something occurs inside humans between the time the stimulus occurs (e.g., Mike Bloggs painting on the artroom door) and the response (e.g., Mary's fury). The something is located between the ears.

Imagine that you are sitting around with a group of your colleagues in a staff meeting discussing stress at your school. Someone says: 'What really gets to me, really gets me angry, is when a student just sits in class daydreaming, not working and not showing any interest. The other students notice and it seems to slow them down.' If we took your colleague's stress temperature in response to 'non-motivated' students he might come up well above 90 per cent stressed. If we polled others on your staff, what do you think the result would be? When I conduct this poll as I have done many times, I find an enormous amount of variation in stress reactions. Some teachers hardly seem to get stressed by non-motivated students, most get moderately stressed, while a few get quite stressed out about it. And further, the type of emotional stress reaction can vary quite a bit. Some of the highly stressed teachers feel furious while others are more down and very worried about it.

The point to be made here is that there are wide differences in the way your colleagues react to the same stressful event. Why? Some might think it has to do with bio-rhythms, political preferences or what people eat for breakfast. A common explanation given is that teachers have different experiences. My response is that it is how you think about what goes on at work that largely determines how stressed you are about it. Your thinking is of course influenced by many events including past experience. However, it seems to me that no matter what has happened to your colleagues previous to confronting one or more students not working, their different stress reactions to the same event will depend on their perception, interpretation and evaluation of the event.

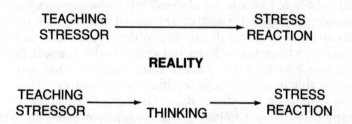

This view is not a new one. Epictetus, a Stoic-Roman philosopher, wrote that 'People are not affected by events, but by the view they take of events'. Shakespeare's observed that 'Things are neither good or bad but thinking makes them so'. In current times, Albert Ellis, the founder of rational-emotive therapy (RET), has written extensively on the topic as have the authors of the many self-help psychology books which have mushroomed in number over the past decade.

The idea that your thinking exerts a large influence over the type and intensity of your stress reactions is an important one. It is the beginning insight to taking control of stress and assuming personal responsibility. You see, it is possible to learn how to change your thinking so that you take control of your emotional stress reactions. This is a powerful tool to use, though it takes a bit of practice.

I'm not saying that what's going on in your school and classroom isn't important in understanding why you're stressed. Of course, the greater and more demanding or threatening your circumstances are at school, the greater the likelihood is that you'll be stressed. However, I am totally convinced that how stressed you become is partly determined by you.

If you want to feel less stressed as a teacher (and in life generally), the first step is to stop blaming the outside world for your stress. By blaming others, you remove any power you have to take control of your stress. You have to rely on the outside world to change before you can change and that might take some time! Mary might say: 'But you really don't understand. The reason I'm so stressed is that I've got the world's worst principal and a class of gorillas. They *make me* so upset.' It may seem that way to Mary, but it is literally impossible for you to be stressed until you produce stress-creating thoughts. Of course, the easiest way for you to feel less stressed is to transfer to one of the 'better' schools with students who want to learn and parents who support them. But you may honestly want to teach 'hard to teach' kids or not be able to change your teaching circumstances.

A colleague of mine, Russ Grieger, explains personal responsibility by employing the concepts of *being at effect* and *being at cause*. He explains *being at effect* as the attitude of a person who believes that one's destiny, well being and behaviour are controlled by circumstances in one's life including one's environment and psychological state. Grieger describes the thought process as sounding something like:

'What happens to me in life, my happiness, my goals being met, even what I do, are dependent on the circumstances of my life working out. If the outside world co-operates, and if my mood holds up, but only if, I can stick to a course of action, act responsibly, and, then, hopefully, have things turn out.'

Being at cause is equal to personal responsibility. It is embodied by an attitude which places you at the centre of your universe, largely in control and responsible for the choices you make in life, and, importantly, the stress you experience in response to certain events. According to Grieger this empowering attitudes sounds something like:

'No one or no thing is put on this earth to make my life work. While circumstances sometimes do thwart me and overwhelm me, I accept the responsibility for and commit myself to giving myself the best life I can regardless of the circumstances. Furthermore, I can make choices about my emotional reactions to the situation I face even if I can't change the situations themselves. I refuse to see myself as a victim of circumstances even though now or in the future I may be victimised.'

I think you'll find it easy to predict how these very different attitudes towards personal responsibility can affect your life as a teacher and your stress reactions. A teacher with low personal responsibility will feel quite helpless and inept in the face of undisciplined students or criticism from a superior. This teacher will experience a great deal of anxiety, depression and bitterness when circumstances at school turn bad. The teacher who sees herself as the cause of events rather than the effect and assumes personal responsibility will not be as likely to reach the levels of negative emotional stress reactions, won't remain as stressed for as long and will be much more likely to initiate positive actions to try to improve her teaching and life circumstances.

The inventory below will help give you a sense of whether your attitude towards life in general is characterised by personal responsibility.

Personal Responsibility Inventory

Directions: Indicate the degree to which you agree or disagree with the following statements. Circle 1 for 'Strongly Disagree' (SD), Circle 2 for 'Disagree' (D), Circle 3 for 'Not Sure' (NS), Circle 4 for 'Agree' (A), Circle 5 for 'Strongly Agree' (SA).

		SD	D	NS	A	SA
1	People at school can realy upset me by what they do	1	2	3	4	5
2	Before I can change, people must change	1	2	3	4	5

71

3	Good things which happen to me are basically caused by luck	1	2	3	4	5
4	I have little control over the good things which happen to me	1	2	3	4	5
5	If bad things happen to me, it's because I am not capable or interesting	1	2	3	4	5
6	It is my past and all its negative influences which makes me the way I am; it is, therefore, almost impossible for me to change for the better	1	2	3	4	5
7	The reason I feel so bad from time to time is because of the unpleasantness of the world around us	1	2	3	4	5
8	I believe there is no real point in trying all the time and never giving up because destiny will determine whether I make it or not	1	2	3	4	5

Total score ＿＿＿
(*Average: 24.22*)

The key point to be energised about is that there are always things you can learn and put into practice to take control of your stress and shrink it down to size!

EMOTIONAL SELF-CONTROL

One of the main ways in which the concept of personal responsibility can be used by you to manage teacher stress as well as general life stress is in taking responsibility for your own emotional stress reactions. Teachers who experience the highest amount of emotional distress about aspects of their job have low personal responsibility. They believe that their stress is directly caused by the 'miserable' things they encounter at school, as when Bill doesn't achieve his goals or when Mary isn't consulted on how to plan for next year's art curriculum. The attitude, which is synonymous with what Grieger calls 'being at effect', is often expressed in the following thought: 'Things at school can really upset me. Students can really make me upset when they don't work. My coordinator can really upset my whole day when he gets stuck into me.' Because they do not take emotional responsibility for their own emotions, they find it hard to imagine how they can do anything about their stress until the situation changes.

Teachers who manage their emotional stress reactions successfully take responsibility for how they feel. Rather than just blaming the situation, they look within themselves for ways they can control their emotional reactions. In 'being at cause', they think: 'Now, what can I do in this miserable situation so that it doesn't get to me'. Some of the solutions they come up with are distraction, not blowing the event out of proportion, relaxation and distancing themselves from the situation. Personal responsibility means learning to control your emotional reactions so that when faced with unpleasant events at work, they don't get you *overly* upset.

Another point to consider is that there are some things at school you will be able to control and some you will not. You will most probably be able to modify Mike's behaviour — although you will always be faced with hard-to-discipline students. There are other aspects of your work such as unfair decisions and policies of the department which you are expected to carry out which will for the most part never change. It is also questionable as to how much success you'll have in changing your principal's decision-making style. By learning how to control your own stress reactions, you will be in a far better position to neutralise the effects of teaching or organisational stressors you cannot change.

'Learn to ignore what you can't control, and learn to control what you can.'
                    Dr Peter Hanson, The Joy of Stress.

Do you want me to become a robot?

The issue of learning to control your emotional stress re-actions is a controversial one to some. When people hear you talking about emotional self-management, they some-times think of 'mind control', 'brainwashing', and doing away with all emotions— including the pleasurable ones. They worry that emotional control is synonymous with not caring about your students and your work. This is not what I mean by emotional control.

Another worry expressed to me is the idea that if you feel less stressed, you will not be motivated to change the stressful situation for the better. To some, 'emotional self-control' techniques are an opiate geared to perpetuate the cruel and harsh aspects of the educational system. This has not been my experience. In fact, I have found that as you come to manage your stress reactions and to develop a higher tolerance for stress, you become more adept at taking effective direct action to change the situation. As already mentioned, Mary will be in a far better position to control Mike's behaviour and modify her principal's actions if she approaches both situations with a less aggravated mind.

What exactly is meant by emotional control? Let's look at the three most common emotional stress reactions: anger, anxiety and depression. While we are all somewhat different in what triggers off our emotions, we can say that when we get emotionally stressed we generally feel one or more of these emotions. Bill Witherspoon gets quite anxious about what his coordinator thinks of him as well as feels down about not being better able to discipline his class. Mary Brunette tends to get quite furious about inconsiderate stu-dents and when she is not more involved in decisions which affect her teaching.

An important point to make here is that *emotional stress reactions vary in intensity from strong to weak*. To illustrate this point, consider the variety of emotional stress reactions Bill could have experienced in response to being publicly harassed by his coordinator and for his class being poorly disciplined. The stress thermometer below is a useful device for representing the point that stress can vary in intensity in response to the same event and also for measuring how stressed you are.

Bill's Stress Thermometer

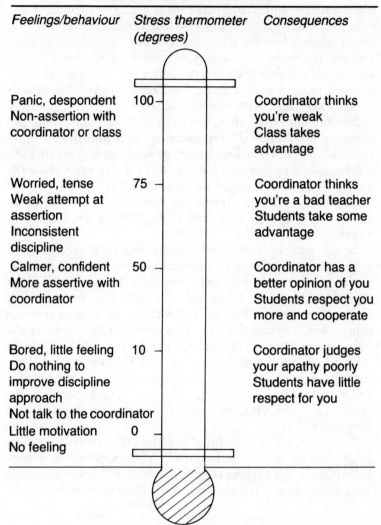

Feelings/behaviour	Stress thermometer (degrees)	Consequences
Panic, despondent Non-assertion with coordinator or class	100	Coordinator thinks you're weak Class takes advantage
Worried, tense Weak attempt at assertion Inconsistent discipline	75	Coordinator thinks you're a bad teacher Students take some advantage
Calmer, confident More assertive with coordinator	50	Coordinator has a better opinion of you Students respect you more and cooperate
Bored, little feeling Do nothing to improve discipline approach Not talk to the coordinator	10	Coordinator judges your apathy poorly Students have little respect for you
Little motivation No feeling	0	

You can see that Bill's emotional reactions to the same events can vary from panic and despondency to no feeling at all. You'll also notice at the higher degrees of stress that Bill's behavioural stress reactions are self-defeating, doing little to bring about a constructive improvement in the situation. At lower levels of stress, Bill's behaviour becomes more constructive and has a greater chance of resulting in consequences which will make his teaching environment less stressful. I have argued and you can see illustrated that low to no levels of stress are actually a bad thing because they remove the emotional energy necessary to motivate Bill to change his circumstances for the better. As you'll see shortly, Bill can make a choice about the degree of upset he experiences when faced with stressors at work.

Emotional control, then, has as its goal the reduction of the intensity of emotional stress reactions to a milder and more tolerable level. To reduce your stress about aspects of your teaching, one option you have is to see if you can reduce the amount of anxiety, anger or 'down' feelings when you are confronted with the stressors at work (and in your life in general) which you find lead to high levels or degrees of stress.

Is the goal of emotional control the total reduction of stress so that in the face of negative events at work you feel nothing? Even if this were possible, I do not think it desirable. As far as I can tell, the only way to reduce all teacher stress is to adopt an 'I don't care' attitude to stressful things which occur at work. This seems to be throwing the baby out with the bathwater for not only would you not be stressed, you would become a non-motivated and non-caring teacher. So I think that the experience of negative emotional stress is inevitable. The key is understanding the extent to which you can control its intensity, duration and frequency.

Now that we've introduced the ideas of personal responsibility and emotional self-control, let's move on to a consideration of the various techniques you can use for managing your emotional reactions when they become over-heated.

ACTIONS SPEAK LOUDER THAN WORDS

For the next week or so, try to become more aware of your emotional and physical stress reactions. Notice the particular situation which appears to be occasioning your stress reaction. Rather than trying to do anything about the situation, see if you can become aware of the dialogue you have with yourself while you are experiencing stress. That is, what are you telling yourself about what's going on? How go you read the situation? Do you believe all teachers would evaluate the situation in the same way? Would some be even more upset than you; if so, what would they be telling themselves?

Try a little experiment. Before doing anything about the situation, try to calm yourself down first, then act. If you find this is a difficult assignment, the material in the next four chapters will present strategies which you can use to help you get control.

RECOMMENDED READING

Albert Ellis and Robert Harper, *A New Guide to Rational Living*, (North Hollywood, CA, Melvyn Powers, 1975).
Richard Nelson-Jones, *Personal Responsibility Counselling and Therapy*, (London, Harper & Row, 1984).

CHAPTER 4
SELF-ESTEEM

'High self-esteem is not a noisy concept. It is a quiet sense of self-respect, a feeling of self-worth. When you have it deep inside, you're glad you're you.'
Dorothy Corkille-Briggs,
Celebrating Yourself: Making Life Work for You,
1977.

It is surprising to me that almost all of the popular books on stress and its management ignore the importance of self-esteem. Stress and your self-esteem are related in at least two major ways. First, if you have high self-esteem, you are more likely to ward off the negative aspects of stress. For example, Bill Witherspoon is more likely to be stressed by the criticism of Mr Gunn because he brings with him low self-esteem. Second, high self-esteem helps buffer you to stress. Not completely, but it certainly can take the sting out of it. If you have high self-esteem, you are more likely to keep bad things which happen at work in perspective and not make mountains out of molehills. High self-esteem seems to go along with not taking negative things which happen to you at school personally.

Low self-esteem can also be seen as an outcome of stress. The more negatives there are at work the more you can feel lousy about yourself. And the more lousy you feel about yourself, the less likely you will be to cope with stress. If you bring low self-esteem into your class, you're a goner!

Without the right attitude, teaching can be a very 'ego deflating' type of work. Why ego deflating? Because your ego is on the line most of the time. You are constantly in the public eye, be it your students, colleagues or principal. And at various times during the year, parents are in a position to judge how well you are looking after their children. Many good teachers — those with high self-expectations — often have their ego wrapped up too much with their teaching performance. They aspire for high levels of success and when they see, as they inevitably will see given the nature of student motivation and ability, that they are not achieving their goals, they put themselves down.

So it's tough emotionally being a teacher. A seemingly intact sense of self-worth can be 'Rambo-ed' over the course of a year. It is vital to insure your emotional survival during the year and to maintain high job satisfaction so that you experience good feelings about yourself and see positive value in yourself as a person when the going gets rough at school. This applies not only to teaching but any job where your ego is frequently on the line.

Let's look at what we mean by low and high self-esteem, what contributes to each and what you can do to take personal responsibility for maintaining good self-esteem or building better esteem.

WHAT IS SELF-ESTEEM?

Self-esteem can be defined in many different ways. Where possible I like to keep things easy so for me self-esteem is defined in two parts. First, *self-concept* is the total picture you have of yourself. Second, it is how you *evaluate your self-concept* which you often do in terms of some ideal stand about the way you think you should be. If your self-concept matches up pretty well with the way you think you should be, then positive self-esteem follows. The greater the discrepancy between the way you see yourself and the way you imagine you should be, the lower your self-esteem.

If you have a negative self-concept, by which I mean that when you examine yourself see mostly negatives, you are prone to low self-esteem. If you have unrealistically high self-expectations which you believe you must achieve, then you are also a good candidate for low self-esteem. If you have a high need for approval you can also be a candidate for low self-esteem where the people who you work with are negative or non-reinforcing.

Characteristics of individuals with low self-esteem

1 *Individuals with low self-esteem tend to withdraw from others and experience consistent feelings of distress.*
2 *People with low self-esteem tend to be intropunitive and passive in adapting to environmental demands and pressures.*
3 *Low self-esteem tends to be equated with inferiority, timidity, self-hatred, lack of personal acceptance and submissiveness.*
4 *People low in self-esteem tend to exhibit high levels of anxiety, depression and frequent psychosomatic complaints.*
5 *People with low self-esteem tend to be isolates who seldom select one another and tend to have great difficulty in forming friendships. The roles they play in social groups are different from people with high self-esteem.*
6 *Low self-esteem individuals tend not to resist social pressures.*
7 *Individuals with low self-esteem are more likely to remain quiet if they feel dissent will evoke personal attack and tend to react strongly to criticism.*
8 *Low self-esteem individuals tend to be invisible members of a group; they, for example, rarely serve as leaders.*
9 *Low self-esteem individuals tend to lack the confidence to respect the critical appraisal of others, and remain defeated and exposed in their real or imagined deficiencies.*

10 Individuals with low self-esteem tend to be self-conscious when talking to others.
S. Coopersmith, **Antecedents of Self-Esteem,** *1967.*

People with high self-esteem have a realistic self-concept with an appreciation of not only their negative qualities but also their positive qualities. While many people with high self-esteem set high standards for themselves, they are not standards that are impossible to reach. Another aspect of high self-esteem individuals is that they seem to have a fairly stable sense of self which doesn't vary greatly from time to time, situation to situation. That is, they are able to feel good about themselves even when they haven't achieved their goals or have been disapproved of or rejected by someone else.

Characteristics of individuals with high self-esteem

1 Individuals with high self-esteem tend to be more effective in meeting environmental demands than those with low self-esteem.

2 People with high self-esteem tend to adopt an active and assertive position in meeting environmental demands.

3 High self-esteem is associated with terms such as self-respect, superiority, pride, self-acceptance and self-love.

4 People with high self-esteem tend to be independent in conformity-producing situations and manifest confidence that they will succeed.

5 High self-esteem people tend to be popular with their peers.

6 An individual with high self-esteem is apt to attend to others only to the extent that he esteems them.

7 High self-esteem individuals tend to participate in exploratory and independent activities.

> *8 High self-esteem individuals possess confidence in their ability to deal with events; anxiety is less likely to be aroused in them and they have greater ability to resist the negative implications of social judgments.*
> *9 High self-esteem individuals tend to be quite capable of defending themselves against threats of their adequacy.*
> S. Coopersmith, **Antecedents of Self-Esteem,** *1967.*

There are a variety of causes of low self-esteem including the following.

1 *Negative self-concept* When you think about yourself or see yourself in a mirror, you see mostly negatives.

2 *Unrealistic self-expectations* Not only do you set too high and perhaps even perfectionists expectations for yourself, but you insist 'I must' achieve them at all times.

3 *High need for approval* You believe that you *need* others' approval to be happy and without it you could never be happy.

4 *Self-downing* When you don't live up to your expectations or when others' disapprove of you, you think of yourself as a 'total' failure.

5 *Low frustration tolerance* When faced with people or events you find frustrating, you tell yourself 'I can't stand it' and you get yourself or themselves away as quickly as possible.

6 *Low personal responsibility* As I have already said, a key to a vital life including a positive self-esteem is believing you are capable of taking charge and creating something good for yourself.

7 *Low self-praise* When you have done something well, you don't pat yourself on your back for a job well done (although you kick yourself hard in the rear when you goof up!).

8 *Low achievement* For many reasons, you rarely perform up to your potential.

9 *Poor recognition from others* Your lack of skilled performance and poor attitude towards yourself invites criticism and lack of positive reinforcement. Or alternatively, over an extended period, people fail to acknowledge you when you are doing a good job.

10 *Little power of influence over others* Because you doubt yourself, you fail to command the respect that is required to win others over, and hence deprive yourself of the satisfaction of personal influence.

11 *Your behaviour is inconsistent with your values* One of the inputs to your low self-esteem is when you observe yourself acting in opposition to what you really believe. For example, rather than sticking up for a student or class in the face of your colleagues' sledging, you go along with the crowd.

GETTING STARTED: SELF-CONCEPT INVENTORY

If you were asked to name your positive characteristics both inside and outside of school, could you in a short period of time come up with such a list? If not, you've got a bit of work to do on the road to developing a higher sense of self-esteem and value as a person.

The starting point is an objective assessment of you—the good *and the bad!* Why the bad? Because it is not your good points which lower your self-esteem, it's how your react to your bad ones.

Start off with making a list of your positive and negative characteristics of you at school. What are things you do well? What are your weaker points? For example, you might be a good communicator of ideas, able to stimulate a good class discussion, but rather poor in disciplining an unruly class. Include both your skills and aspects of your personality. You might be a hard worker but not particularly supportive or sensitive to your colleagues' concerns. Make the list a long one. Include positive things which you might feel are unimportant or that come easily to you and, therefore, you believe you deserve no credit for. For example, you might be good at organising events, but because you've always been that way and don't think it's very important, you might not credit yourself for it.

Once you've completed your 'in-school' self-assessment, turn your attention to yourself outside of school. Once again, write down your positive and negative qualities. Consider your positive and negative competences and traits in your home life and significant personal relationships, in your recreational life, in community affairs and, if appropriate, as a practising member of a religion. What do you like about yourself; what could be changed for the better?

Separating your self-concept in terms of yourself in work and outside of work has a definite purpose. It is all too easy — especially when you're just getting started as a teacher — to focus too much of yourself on your work. (The same problem arises if you are a Type 'A' personality or workaholic.) To have good self-esteem, it is often important to have a positive regard for the things you do outside of teaching and to look for sources of self-esteem outside as well as inside school.

RATIONAL SELF-ACCEPTANCE

How do you decide the worth of a person? Is it by specific actions or characteristics? Do people who succeed at work have more value than a person who raises a successful family?

In our Western culture, many if not all of us have grown up with very much of an 'external' locus for our self-esteem. You feel worthy and esteem yourself either when you are performing well and/or when others approve of you. If you perform well as a teacher you think you're pretty good. The same goes for when others acknowledge your performance. Your self-esteem tends to go up.

The equation for determining your self-esteem — *good achievement + approval/recognition = high self-esteem* — is a very common one. And it works fairly well when you are in an environment where your chance of constant success is pretty good and when the amount of approval and recognition is frequent. Unfortunately, teaching provides for somewhat limited opportunities for success, let alone constant success. Moreover, research indicates that good feedback and acknowledgement are somewhat rare species in schools. Another problem with the above formula is that the reciprocal of the self-esteem equation also holds, namely: *bad achievement + disapproval/little recognition = low esteem*. With this equation, your level of self-esteem can resemble a bit of a roller-coaster. When things are going well your self-esteem goes up. When things are at school are going badly, down you come.

There is another way of arriving at a positive and stable sense of positive self-esteem than getting hooked into using external signs. Look back over your self-concept inventory paying attention to both the positive and negative aspects of you. Your value as a person is represented by all of you — both the good and the bad. Some things about you are good and sure, others not so good. But taken all together they represent your value; the sum total of you, personality and experience over the years you have lived.

From this perspective, isn't it ludicrous (and self-defeating) to use someone else's opinion of you as the basis for you valuing yourself? Suppose Mr Gunn thinks Bill is a loser, does that make Bill a loser? It can only if Bill lets himself be persuaded it is so. And suppose one of your classes performs poorly on their end of year exams. Does that mean you are hopeless because they haven't performed very well? Of course not, only that they didn't go as well as you would have liked and that, perhaps, with a similar group you'd do it differently the next time.

So an 'internal' locus of self-esteem has you accepting yourself warts and all and saying that 'I have value because I am alive and because of the good things about me'. It refuses to use any one event, or even an extended series of negative events, at work or at home as the sole input to your self-esteem.

Does this mean that you simply accept the way you are? No. It says once you can accept who you are then you are more able to acknowledge your bad points and try to correct them for the better.

Rational self-acceptance means that you are the determiner of your value as a person. It also means that you carry around with you a stable sense of positive self-worth into situations which might be negative and stressful, like a misbehaving class or critical colleague, and that it remains unchanged throughout.

Rational self-acceptance means an end to self-rating and self-downing. It means an end to looking to others and your achievements as 'necessities' in order to feel good about yourself. Sure it feels good to achieve well and to receive recognition, but that doesn't mean you *need* achievement and approval to value yourself. The valuing of yourself needs to come from within, from a sense of who you are and an acceptance of your value because of who you are and because you are alive.

The notion of personal responsibility has a direct application here. You can start to take control over your own self-esteem rather than having the control rest in things frequently outside you and your influence by adopting an attitude of rational self-acceptance.

Countering 'self-depreciating' attitudes

One of the killer attitudes to your self-esteem is when you tell yourself that 'I am a hopeless failure of a teacher'. This attitude generally tears strips off your self-esteem at those times when you have failed to achieve something at school, such as when a student or class of yours behaves or perform poorly or when you are 'Rambo-ed' by a negative colleague or parent. The idea that you are incompetent and the other thoughts that follow on from this attitude — like it's time to take the job at the ice cream parlour or have another child — will rot the very foundations of your self-esteem if you do not counter it with swift and effective retaliation.

Look at the Teaching Skill Inventory opposite which shows the characteristics of a good teacher. After adding some other teacher attributes which you believe go into making a good teacher, you may want to complete the checklist below.

Teaching Skill Inventory

(Place a tick in either the 'Yes' or 'No' column.)

		Yes	No
1	Prepares lesson		
2	Good classroom management		
3	Is able to motivate students		
4	Cares/supportive of students' welfare		
5	Gives good feedback to students on work		
6	Modifies curriculum to cater for individuals		
7	Keeps abreast of new developments in field		
8	Good at assessing student performance		
9	Students learn what they are taught		
10	(You fill in)_____		

Your answers hold the solution to countering the idea that you're a hopeless teacher. 'I'm a hopeless teacher' literally means that you are hopeless at everything you do as a teacher. Otherwise, you would just say 'I'm a hopeless classroom disciplinarian' or 'I'm hopeless at modifying the curriculum for individual students'. These latter two attitudes, even if they are true, will do little to damage your self-esteem. It is the all-embracing nature of 'I'm a flop as a teacher' which will do you in.

In completing the inventory, you will get a sense of your strengths and weaknesses as a teacher. You will see the areas which require self-improvement if your goal is to be a better teacher.

If your answers to all ten questions are 'no', and if you anticipate that your teaching will remain the same in the future, you probably should seek out a new line of employment. (And remember, ten 'no's' would say nothing about your value as a person. Just that you are possibly not suited to teaching and that haven't you selected a profession suitable to someone with your characteristics).

Let's now turn to another major way of taking responsibility for creating your own sense of positive self-esteem and value. The key is in making a plan to do things which will bring you more pleasurable and constant good feelings about yourself.

INCREASING YOUR SELF-ESTEEM

Rather than waiting for the Good Ship Lollypop to sail past your shores and leave you with some glittering treasures (achievement, recognition) which will enhance your self-esteem, you can take some positive steps to influence your outside world so that the feedback you receive about yourself from yourself and others is reinforcing and personally enhancing.

Sources of self-esteem

Whether you have an internal or external locus for your self-esteem, there are certain sources in your outside teaching world and greater life which make it easier or more difficult to experience high self-esteem. The three main sources are achievement, affiliation (acceptance recognition by others) and power and influence over others. Let me briefly discuss these sources one at a time.

When you achieve a goal you have set for yourself in your teaching, you will normally experience an elevated sense of self-esteem. For example, if you spend some time learning about a new curriculum approach to teaching your subject and successfully introduce it to your students, you will not only have upgraded yourself professionally but also taken control over events which positively enhance your self-esteem. If your professional self-esteem needs a shot in the arm, it is a good idea to identify some professional goals for yourself in different teaching areas and work hard to achieve them.

Your personal achievements will also increase your self-esteem when they bring with them, as they sometimes do, the admiration and recognition of significant others at work be they students, colleagues or someone in administration.

Personal achievement which is motivated out of your

desire for self-actualisation — bringing out more and more of your talent — also brings with it a strong element of intrinsic reinforcement and feeds your self-esteem. You don't need anyone including yourself to pat yourself on the back. It just naturally feels good.

Affliation with people at school means team building, giving and receiving support, including participation in support groups, recognising the contributions of individuals, sharing plans, and forming supportive, cooperative and cordial working relationships. The more closely affiliated you are with others, the more likely your contributions will be seen and, therefore, acknowledged by others. Additionally, giving your time and support to people you work with and your students *without expecting anything in return* brings with it feelings of satisfaction and fulfilment.

It is certainly the case — especially as you get older — that exerting influence and power over others in order to achieve positive outcomes is very reinforcing, especially for some people. Giving and receiving feedback, making decisions which positively influence things which happen at school and acknowledging your own areas of influence can definitely support your sense of self, your competence, and the respect others have for you.

In order to see how these three sources can influence your self-esteem, complete the self-esteem shield below.

It sometimes can be useful to replay past experiences which have been associated with your feeling good about yourself in order to learn how to repeat the experiences in the future. By completing the following form, you will become more aware of the importance of the above three sources of self-esteem in your life (achievement, affiliation/recognition, positive power and influence).

Personal Sources of Self-esteem

1 Write down a time when you felt especially good about your job. What happened (brief description)?

_____

_____

Self-esteem Shield

1 What for you has been your most significant achievement so far this year at work? (One word is enough; it doesn't have to be an essay.)

2 Write down some time in the past two weeks when you can recall having set yourself some kind of task and achieved it. Three words (adjectives or adverbs) that best describe how you felt at that time.

3 Write down some time in the past couple of weeks at work when you can recall having exercised some power, control or influence over people and/or events of significance to you at work.

4 Write down some time at work in the last two weeks when you felt valued and cared about as a worthwhile person for who you are and not necessarily for something you had just done.

5 Write down some time in the past couple of weeks at work when you can recall acting consistently with some deeply held value or belief (something which you feel is really important and which you can look back on and say, 'That shows how much I value...')

6 Write your own definition of self-esteem.

2 At this time what did you do that helped you to feel good?

_____

_____

3 What did others do that helped you at this time?

_____

_____

4 Which of the three main sources of self-esteem were involved?

_____

_____

5 How do you feel about your job now?

_____

_____

6 How often do you feel good about your job?

_____

_____

7 Are the three sources of self-esteem enhancement available from each of the three sources? Which of the sources are available, which are not?

_____

_____

_____

_____

Goal-setting

Now that the three main sources of self-esteem enhancement and, in particular, which ones turn you on, are clear to you it is possible for you to take more control over your self-esteem by planning what you do at school to enhance the availability of these sources.

The way to enhance your self-esteem involves doing things which for the most part you already know, especially if you have been teaching for a few years.

If you are a new teacher you may feel that you are at the bottom of the totem pole with very little power to control things at school which might affect your self-esteem. But there are in fact many things you can do—and probably already do. 'Putting in more', 'showing you're keen' is one of the basic rules of thumb. By going beyond what's expected of you, others will take notice and offer recognition for your efforts. Examples might include extra-curricular activities such as taking after-school sports, directing the school play, editing the school magazine and looking after school camps.

If you are a more experienced teacher, you could work on improving areas of your teaching practice including the traditional ones of classroom management, report writing, record keeping, establishing parent rapport and getting good results. Choosing to expand your knowledge of your curriculum area including new curriculum programs adds to your 'professional' self-esteem. Finding out more about what makes your students tick, how they actually think and learn, and integrating knowledge of students with the most current ways of teaching your subject are bring important additions to your self-esteem.

Your experience may also enable you to take on positions of responsibility including year level coordinator, subject matter coordinator, head of subject, head of department and other positions of influence in your school.

Indeed, it would seem sensible to use 'career tracking' as part of the process of continuing to develop professionally and personally at work and, in the process, continue to feel good about yourself. The more you 'grow' professionally and personally, the more likely it is that you will maintain a stable sense of positive self-esteem.

So consider what career paths lie ahead of you in teaching and where you'd like to go. You might aspire to be a senior teacher recognised for teaching excellence or you might have your long-term sights on administration.

Another area to consider is the further education offered to you both in in-service activities and post-graduate degrees. Whether there are tangible rewards for your further study depends on your school system and school. Even if further study does not result in higher salary or positions of responsibility, there can be little question that by furthering your professional knowledge and skills, you will become a more competent teacher in your own and other's eyes.

So setting long-term and short-term professional goals for yourself is a good starting point to taking positive control over the development of your own professional self-esteem rather than relying on the winds of chance. Goals can refer both to career/ position goals (e.g., senior teacher, curriculum coordinator, principal) as well as professional skills you'd like to acquire over time.

'Gosh, you're a wimp, Bill,' offered Mary as Bill was getting ready to leave for the day. 'Why didn't you put in for head of department. You can run rings around anyone around here.'

'Naw, not for me. Somebody else... I'm too busy.'

'Busy, smizzy. I'd say you have a self-image problem, old boy. You don't think you're up to it.'

'What do you mean, self-image? What would you know about self-image? If you did, you wouldn't dress like a slob.'

'Hey, what would you know? It's French. And anyway, we art teachers are supposed to look a bit non-conventional. But my image is not the problem, yours is. I reckon you're afraid you might not get the position.'

'Well, I probably wouldn't. There are others who command an audience better than me. I can see it when they speak and I speak in staff meetings.'

'That's because you doubt yourself too much. You've got the points on the scoreboard, but don't give yourself enough credit. It's about time you took stock of what you've done. Why, last year your classes performed better than ever. Even the principal acknowledged that—and that, my friend, was a miracle.'

'I'll think about it. I've still got a few days.'

'C'mon. It'll do you and your poor image the world of good.'

Bill drove off wondering how he was going to face Mary with the news that he wasn't going in for it. 'I've made up my mind. Too much to do. Looking after the school magazine. Someone's got to do that. But why does it always get left to me? Maybe I am a wimp. Maybe I could put in for the position. She's right. Might give the old esteem a bit of a lift.'

ACTIONS SPEAK LOUDER THAN WORDS

The following goal-setting activity may help formalise what you already do or are planning to do in the context of your own personal self-managed blueprint for positive self-esteem. It may also stimulate you to start doing new things which themselves will feed your sense of personal esteem, mastery and fulfillment.

Do not be surprised if you do *not* find this an easy exercise. If you haven't done career tracking or thought about the kind of teacher and educator you would like to be, you may have to slowly add to this activity over time.

The last two parts to the activity will help alert you to obstacles which might stand in your way to achieving your plan for self-esteem enhancement, and offer you an opportunity to think about ways to overcome them.

Goal-setting for Self-esteem Enhancement

A *Long-term goals (5–10 years)*
    1 Level of teaching responsibility/administrative responsibility.

    2 Further educational qualifications.

    3 Professional competencies (things I want to be good at).

_____

_____

_____

_____

B *Short-term goals (within this teaching year or next twelve months).*
1 Promotion/assuming new position of responsibility.

_____

_____

2 Beginning/completing further educational course/in-service.

_____

_____

3 Professional competencies (skills/knowledge I want to acquire).

_____

_____

_____

_____

4 'Extra' involvements in school activities.

_____

_____

C *Activities for achieving short-term goals*
Goal 1 (re-state): _____
Activities

_____

_____

_____

_____

Goal 2 (re-state): _____

Activities

_____

_____

_____

_____

Goal 3 (re-state): _____

Activities

_____

_____

_____

_____

D Obstacles to achieving your short-term goals.

_____

_____

_____

_____

E Solutions for overcoming obstacles.

_____

_____

_____

_____

RECOMMENDED READING

Diane Frey and C. Jesse Carlock, *Enhancing Self-Esteem* (Muncie, Indiana: Accelerated Development Inc., 1984).
Bob Hoffman, *No One Is To Blame* (Palo Alto, CA: Science and Behavior Books, 1979).

Mathew McCay and Patrick Fanning, *Self-Esteem* (Oakland, CA: New Harbinger Publications, 1987).
Andrew M. Mecca, Neil J. Smelser and John Vasconcellos editors, *The Social Importance of Self-Esteem* (Berkeley: University of California Press, 1989).
Freda Parot, *Self-Esteem: The Key to Success in Work and Love* (Saratoga, CA: R & E Publishers, 1988).

CHAPTER 5
STRESS-REDUCING ATTITUDES AND THOUGHTS

'You are what you are and where you are because of what has gone into your mind. You can change what you are and where you are by changing what you put into your mind.'

Zig Ziglar, See You At The Top, *1974.*

In this chapter, stress-creating as well as stress-reducing attitudes and thoughts will be described and illustrated. You will clearly see how much influence your thinking has in determining the emotional stress you experience. Just as it is possible to list unhealthy aspects in our lifestyle (e.g., no exercise, poor diet), it is also possible to pin point unhealthy thinking habits which are associated with emotional distress. Once you become more aware of stress-creating attitudes and thinking, you are halfway there to doing something about them.

A format that will help you develop new ways of thinking is the Stress Script described on page 106. Planning and practising what to think before you enter a stressful situation is one of the ways you can innoculate yourself against stress.

USING YOUR HEAD

Bill W. is walking down the corridor and sees his coordinator emerging from his office. He immediately feels panicked and

notices his breath shorten and quicken. Rather than pro-
ceeding towards his destination, Bill turns to pick up some
imaginary litter and, while trying to drive in reverse, crashes
loudly into the locker, only to be greeted by Mr Gunn's icy
glare.

'Oh shoot, he's going to have another stab at me. I can't
stand it when he criticises me. This is going to be terrible! I
could explain why I was a little late and even ask him not to
criticise me in front of the kids. No, I'd better not. I'd be too
uptight and I couldn't hack it.'

In the above situation, Bill quickly feels very stressed
because his head is filled with stress-creating thoughts. Even
though the confrontation situation with Mr Gunn is objectively stressful, it is not the situation which causes Bill's
extreme stress but rather what he is telling himself about the
situation. How do we know this? Not only from substantial
research which shows a strong relationship between certain
types of thinking and stress, but also because it is apparent
that if Bill changes his thinking, he will feel less stressed
about approaching Mr Gunn.

A more realistic and less stress-creating set of thoughts for
Bill would be: 'Oh shoot, he's going to talk to me about
what happened this morning. I won't like it, but it's not the
end of the world. It'll only last a minute or so. I can hack his
criticism. I might mention that I agree with him that it's bad
to be late and that next time I'll try to avoid the distractions
of parents who come up to me before class. I might even add
that I would appreciate it if he could talk to me about his
concerns without students being in earshot of the conversation. That's what I'll do!' In this second scenario, Bill's
thoughts would definitely lead him to experience some unpleasant arousal, but not nearly the amount of anxiety as
earlier. Bill's confidence in confronting Mr Gunn would also
have been increased as a result of his pattern of thinking.

In the two examples following, you will not only observe
how the same potentially stressful event can lead to different
types of stress reactions but also how a different point of
view can radically modify the type and amount of stress you
experience. In reading through the examples, pay particular

attention to the differences between stress-creating and stress-reducing thoughts. (These two illustrations have been developed by Professor Susan Forman, University of South Carolina.)

Teaching stressor 1: almost the entire class fails a test (twenty-four out of twenty-eight).

Stress-creating thoughts

Teacher A
1 I must be a terrible teacher.
2 I'm so dumb and incompetent.
3 It's my fault they didn't learn the material.
4 I'm just useless.
5 The principal will probably find out and I'll probably be fired.
6 I might as well quit.

Stress reactions: depressed, anxious

Teacher B
1 Those stupid kids.
2 I shouldn't have to work with dumb kids.
3 They never learn anything.
4 All they do is take up space.
5 It's their own fault they failed the test.
6 They never do anything but play around.
7 It's impossible to do anything with kids like this.

angry

Stress-reducing thoughts

Teacher C
1 Twenty-four out of twenty-eight failed—that's not good.
2 I guess I'd better look what's going on here.
3 All my other classes did well, I thought I taught the material well and I went over it several times.
4 Maybe the material was too hard for them.
5 Maybe these kids are not as bright as the others I've had.
6 Maybe the test was too hard.
7 Well, instead of guessing, maybe I could get some feedback from the class.
8 It is possible they need some help on developing study skills.
9 I could also talk to their previous teacher to get some information about them.
10 This isn't going to be easy.
11 Oh well, if all the kids were exactly the same I guess this job wouldn't be interesting.

Stress reactions: concerned, calm
Teaching Stressor 2: It's the second week of school. Johnny just hit Mark in the face and threw a book across the room. He has been out of his seat, running around the room and hasn't completed any of his work.

Stress-creating thoughts

Teacher A
1 This is terrible.
2 I'll never be able to control this kid.
3 He's going to destroy the entire class.
4 The other teachers are going to hear about this.
5 They'll probably all be talking about me.
6 The principal will probably fire me.
7 I'm so useless.
8 I can't do anything right.

Stress reactions: depressed, anxious

Teacher B
1 This is awful.
2 What a little monster.
3 Kids like that shouldn't be allowed in school.
4 I shouldn't have to deal with this.
5 His parents should do something about him.
6 By this time, he should know how to behave.
7 He's a hopeless case.

angry

Stress-reducing thoughts

Teacher C
1 Looks like I have a problem here.
2 This situation isn't good for Johnny, the rest of the class or me.
3 He doesn't seem to respond the way most other kids do.
4 Oh well, I know I'm not the only one with this type of classroom situation. I hear other teachers talking about it all the time.
5 Since I don't like it and I really want things to change, I guess I'll have to do something about it if I want things to be different. Getting upset at myself or at him isn't going to help.
6 He just hasn't learned how to behave appropriately and I'm going to try to teach him how.
7 I don't like this but he is part of the class, and if I want him to act differently in class I'll have to try some different approaches with him.

8　I think I'll talk to some of the other teachers to see what's worked for them. Maybe I'll talk to the school psychologist.

Stress reactions: concerned, calm, motivated

You will have noticed that the stress-reducing thoughts are less emotionally laden. They do not exaggerate the unpleasantness of the stressor. They also do not involve you taking the event personally. As well, they tend to identify the stressor as a problem to be solved, orient you to ways of dealing with the problem and communicate a sense of optimism and confidence.

One important point on trying to locate your negative stress-creating thoughts. It is not a skill many people have ever practised or developed. You may have difficulty indentifying what it is you are saying to yourself which is increasing your stress level. From experience, I can say with almost 100 per cent certainty that if you find yourself getting emotionally distressed about something at school which is bad, such as student behaviour problems, unfair actions or criticism from administrators, excess time and workload pressures, you will be helping your stress along with some unnecessarily stress-creating attitudes and thoughts. However, don't take my word for it. See if you agree after reading on in this section.

There are two further explanations as to why it is sometimes difficult to be aware of your thoughts. The first is that some of your stress-creating thoughts are sub-conscious. That is, they are away from your immediate powers of self-observation. The second reason is that when you think to yourself, you think more rapidly than when you are talking to someone else. It can be difficult to slow your thoughts down long enough to recognise them. When you know what to look or listen for in your thinking and when you have had some practice in discovering stress-creating attitudes and thoughts, you will find the process much easier.

TYPES OF STRESSFUL THOUGHTS

Let's briefly examine four different aspects of thinking which can contribute to reduce your teacher stress. Such a review will make it easier for you to recognise your own stress-creating thoughts and will provide guidance for helping you modify your thoughts to more stress-reducing ones.

Rational versus irrational thinking

'A fundamental premise of RET (rational-emotive therapy) ...states that stressful conditions do not exist in their own right but vary significantly in relation to the perceptions and cognitions of those who react to these conditions... In the case of ordinary or moderate 'stressful' situations, people choose, decide, or create their own feelings of anxiety, depression and self-downing by picking a certain kind of belief about the stressful situations that happen to them. Their stressful reactions follow directly from their beliefs and although what happens to them significantly contributes to it, it hardly causes the stressful reaction.'

Albert Ellis,
'What People Can Do For Themselves To Cope With Stress', 1978.

The founder of rational-emotive therapy, Albert Ellis, has made some important discoveries about why certain teachers feel moderately stressed about such events as when they fail to achieve their goals with a student or class, are unfairly criticised or when they are forced to implement too many new changes to their teaching in too short a period while other teachers feel extremely distressed about the same events. He has proposed—and my research has strongly confirmed it—that it is the irrational thoughts you have about teaching stressors which cause you to feel *overly* stressed. Rational thoughts lead to a lower amount of stress and help you to control the amount of stress you experience.

Now, don't be put off by the term 'irrational'. It doesn't mean you're a 'psycho'. It is a term Ellis has coined to describe a type of thinking which is characteristic of all humans. That is, all of us from time to time, in different situations and in different degrees, tend to be unrealistic and subjective about the negative stress-creating events in our lives. The key to stress-management, according to Ellis, is to recognise when we are thinking irrationally and then counter our irrational thinking with more rational attitudes and thoughts.

What's the difference between an irrational and rational belief? Let me explain by way of an illustration. When confronted by a poorly behaved student who is being continually disruptive most teachers would think to themselves: 'I don't like this behaviour one bit as I am unable to achieve my goals for this class and for this student. I really want him to behave better and it's a pain in the bum when he acts this way and I can't seem to control him. Now is there anything else I can do to get on top of this situation or do I just grin and bear it?' Teachers thinking in this fashion will feel disappointed, concerned and irritated but they won't be totally stressed out.

What distress-prone teachers think is somewhat different. They take what is preferable—which in the above situation is getting control of a student and achieving some teaching goals—and they tell themselves: 'Because I prefer to have control and be successful, I *must* have control and be successful; it's really *awful* that I am not succeeding here; *I can't stand it*; I'm a *failure* for not being a better disciplinarian and that student is a *total ass* for acting that way'. These irrational thoughts lead to extreme emotional stress such as rage, high anxiety or feeling very down.

Albert Ellis has identified five characteristics of irrational thinking that we need to look for in learning to recognise some of the thoughts which change our stress into distress.

1 *Absolutistic thinking* is frequently expressed by the words 'should', 'ought', 'need' or 'must'. Absolutistic thinking involves you taking a value which you would prefer to have, such as being successful as a teacher, receiving approval from others for a job well done, consideration and respect from your students and a reasonable work load for the time available, and converts the value from a rational preference into an irrational command or demand.
– 'I *should* be able to discipline more effectively.'

– 'Students *should* always behave well.'
– 'Things at school *should* be easier than they are.'
– 'Schools *should* always consult with teachers about decisions which effect them.'

2 *Awfulising thinking* which reflects the belief that 'bad things which happen at school are horrible and terrible'.
– 'It's awful to have to teach in a class with so many problems.'
– 'It's terrible not to be consulted.'
– 'It's horrible to be criticised.'

3 *Low frustration tolerance thinking* involves you telling yourself that because something is bad, you cannot tolerate it and can never be happy.
– 'I can't stand it when students come in late.'
– 'It's unbearable to have so much work to do and not enough time to do it.'
– 'I can't tolerate being treated disrespectfully by my coordinator.'

4 *Self-downing thinking* involves you taking one aspect of your teaching which might be going badly or not as well as you would like and thinking that because you haven't done very well in that area that you have failed and are hopeless.
– 'Because my class didn't perform as well as last year's class, I'm a failure.'
– 'I'm so dumb and incompetent.'
– 'I'm really a hopeless character.'

5 *Other-downing thinking* involves you telling yourself that because one or more aspects of another person or an organisation are bad, the whole person or organisation is bad and rotten.
– 'He'a a real monster.'
– 'This places totally stinks.'
– 'My principal is a total moron.'

Irrational thinking can be defined as thinking which is not true, illogical and unrealistic, is expressed generally as some personal command, leads to extreme distress and does not help you achieve your goals. On the other hand, rational thinking is true, logical and realistic, is not absolutistic, and leads to moderate levels of stress and helps you achieve your goals.

There are many reasons why we think irrationally. Albert Ellis believes it's largely innate. That is, it's just a natural thinking tendency which is basic human nature. Others believe that society and cultural influences including our childhood upbringing teaches, models and reinforces irrational thinking. It also seems pretty clear to me that, when you are under a great deal of pressure and begin to feel very stressed, your thinking starts to become more and more irrational. Little hassles become huge horrors. You really give yourself and others a harsh evaluation. Your ability to tolerate frustration takes a nosedive. Whatever the causes, the fact remains that by recognising your irrational thinking and changing it to become more rational, you will reduce your stress.

While a more complete model of rational self-management will be presented in full in the following chapter, let me briefly describe how to counter irrational attitudes and thoughts. By changing your irrational thinking to more rational thinking you will reduce your emotional stress in the face of the same threats and demands. You will also be in a better state of mind to do something about changing the situation if you can.

To counter unrealistic demands ('absolutistic' thinking) you make of yourself, others at school or your school itself, ask yourself, 'Where is the evidence that I (others, school) *must* be the way I demand?' The rational answer is nowhere. Instead, Ellis advises changing unrealistic demands to *preferences*. For example, 'I strongly prefer to achieve or be approved of, but I don't need success or approval'. 'I strongly desire people at school and school itself to be fair, considerate or professional, but I know that it will not always be that way. That's the way life is.' It is really a matter of being more realistic in what you expect, given that you know from time to time people (including yourself) will not think the way you would like.

To counter 'awfulising,' you need to put the stressful events which happen at school into perspective. Using the 'catastrophe scale' illustrated near the beginning of the book, remind yourself that just because something might be bad doesn't make it awful or a catastrophe. Compared to having a heart attack or a bad car accident or losing a loved one, how bad is student misbehaviour or not being consulted by your principal about a decision which affects you?

'Low frustration tolerance' can be countered by asking yourself, 'Where is the evidence I *can't* stand it when something stressful at school happens?' The evidence generally is that while you don't like it and you feel crummy, it hasn't killed you nor is it likely to in the future. The more rational attitude is 'While I don't like what's happening, I can cope.'

To counter 'self-downing', you have to keep in mind your other good qualities both inside and outside of teaching— especially at those times when you are not achieving your goals at school or are being criticised by someone important. Ask yourself, 'How does doing badly in something at work take away all my other good qualities both inside and outside of work and make me a failure?' Answer: it doesn't. It only means you are fallible and sometimes will not do as well as you would like. The role of 'self-downing' was discussed in more detail in Chapter 4.

'Other-downing', which almost always leads to excessive anger, can be countered by asking yourself, 'Does this person's bad behaviour(s) make this person *totally* bad?' Of course it doesn't. The key here is to keep the other person's good qualities in mind at the time they are acting badly. That is, if your goal is to reduce your emotional stress.

Pessimistic versus optimistic thinking

'It's not reality itself which that's the problem. We all suffer tragic realities, but it's how you see reality that makes the difference.'

Martin Seligman, psychologist.

Consider the example of Bill Witherspoon being criticised by his coordinator, Mr Gunn. There are two very different ways he can explain this potentially stressful event. An optimist would think it's not a big deal, everyone gets in bad moods. However Bill, a pessimist, thinks he's hopeless.

Basically, optimists see themselves in control of events or, at least, not at the mercy of events. Pessimists feel victimised by events and powerless to do anything about them.

Martin Seligman, a professor at the University of Pennsylvania, has developed the idea of 'attributional style' which he defines as the way people explain both good and bad things which happen to them. According to Seligman, there are three different dimensions which describe a person's 'attributional style.'

Stable Do you see events at school as controllable or do you feel events are basically out of your control? Take two teachers who find their current class is performing significantly better than last year's class. An optimist would say he or she was becoming more effective as a teacher. A pessimist would say it's just luck, like winning the lottery. If on the other hand, a class's performance deteriorates from the previous year, the optimistic would deem it bad luck while the pessimist would think it could not have happened any other way.

Global Optimistic teachers believe that their good teaching is general proof that they are successes in life. But to the pessimist it's just an isolated case of luck. In the face of stressful teaching events, the tables turn. Optimistic teachers dismiss each stressful event as an isolated occurrence, while for pessimists bad events bring doom and gloom into their lives.

Internal Optimistic teachers cast off the bad and take credit for the good things which happen at school. Pessimistic teachers attribute the bad events to themselves while crediting good things which happen to luck.

Seligman's research has shown clear relationships between your 'attributional style' and achievement, happiness and the ability to manage stress. Specific findings indicate that optimists live longer, have better health, fulfill their potential, persist towards their goals rather than giving up and, because of their faith in their own abilities, are more likely to take risks.

Seligman believes that people begin to learn their attributional style at an early age. As they grow older, it becomes more entrenched as part of their belief system.

However, he believes it is possible to learn to change your attributional style. The general approach involves adopting a more optimistic framework towards the good and bad at work. Specifically, you need to start to take full credit for the good things which happen, attributing them to your own effort and skill. And when faced with bad things, get in the habit of seeking explanations in terms of outside forces frequently beyond your control. There are many things which happen at school which are really beyond your control such as a student not achieving after all your hard efforts. It is almost impossible to do anything about these factors. You sometimes simply cannot over-ride the effects of parental conditioning, peer group pressure, modest intellectual ability, etc.

An optimistic style can be developed by changing the way you think about, describe and explain events in your life. This is ideally combined, of course, with other people at work such as your principal and senior administrators giving you credit, reinforcement and recognition for a job well done.

Low versus high self-efficacy

'The strength of people's convictions in their own effectiveness determines whether they will even try to cope with difficult situations. People fear and avoid threatening situations they believe themselves unable to handle, whereas they behave affirmatively when they judge themselves capable of handling successfully situations that would otherwise intimidate them.'
Albert Bandura, **Social Learning Theory**, *1977.*

There is little question that if in doubt whether you are skilled enough to manage a situation at school you find stressful, you will not only be less able to cope successfully with the stressor but you will tend to feel more stressed. If Bill Witherspoon does not believe in his ability to discipline a class, then he will experience a misbehaving student or class as much more stressful than if he believed in himself. He would also be in a better position to manage the situation.

Examples of low self-efficacy thinking include:
'I'm lousy at classroom discipline.'
'I can't deal with negative parents.'
'I simply can't assert myself.'
'I am a totally disorganised person; I simply can't manage everything I have to do.'
'I'm hopeless at computers, I'll never be able to learn this.'

Combating low self-efficacy is not easy. It's not simply a matter of telling yourself 'I can do this', although changing your thinking is a step in the right direction. The key to increasing self-efficacy is to counter your low self-efficacy with positive self-efficacy thinking and to work out a plan developing and strengthening your skills (e.g., discipline, communication, problem solving, time management). Employ these skills over and over again until you begin to get the evidence that you are capable and that with effort you can do something to improve the situation.

Coping self-statements

'How one responds to stress in large part is influenced by how one appraises the stressor ... and how he assesses his ability to cope.'

Donald Meichenbaum,
Cognitive-Behavior Modification, 1977.

As I have suggested, one of the common characteristics when you are experiencing stress is the lack of effective thoughts or self-statements. If you experience high degrees of emotional stress when faced with a threatening situation, you tend to overestimate the degree and consequences of the threat and underestimate your coping resources.

Donald Meichenbaum, a well-known psychologist, has popularised an approach to stress-management which is called 'stress innoculation training'. In this approach, individuals are presented with a set of skills to enable them to deal with stressful situations. The basic skills taught within this approach are ones which are presented later on in this book and include relaxation and other measures which can help you manage the outside stressors (e.g., discipline techniques, assertiveness, communication, time management). Of particular interest here is his provision of a list of coping self-statements which you can use in the face of threats or provocation.

Meichenbaum offers an interesting insight into the nature of our stress arousal when confronted with stressors. He indicates that rather than being in a state of no stress or full-on stress, in fact, you experience a gradual build up of stress beginning when you are preparing to face the threat or demand, experiencing its impact, then coping with your arousal and, finally, reflecting on the effects of the threat or demand. Experience and research have shown that you can decrease your reaction to stress by learning how to employ coping self-statements at various times before, during and after you have been exposed to stress.

In preparing for stressful situations where you experience high anxiety, Meichenbaum recommends that you use the following set of coping self-statements. (From Donald Meichenbaum *Cognitive-Behavior Modification*, New York: Plenum Press, 1977, pp 155, 166, 167.)

Preparing for a Stressor
What is it you have to do?
You can develop a plan to deal with it.
Just think what you can do about it. That's better than getting anxious.
No negative self-statements; just think rationally.
Don't worry; worry won't help anything.
Maybe what you think is anxiety is eagerness to confront it.

Confronting and Handling the Stressor
Just psyche yourself up—you can meet this challenge.
One step at a time; you can handle the situation.
Don't think about fear; just think about what you have to do.
Stay relevant.

This anxiety is what the doctor said you would feel.
It's a reminder to use your coping exercises.

Coping with the Feeling of Being Overwhelmed

When fear comes, just pause.
Keep the focus on the present. What is it you have to do?
Label your fear from 0 to 10 and watch it change.
You should expect your fear to rise.
Don't try to eliminate fear totally; just keep it manageable.
You can convince yourself to do it. You can reason your
fear away.
It will be over shortly.
It's not the worst thing which can happen.
Just think about something else.
Do something which will prevent you from thinking about
the fear.
Describe what is around you. That way you won't think
about worrying.

Reinforcing Self-statements

It worked; you did it.
It wasn't as bad as you expected.
You made more out of the fear than it was worth.
Your damn ideas — that's the problem.
When you control them, you control your fear.
It's getting better each time you use the procedures.
You can be pleased with the progress you're making.
You did it!

While the above sets of self-statements can be used for dealing with threatening situations which can trigger off anxiety, a different set of self-statements can be employed when faced with difficult and provocative situations and people at school when you decide you want to stay calmer, rather than getting very angry.

Preparing for a Provocation

What is it you have to do?
You can work out a plan to handle this.
You can manage this situation. You know how to regulate
your anger.
If you find yourself getting upset, you'll know what to do.

There won't be any need for an argument.
Time for a few deep breaths of relaxation.
Feel comfortable, relaxed and at ease.
This could be a testy situation, but you believe in yourself.

Confronting the Provocation
Stay calm. Just continue to relax.
As long as you keep your cool, you're in control here.
Don't take it personally.
Don't get bent all out of shape; just think of what to do here.
You don't have to prove yourself.
There is no point in getting mad.
You're not going to let him get to you.
Don't assume the worst or jump to conclusions. Look for the positives.
It's really a shame this person is acting the way she is.
For a person to be that irritable, he must be awfully unhappy.
If you start to get mad, you'll just be banging your head against the wall.
So you might as well just relax.
There's no need to doubt yourself. What he says doesn't matter.

Coping with Arousal and Agitation
Your muscles are starting to feel tight.
Time to relax and slow things down.
Getting upset won't help.
It's just not worth it to get so angry.
You'll let him make a fool of himself.
It's reasonable to get annoyed, but let's keep the lid on.
Time to take a deep breath.
Your anger is a signal of what you need to do. Time to talk to yourself.
You're not going to get pushed around, but you're not going haywire either.
Try a cooperative approach. Maybe you are both right.
He'd probably like you to get really angry.
Well, you're going to disappoint him.
You can't expect people to act the way you want them to.

Self-reward
It worked!
That wasn't as hard as you thought.
You could have gotten more upset than it was worth.
Your ego can sure get you in trouble,
but when you watch that ego stuff, you're better off.
You're doing better at this all the time.
You actually got through that without getting angry.
Guess you've been getting upset for too long when it wasn't
even necessary.

Learning to use coping self-statements in conjunction with practical coping and problem-solving skills in the various teaching situations you find stressful is the Meichenbaum formula for stress reduction.

STRESS SCRIPTS

Now that you have seen illustrated the wide variety of thoughts and attitudes which can both exacerbate and alleviate stress, you are in a good position to begin to not only recognise your own stress-creating thinking but also to modify it.

In order to recognise stress-creating thinking, be on the lookout for irrational thinking, pessimistic thinking, low self-efficacy and negative coping self-statements. Stress-reducing thoughts are characterised by rationality, high self-efficacy, optimism and coping self-statements.

Susan Forman employs Stress Scripts as a way of preparing teachers to cope with on-the-job stress. As you see illustrated below, a Stress Script has you initially identifying stress-producing thoughts, your emotional stress reactions, and your typical behavioural stress reactions. The next step is to develop a list of stress-reducing thoughts which counter the stress-producing ones and specify how you would like to feel and act in the stressful situation (from S. G. Forman & M. A. Cecil, *Teacher stress: causes, effects, interventions* in T. R. Kratochwill (ed.), *Advances in School Psychology*, Vol. 5 [Hillsdale, New Jersey: Lawrence Erlbaum, 1986]).

Stress Script 1

Teaching stressor: you get a message from the principal that says he's going to be observing your class tomorrow.

Stress-producing thoughts
1 I must be doing something wrong.
2 I must be doing a bad job.
3 He probably thinks I'm incompetent.
4 I'll be so nervous. I'll do everything wrong.
5 He probably doesn't like me.
6 The kids will act up and I don't know what to do.

Emotional stress reactions
Very anxious and depressed.
Behavioural stress reactions
May teach a lesson and interact with students inappropriately.

Stressreducing thoughts
1 I don't like having people observe me, but the principal has to observe everyone, so I guess I can get through this as everyone else.
2 I'll make sure I'm prepared tonight and do the best I can.
3 I think I'm doing a good job so far and he's never indicated otherwise.
4 Since I've been doing well all along, there's no reason to think I won't do well tomorrow.
5 If I relax and stay calm things will go well, just like they have been going.
6 I have always been able to handle this class before, so there's no reason for me not to handle it well tomorrow. Even if a student does become disruptive, if I can remain calm I'll be able to use a classroom discipline method that will help the situation.

New emotional stress reactions
Calm and confident

New behavioural stress reactions
Will do a good job with the planned lesson and handle any problems arising.

115

Stress Script 2

Teaching stressor: you give a student an assignment. He looks at you and belligerantly says 'I'm not gonna do that.'

Stress-producing thoughts
1 You little monster.
2 How could he say this to me?
3 He's getting me really upset.
4 He's stupid. He doesn't want to learn.
5 This is going to destroy the class.
6 Why hasn't he been helped before? He's in high school already! I shouldn't have to deal with these problems in the high school.
7 I've got to find a way to motivate him. I should be able to do it.
8 Why should I?

Emotional stress reactions
Angry and anxious

Behavioural stress reactions
Yell at him. Tell him to leave the class.

Stressreducing thoughts
1 He's not a monster.
2 I want to know why he said that, so I guess I can talk to him about it.
3 I can stay calm if I want to because I can control how I feel.
4 Most kids want to do well. He's probably just afraid he can't do the work.
5 The rest of the class is doing all right. Most kids are smart enough to understand why some kids act out. This class has been going pretty well for two months. One comment won't destroy it.
6 It would have been nice if he had been given remedial help before and it would be more pleasant if I didn't have to deal with this. But just complaining won't make things better. Since I don't like this situation I will decide where to go from here. No one ever said this job would be easy.
7 I'm going to try to find a way to motivate him. But I also want to remember that it's difficult to find motivators for all kids. We can't have complete control over their lives and we have limited amount of materials. I'll just do my best. I'm doing fairly well with the other twenty-seven kids in the class.

8 I will calmly consider the options and then consider which is best. I can talk to him about why he doesn't want to do the work. I can give him something I know he can be successful at. I can reward him for what he does and gradually make his assignments more difficult. I can ask other teachers or special services staff for suggestions.

New emotional stress reactions
Calm, confident and somewhat optimistic.

New behavioural stress reactions
Will relax. Will act on the thoughts in statement 8.

ACTIONS SPEAK LOUDER THAN WORDS

Over the next week, continue to monitor your stress levels using your stress thermometer. As well, record as concretely and specifically as possible the stressful event and your behavioural reaction.

In addition, single out one or two stressful events and, using the format below, complete a Stress Script. In doing this, keep in mind that the first few times or even more that you write a Stress Script you may find that you are only able to come up with a few stress-creating or stress-reducing thoughts. That's quite 'normal'. You may find that by going through the material in this chapter and the various lists of thoughts that you will be able to expand your own list. Remind yourself that the goal of emotional self-control is not the total elimination of all stressful feelings but rather a reduction in their intensity, duration, and frequency.

Outline of Stress Script

Teaching stressor: _____

_____

Stress-creating thoughts

_____

_____

Taking the stress out of teaching

Emotional stress reactions

_____

_____

Behavioural stress reactions

_____

_____

Stress-reducing thoughts

_____

_____

_____

_____

New emotional stress reactions

_____

_____

New behavioural stress reactions

_____

_____

RECOMMENDED READING

Elwood Chapman, *How to Develop a Positive Attitude* (London: Kogan Page, 1988).
Ernest Feist, *The Winning Edge* (Chatswood, NSW: Golden Spurs Publication, 1989).
Stephon Kaplan-Williams, *Changing Your Life* (Berkeley: Journey Press, 1984).
Arnold Lazarus and Alan Fay, *I Can If I Want To* (New York: Warner, 1978).
Maxwell Maltx, *Psycho-Cybernetics* (New York: Pocket Books, 1970).
Maxie C. Maultsby, *Coping Better Anytime, Anywhere* (New York: Prentice-Hall, 1986).

Richard Nelson-Jones, *Thinking Skills: Managing and Preventing Personal Problems* (Melbourne, Vic.: Thomas Nelson, 1990).
Mike Pedler and Tom Boydell, *Managing Yourself* (London: Fontana, 1985).
John Pepper, *How to Be Happy* (London: Arkana, 1985).
Penelope Russianoff, *When Am I Going to Be Happy?* (Sydney: Transworld, 1989).
Haydn Sargent, *Power to Choose* Brisbane, Qld: Boolarong Publications, 1989).

CHAPTER 6
RATIONAL EFFECTIVENESS TRAINING

'RET is directed at helping people overcome inefficient ways of handling their problems at work, the emotional hangups they have about these problems (hostility, anxiety and depression), and how to reduce the inevitable and, potentially, overwhelming amounts of job-related stress.'

Michael E. Bernard,
Staying Rational In an Irrational World, 1986.

This chapter presents a more detailed analysis of the relationship between irrational attitudes, thinking and teacher stress and shows how rational thinking skills can be applied by you to gain additional control over your own emotional stress reactions. If you want to continue to see how you can use your head to manage stress, read along. Otherwise you may wish to come back to this chapter after you've read other sections of this book.

ATTITUDES AND THOUGHTS

I define attitudes and thought as being related but somewhat different in character. 'Attitudes' are general rules or values about yourself, other people, your work, your school and the wider community and world. Attitudes provide you with a framework for understanding and evaluating your world. They also tend to be more general than thoughts.

'Thoughts' are what you actually tell yourself in a certain situation where you are evaluating yourself, people, your work, your school, and the wider community and world. Synonyms for thoughts are 'self-talk', 'self-statements', and 'private thoughts'.

An example of the relationship between attitudes and thoughts can be seen in Alyce, who has the *attitude* 'I must be successful in things that I do at school'. When Alyce is confronted with situations at school where she hasn't succeeded, such as having an undisciplined class or having a student do poorly on an important test, her *thoughts* in these situations include: 'It's terrible to have such an undisciplined class. I can't stand it knowing that my student did so poorly. I'm a hopeless teacher.' In order for Alyce to de-stress herself about situations at school where she hasn't achieved her goals, she needs not only to change her stress-creating thoughts but her stress-creating attitudes as well.

Put another way, attitudes can be compared to computer programs which direct a computer to perform in the desired fashion. Unlike the computer, your attitudes via your thinking have a strong influence on your emotional stress reactions. As you know, what you put in is what you get out and bad computer programs produce bad results. And the more junk you put into your own computer (your head) in the form of stress-creating irrational attitudes, the more stress-creating thoughts and feelings you get out. So you have to become more aware of your attitudes and your thinking which turn a stressful situation at school into teacher distress.

A MODEL OF RATIONAL
SELF-MANAGEMENT

I have developed a five-stage model which can help you gain emotional control over your stress reactions at work. It is one which I have introduced to people who work in a variety of occupations including public servants, insurance salespeople, real estate agents, hospital administrators and professional athletes to name but a few. The basis of the model lies in the work of Albert Ellis and his theory and practice of rational-emotive therapy. Dominic DiMattia, the director of Corporate Services at the New York Institute for Rational-Emotive Therapy, is a colleague who has helped me with the development of this model under the workplace derivative of RET which has been coined 'Rational Effectiveness Training'. The model is being increasingly used throughout the world in a variety of business organisations and governmental agencies as a way of not only reducing stress but increasing work performance and satisfaction. Let me briefly describe the five steps to rational self-management.

1 *Identify teaching stressor* The first thing to do to reduce stress is to identify for yourself as clearly and specifically as possible something which happens at work which creates in you a great deal of emotional stress.

2 *Identify your stress reactions* It is important to be clear in describing your feelings such as anxiety, feeling down or rage in reaction to the stressor. You also need to rate the amount of emotional stress you experience. You can use the Stress Thermometer presented below to measure your 'emotional temperature' on a 0 to 10 point scale. Be sure to indicate all the different feelings you experience. In step two you should describe your typical behavioural stress reactions (what you do) when confronted with the teaching stressor.

Stress Thermometer

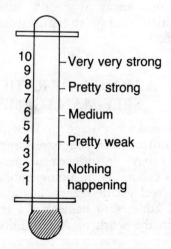

10	
9	– Very very strong
8	– Pretty strong
7	
6	– Medium
5	
4	– Pretty weak
3	
2	– Nothing
1	happening

3 *Stress-creating thoughts*   Write down the kinds of different thoughts you have when you are experiencing emotional stress.

4 *Goals*   How would you like to feel and behave the next time you are confronted with the *same* teaching stressor?

5 *New stress-reducing thoughts*   Identify some thoughts which you can use the next time the stressful situation arises which counter your stress-creating thoughts (step four) and which will help you control and reduce your emotional stress reactions and engage in more constructive, coping behaviours.

Presented below is the Rational Self-Management Form I have developed which you can use to help manage your stress.

Rational Self-management Form

1 *Teaching stressor* (be specific):

_____

_____

2 *Stress reactions*

My feelings _____   How strongly 1 2 3 4 5 6 7 8 9 10

My feelings _____   How strongly 1 2 3 4 5 6 7 8 9 10

My behaviour _____

3 *Stress-creating irrational thoughts*

_____

_____

4 *Goals (how you would like to feel and act)*

New feeling(s) _____

New behaviour(s) _____

5 *New stress-reducing thoughts*

_____

_____

_____

This approach to self-management is not that much different from the steps involved in the Stress Scripts introduced in the last chapter. The difference lies in a more careful analysis of the types of situations at work you find stressful and in your use of rational beliefs and thoughts to modify your stress.

In the following sections, four categories of stressful situations at work which we know can lead to extreme teacher stress are described: 'Being evaluated', 'Difficult People', 'Organisational Mismanagement' and 'Frustrating Work Tasks'. For each of these categories, common examples of teaching stressors, typical stress reactions, stress-creating attitudes and thoughts, and new stress-reducing attitudes and thoughts are provided.

BEING EVALUATED

Bill was chomping on his tuna and vegemite sandwich when out of the corner of his eye he saw Alyce Greenway sneaking into the staff room. It was her first year of teaching and he knew she was going through a tough period.

'Come sit over here, Alyce,' grunted Bill as he wolfed down the remainder of his third sandwich. 'How's it going?'

Alyce looked like she had just pulled herself out of the trenches at Gallipoli. 'Huh?' was all she could manage.

'Do you like teaching?'

'I guess I do,' said Alyce after a long pause while she considered the question. 'But I find it a big strain.'

'Yeah, I know what you mean. It gets easier after a while, but I still have some horror days.'

'You do? I always thought you looked...I guess confident.'

Bill scratched his head, realising that compared to Alyce, perhaps, he didn't appear so unsure to himself as he thought.

'What exactly is it about teaching that you find a strain?'

Alyce was pleased to be able to talk to someone beside herself and her cat. 'I find the psychological and physical confrontation with the kids very hard. I guess because I care so much, I find the strain immense. I sometimes feel, especially earlier in the year, that I am really going insane. I seem to lose my sense of judgement. Tiny incidents become terrible catastrophes. Last night I thought I was going off the rails mentally and emotionally. I actually burst into tears.'

Alyce stopped herself, fearing she had said too much already.

Sensing her discomfort, Bill replied: 'Oh don't worry. Sometimes everyone needs someone to talk to. Otherwise, you will go crazy!'

Alyce smiled and then asked: 'What did you do to, y'know, cope with it all?'

'I'm not expert, mind you. I'm probably a bit like you. I care a little bit too much about what others think of me and put too much pressure on myself to succeed. I guess I'm learning not to blow things out of perspective and not to take everything all the time so personally. I've learned a bit about how to change my attitudes so that my thoughts don't make things any worse than they are.'

'You mean like not getting my knickers in a twist when my team loses a game?'

'Huh, ah yes, Alyce, something like that,' said Bill grabbing his books wondering about the connection between sport and teacher stress. 'Something like that.'

'Evaluation' stressors

One of the reasons teaching is so stressful is that your 'ego' is publically on the line every day in many ways for many to see. Your students evaluate you from the moment they see you on the first day of school. Your performance and teaching ability are reflected in your students' performance. As well other teachers, administrators and parents stand in judgement of you at various times in the school year. Not only that, your ability to deal with 'difficult' students students with special needs, your discipline skills, your organisational skills, etc. are also being judged. When you want to make a point at a staff meeting or to a colleague or administrator, your public speaking performance is also being judged. Occasionally, you may even receive a formal face-to-face evaluation of your teaching performance.

The impending changes which you may face in assessment procedures, curriculum and in amalgamating with other schools bring with them the threat that you may not perform as well as you would like. Given the complexity, diversity and difficulty levels of the many tasks you perform at school, the likelihood of you achieving *all* your goals *all* of the time is small. And the possibility of students, colleagues and administrators disapproving of some aspect of your teaching is quite high.

Common stress reactions

In a nutshell, the common emotional stress reactions to situations where you do not achieve your goals and where others might be evaluating you negatively are feelings of anxiety about what might happen tomorrow, about what others are thinking of you, and feeling down about yourself because of what's happened. It is also true that sometimes you can get quite angry with yourself or others for not allowing you to achieve what you set out to do or for unfairly, perhaps, criticising you.

Behaviourally, there are an almost infinite number of expressions of 'ego anxiety' and 'self-downing' including giving up, unsteady and uneven performance, aggression, social isolation and detachment.

Stress-creating attitudes and thoughts

There are two stress-creating attitudes which you need to be on the look out for which give rise to excess stress in the above situations. One has to do with *your unrealistic demand for achievement* and the other has to do with your *need for approval*. The former has to do with how you evaluate yourself when you have not achieved your goals while the latter involves how you evaluate yourself when others devalue or criticise your teaching. Let's look at the first of these attitudes: 'I must always be successful at things I do at work and never make mistakes; if I do, I am a failure'.

Many teachers who are very stressed are excellent teachers.

They have very high standards both for themselves and for their students. Their excellence is often recognised by the awards they win. Over time, however, they slowly begin to be burned out because of the impossibility of themselves and their students ever satisfying their *need for achievement*. If you are a teacher who *demands* to be achieving, you will slowly tyrannise yourself when faced with your own and your students' lack of accomplishment. Each time a student or class fails to achieve what you have thought they *should* achieve, your doubts about yourself increase. You start to feel anxious and, perhaps, even depressed about your teaching. And the cause of your despair is partly due to your own irrational demands of yourself that you must be successful all the time.

Why irrational? Because there is no law of the universe which says you must be successful at all the important things you do at school. It is obvious from what we observe in student behaviour that some students will not perform satisfactorily no matter what teaching approach they have been exposed to. Further, demanding of yourself success all the time is unrealistic. It denies your own fallibility as a teacher and human being who makes mistakes and who cannot perform at a top level all the time.

This attitude is also irrational because it is not logical. It does not logically follow that because you desire and like to be successful that you must be successful and that you are a failure when you are not. Further, just because it is bad to not achieve your goals, doesn't mean that it is terrible or a catastrophe.

A variation of this theme can be seen in the teacher who demands perfection. *Perfectionism* is expressed in the stress-creating teacher attitude: 'I must perform perfectly at important things I do at work; I cannot accept it when I don't; I am a failure when I do things imperfectly'. This attitude is even more unrealistic than the simple need for achievement because with this attitude you are insisting that things at school be done perfectly. And no matter how good you are, it simply is not possible for you to do things perfectly all the time.

How will you know if you have a high need for achievement or are even a perfectionist? You can tell by thinking about how anxious and down you feel and how often you feel that way when faced with situations at work where you haven't achieved your goals. These can include when you are confronted by a sea of blank faces, lack of student enthusiasm, students not showing up for an elective, a student or students not performing well on the end-of-year exam, students not responding to your discipline and any other situation which implies to you that you haven't achieved or performed perfectly. Excess stress at these times goes hand-in-hand with the unrealistic standards and expectations you have of yourself.

Here are some specific examples of stress-creating thoughts which stem from a high need or demand for achievement.

'I should be able to solve my students' problems.'
'I must never make mistakes.'
'I should be able to have good classroom discipline.'
'I should do this perfectly.'
'I ought to know better how to handle this situation.'
'It's awful to make mistakes.'
'It's terrible that I can't get this class to settle down.'
'It's horrible that my class did so poorly.'
'I'm a hopeless teacher.'
'I've failed.'
'I'll never be a good teacher.'

The attitude involving excessive approval seeking can be stated as follows: 'I need to be recognised and approved of by important people that I work with; it's awful to be criticised or rejected. I think I'm no good when people think badly of me.'

Some teachers have a higher need for approval than others (as do people in all professions). Some have a great deal of trouble tolerating criticism of disapproval. These 'approval seekers' get quite high when they are positively evaluated by someone at school whom they value and conversely get quite anxious and down when their lack of performance brings with it disapproval or criticism. Now all of us like to be approved of and dislike disapproval. The issue here is the strength of the need, which you can largely determine by how stressed you get when your colleagues at school, the principal and parents seem to be devaluing your teaching performance and are either implicitly or explicitly negative towards you.

Here are some examples of thoughts which are caused by having a high need for approval. This list might also be helpful in assisting you locate stress-creating ideas for your rational self-management analysis.

'I need people to approve of my work.'

'It's awful to be criticised.'

'I can't stand it when someone tells me I didn't do something very well.'

'Because important others disapprove of the job I'm doing, I'm no good.'

New stress-reducing attitudes and thoughts

The rational counter attitudes to a *high need for achievement* and *perfectionism* can be expressed as follows: 'Doing things well at work is satisfying but it's human to make mistakes. There is no law of the universe that says that I must do well.' 'While it's desirable to be the very best I can be in my work because excellence brings with it satisfaction, I can accept myself even when my work is imperfect.'

Changing your attitude does not involve throwing out the standard of achievement nor, even, the desire to be perfect. Both of these values and goals will, when achieved, bring you (and others) a great deal of pleasure and satisfaction. The solution is to drop the command you are making of yourself that you *must* be successful or even perfect most if not all of the time. The idea is not to be so hard on yourself. Try the best you can at work and even strive for perfection if that turns you on, but don't dump on yourself when you or events outside you conspire against you and you are not the success you want to be. Stay confident in yourself and believe that things will soon change for the better. They tend to when you don't overly stress yourself out by blowing things out of proportion.

To counter the attitudes and thoughts surrounding approval seeking and low disapproval tolerance, consider the issue of whether you really *need* approval and recognition like you need food, shelter and clothing. Sure, it's preferable to have approval than not to have it. But is it a life necessity?

The facts are that many teachers—including you and me—survive periods when others think we're pretty hopeless at what we do. We feel crummy at those times, but we survive. You can still be happy, though not as happy, without it. Once you realise that you have survived without it, you'll panic less about doing without it again. A rational counter to the need for approval can be expressed along the following lines: 'While it's definitely nice to have the approval of the people I work with, I don't need it in order to accept myself and I can still enjoy myself without it'.

It sometimes is difficult to come up with some new thoughts which can counter the old stress-creating ones. Below is a list of ones which can be employed when you are experiencing feelings of anxiety and being down in situations where you and/or others are negatively evaluating your performance.

'Just because things are not succeeding today does not mean I'm a "no hoper" or that I will not succeed tomorrow.'

'Striving for a perfect solution can drive me crazy.'

'While it is very desirable to achieve well and be recognised by others, I do not *need* achievement or recognition to be happy.'

'Mistakes are inevitable. I will work hard at accepting myself while disliking my mistakes.'

'My performance at work—imperfect or otherwise—does not determine my worth as a person.'

'It's definitely nice to have the approval of people I work with, but even without it I can still accept myself.'

'I accept who I am.'

'There are many things about me that I like and do well.'

'Doing things well at work is satisfying—but it's human to make mistakes.'

'I am confident that everything will turn out okay given that I have my goals, know what to do and work hard.'

DIFFICULT PEOPLE

The rational self-management model can be applied by you

equally in learning to control your emotional stress reactions to people or groups of people you find difficult.

Common people stressors

Schools literally abound with difficult people. Difficult difficult people. Difficult people can be identified by their inconsiderate, disrespectful, unprofessional and unfair behaviour. Have you any of these in your school?

Descriptions of difficult people could literally take up the rest of this chapter if not the book. Let's target a few of the most common offenders.

Students All students are difficult some of the time and a few are difficult most of the time. Desciptions of their difficult behaviour are many. A few of the most common examples would be students who swear, bully, cheat, fight, call out, lie, don't do their work, talk too much and who deface school buildings.

Other teachers Difficult staff members to work with are those ones who are negative, critical, unprofessional, incompetent, lazy, non-supportive, judgemental and who play games.

Administrators Difficult administrators are the ones who yell, manipulate, are sexist, racist or ageist, authoritarian, non-communicative, indecisive, non-supportive, critical, incompetent or who lack leadership including a clear direction.

Parents Difficult parents are ones who are either totally disinterested or too involved. They can be excessively negative and non-supportive of your efforts. Difficult parents are also ones who exert an obvious negative impact on their children. They're the ones whose kid goes home on Friday reasonably shaped up from a week of your effort and comes back Monday morning a mess.

Common stress reactions

The most common emotional stress reaction when confronted with a difficult person is anger. The more provocative, unfair and inconsiderate the difficult person's actions are, the more fury you experience. It is also not uncommon to feel put down and inferior in the face of unfair and negative treatment.

Behaviourally, the more anger you experience, the more you would like to throttle the difficult person. Some of the things you might elect to do, depending on who it is, include: yelling and screaming, resisting direction, undermining, criticism, not helping or supporting, and back stabbing.

One of the important questions to answer in order to lessen your anger towards another and thereby reduce your stress is whether your behaviour is helping you get what you want. Does it help change the situation so that the next time the person is likely to act differently? If your behaviour doesn't help and either prolongs your anger or makes the situation worse, you have to decide whether there is a better way to handle the person. If there is, then learning to reduce your anger is an important first step.

Stress-creating attitudes and thoughts

The general irrational attitude which increases your stress level in the face of inconsiderate, unfair or unprofessional people can be stated generally as follows: 'People must treat me considerately, respectfully, fairly; I can't stand it when they don't; if they don't, I consider them totally bad and deserving of punishment'.

You can hold this idea with respect of one type of person such as a student, colleague or parent, or hold it about everyone. Here are some sample irrational thoughts which stem from this attitude. 'I can't stand students who are constantly rude and misbehave.'

'Parents should be more interested in their children work.'

'It's really terrible to have to teach with someone who doesn't care about their work. They really should.'

'My coordinator should know better than to criticise me in public. He's a real ass.'

The most stress-creating thought which seems to result in rage rather than just irritation is when you condemn someone for what they have done. Think about the last time you were furious with someone. What choice word did you use to describe the person? I'm sure it wasn't 'He's a little angel for treating me so badly'.

New stress-reducing attitudes

The rational attitude to combat the irrational demand that people act considerately sounds something like: 'I accept that people are fallible and make mistakes. They are the way they are because that's the way they are. While I don't like it when they are negative, unfair or unprofessional, I can definitely stand it and still accept them.'

Once again, modifying and revising your irrational expectation that people *must* behave well does not mean you simply accept their behaviour. The way to lower your stress level in the face of behaviour which you find unacceptable in others is to begin to expect that they will from time to time act unfairly, inconsiderately and not in the way you expect. Once you tell yourself that you can tolerate their miserable behaviour, that it's not the end of the world and that they are not total asses for their ass-like behaviour, you will be in control of your anger and you will be more likely to figure out and employ the most effective means for modifying their behaviour in the future.

Here are some examples of rational thoughts which you can employ in the face of another's difficult behaviour which will counter your old stress-creating irrational thinking.

'While it is preferable to be treated fairly, kindly and considerately, there is no law of the universe which says I must.'

'People who act unfairly, inconsiderately or unkindly may deserve to be penalised, but never to be totally condemned as rotten no-goodniks who deserve to be eternally damned and punished.'

'Anger does not help in the long run, it is only temporarily effective at best.'

'Anger towards others frequently prevents me from getting what I want.'

'While it is undesirable to fail to get what I want, it is seldom awful or intolerable.'

'I can cope successfully with unfair people though I strongly wish they would act better.'

'I wish others would treat me better, but they never have to.'

'I do not need other people to act well, I only prefer it.'

'People are the way they are because that's the way they are, tough.'

'I can live and be happy — though not as happy — with his/her fallibility.'

'My superior (colleague, student) is fallible and will often, not always, do the wrong thing; tough, that's the way fallible human being work.'

'I can put up with this negative and hostile person, though it would be better if he/she acted better.'

ORGANISATIONAL MISMANAGEMENT

Many aspects of the ways both the Department of Education and your own school organisation operate are known to lead to teacher stress. Once again, the key is to learn how to control your emotional reactions to these organisational stressors so that they do not become intolerable.

Organisational stressors

As discussed earlier, there are aspects of the way the Department of Education makes policy and executes policy which are negative. Recent changes in ministerial policy involving amalgamation, curriculum, assessment and job conditions have had a negative short-term impact on teachers. (It is to be hoped in the long run that the wrinkles will be ironed out, but this knowledge doesn't make your life any less stressful.)

At the same time, the way in which your school organisation is run can have a negative impact on you. You may have little say over decisions made by higher-ups which affect you and in which you could be involved. The choice of class, scheduling of classes, the distribution of free periods, the frequency of assessment, the specific extra-curricular activities selected as the year's priorities, and the number and timing of meetings are decision areas which if made by others can have a negative impact on you. You may find yourself having to work with a year-level coordinator, vice principal or principal who lacks effective interpersonal, decision-making and leadership skills. You might find that your school is excessively conservative or liberal. The distribution of workload may also be something you find inequitable, unsatisfactory and stressful.

Common stress reactions

As much organisational mismanagement and bureaucratic bungling is not directed at you personally, in the majority of instances your emotional stress reaction will be one of frustration, anger and alienation. Your enthusiasm and satisfaction will also tend to be greatly reduced unless there are compensating factors.

Behavioural stress reactions can be either passive or aggressive. You may decide to confront aggressively those in positions of authority and ventilate your displeasure and rage. Or you may simply decide to go into a work slow-down mode, show less interest in your work, have more days of absenteeism or, eventually, even decide to get out of teaching altogether.

Stress-creating attitudes and thoughts

One of the main stress-creating attitudes which exacerbates the effects of organisational mismanagement is similar to the one which causes excess stress in response to difficult people: 'Organisations should be fair in carrying out decisions which affect the working conditions of teaching. Schools should consult with teachers and should never act in self-serving ways.'

Typical thoughts which reveal this attitudes include:

'I can't stand it when I am not consulted about something which effects me.'

'It's awful to have to teach here.'

'It's not fair that I am expected to change what I'm doing.'
'I despise the fact that our principal is so insensitive.'
'I can't teach when I have no say.'
'One of the things I find horrible is the lack of communication between teachers and central administration.'
'Without good communication and support, school is a disaster.'

Once again, by referring to the Teacher Irrational Belief Scale you completed in Chapter 2, you will get an idea how your attitude towards your school's organisation compares with other teachers. My own research suggests that while these attitudes and thoughts are not sufficient to produce a debilitating stress reaction, they do add to your overall stress level.

Stress-reducing attitudes and thoughts

The key to managing stress related to the way the department or your school operates is to increase your tolerance for the 'miserable' actions of your organisation. Once you fall into the trap of thinking that you can't stand things you do not like, you will increase your stress dramatically.

The rational attitude acknowledges that there are bad things which characterise your school's organisation and that, indeed, just about any organisation has its problems. Learning to tolerate (but certainly not like) your own school's failings as well as the 'miserable' actions of the education department or your school board has you adopting an attitude: 'School organisations are inherently fallible, some more than others. It's their nature. While I definitely do not like working in an environment which makes bad decisions and for people who initiate and carry out the decisions, I can definitely work in such an environment. By learning to tolerate bureaucratic "glitches", I will be in a stronger position to make changes where I can as well as continue to be the best teacher possible.'

I hope this doesn't sound like selling out or contributing yourself in the perpetuation of a bad system. It doesn't result in this end. This attitude does enable you to clearly see your school and the educational system for what it is—its good points and its not so good points—and, as a consequence, be realistic in what you can expect. You may decide in your realistic appraisal that it is not the system you want to work in. That may be a decision which is in your best interests. At least, however, you will have arrived at the decision weighing up the pros and cons without letting your emotional distress reaction magnify the negatives and negatively influence your own decision-making process.

Some of the thoughts which can help you remain sane when things around you appear insane are:

'Why *must* this place be any different than it is? It's desirable, but is it realistic, given what I know about school, to demand that it be better?'

'I can put up with organisational miserableness, even though I don't like it.'

'What are the good things about working in this school?'

'While not being consulted is bad, it is not the end of the world.'

'My principal's lack of communication is a real negative. I can be happy— though not as happy—working under these circumstances.'

'Rather than blaming my school's conditions for how stressed I am, what can I do over the next few months to make things better for myself?'

'I don't have to let this get to me.'

'Where is it written that my school should be a fair place to work all the time?'

FRUSTRATING WORK TASKS

My experience and research are clear in showing that your ability to maintain self-control in the face of time and workload pressures as well as when doing certain frustrating work tasks is a vital barrier between you and job distress. The more you can marshall your own resources, including staying calm, working out an efficient time management plan (see Chapter 9) and getting support from those around you at school and at home, the more they will help innoculate you against stress.

Common task stressors

Teachers, as do people in all other professions, find that there are certain things they have to be done in their job that they find especially frustrating. It might be grading, writing reports, long-term planning, preparing exams, returning phone calls, attending meetings, preparing new work units or revising old work units. Any one of these alone is generally not that difficult to do. It's when you have to do the tasks along with all your other teaching and at-home responsibilities that you might find them especially demanding and stress-creating.

Common stress reactions

When faced with doing tasks we find frustrating, boring, tedious and hard we tend to experience varying degrees of frustration. Some of us get more frustrated more quickly. This is especiallly the case when we have quite a bit to do and not enough time to do it. It's not the frustration or even the high level of frustration experienced under these conditions which is the problem. It's normal to feel very frustrated. It's how you feel and react when you get frustrated that represents the distress. The common emotional distress reactions to frustration are extreme anger, resentment, tension, confusion and often anxiety and depression.

Intense emotional stress reactions to frustrating tasks, especially if you're under time pressure, often lead to a variety of self-defeating behavioural stress reactions including procrastination, spending too much time on unimportant tasks, and becoming generally disorganised. An accompanying set of behavioural reactions which serve to reduce our discomfort and frustration include excessive drinking and taking days off from school.

Common stress-creating attitudes and thoughts

Your attitude towards difficult and frustrating tasks, particularly when you are pressured, can decrease your tolerance of frustration and increase your need for immediate stress reduction. Some of the main irrational attitudes leading to low frustration tolerance include: 'Conditions at work shouldn't be so hard; I can't stand the frustrations of work; things at work should be easier than they are'; 'I must have a pleasant life, a comfortable time and I cannot accept it when things at work are a hassle.'

While these attitudes may seem at first glance to be reasonable, a closer examination finds them to be irrational. The irrational part is in expecting things at work to be easier than they are and expecting that your life shouldn't be so hard. If you know from all the evidence around you that from time to time things are going to be hard slogging at work and that your life will be hassle-ful, it is quite unrealistic to expect things to be otherwise.

I'm not saying that it isn't bad when you've got to put with frustrating tasks at work and when there simply isn't enough time to accomplish everything that everyone expects of you. It is bad. And it's probably unfair, too. No disagreement. However, sometimes, especially in teaching, that's the way life is.

Some of the thoughts which reveal low frustration tolerance are:

'I shouldn't have to work so hard.'

'I can't stand having to put in so many hours at work.'

'It's really terrible to have too much work to do and not enough time to do it.'

'I really need my life to be more relaxing.'

'I can't put up with having to do all this work.'

Common stress-reducing attitudes and thoughts

Developing high frustration tolerance to things you have to do that you find frustrating or tedious is one of the keys here to sttress management. A rational attitude which can help you further develop your tolerance for frustration is: 'Things I do at work will often be hard, unpleasant and frustrating. Even though I don't like being frustrated, I can stand it.'

This attitude is realistic. It acknowledges the nature of your job which for the most part is not going to go away.

Here are some examples of rational thoughts which you can use when faced with difficult tasks or time-work load pressures:

'While it may be unfair that I have to work so hard, why *must* my life be easy?'

'What makes this task *too* hard?'

'No matter how onerous a task is to do, it is tough to do it now, but it is much tougher to do it later.'

'While things I have to do may be difficult, unpleasant and boring, they are rarely *too* difficult unpleasant and boring.'

'Even though I don't like frustration, I *can* stand it.'

'Yes, it is a pain to do this now, but I'd better because it's much harder and I get worse results if I do it later.'

'I can cope with feeling stressed and strained.'

'In order to obtain pleasant results, I often have to do *un*pleasant things.'

'The more I keep at this, the better I'll get.'

'Hey Mary, come over here for a moment.'

Mary looked over at Bill, wondering what he was up to.

'Come over here, I said!'

'What's up with you?'

'Listen, I want you to fill out this RET form. It'll fix your stress up quick smart.'

'I'll pick who or what's going to fix me up, thank you very much.'

'C'mon, you look like you've been rode hard and put away wet! This place is really getting to you.'

'It's all right for you. No one is telling you how to teach science.

I can't stand having to re-do my course for next year simply to please some bureaucrat—or even the principal for that matter.'

'Well, where's all that aggro getting you? Closer to early retirement.'

'Okay, let's have a look at this form.'

Example of Mary's Rational Self-management Form

1 *Teaching stressor (be specific)*:
Not being consulted over curriculum changes. Lack of communication from principal.

2 *Stress reactions*
Your feelings furious   How strongly 1 2 3 4 5 6 7 8 9 ⑩
Your feelings resentful How strongly 1 2 3 4 5 6 7 ⑧ 9 10
Behaviour Smoke too much, take it out on the kids, cold-shoulder the principal

3 *Stress-creating thoughts*
I can't stand it. Schools should be better places to work. The principal is a no-hoper. I can't work under these conditions. I shouldn't have to put up with this.

4 *Goals (how you would like to feel and act)*
New feeling(s) Calmer, less irritated
New behaviour(s) Discuss matter calmly with principal. Investigate how much new work I really have to do.

5 *New stress-reducing rational thoughts*
I don't like what's happened but it's fairly typical of the way things work. I don't like it, but I can put up with it. I guess the principal isn't totally bad; he did give me time off to study last year

ACTIONS SPEAK LOUDER THAN WORDS

Select a work stressor from one of the above four categories (being evaluated; difficult people; organisational mismanagement; frustrating work tasks) which you find particularly stressful. From the above discussion, see if you can identify which irrational attitude(s) you hold which leads to your high level of stress and which rational attitudes you can employ to reduce your stress. Then, using the form below, complete a rational self-analysis.

Rational Self-management Form

1 *Teaching stressor (be specific):*

_____

_____

2 *Stress reactions*
   Your feelings _____ How strongly 1 2 3 4 5 6 7 8 9 10
   Your feelings _____ How strongly 1 2 3 4 5 6 7 8 9 10
   Your behaviour _____

   _____

3 *Stress-creating thoughts*

   _____

   _____

   _____

4 *Goals (how you would like to feel and act)*
   New feeling(s) _____

   New behaviour(s) _____

   _____

5 *New stress-reducing thoughts*

   _____

   _____

   _____

   _____

   _____

   _____

RECOMMENDED READING

Michael E. Bernard, *Staying Rational In an Irrational World* (Melbourne, Vic.: McCulloch Publishing, 1986).

Wayne W. Dwyer, *Your Erroneous Zones* (New York: Avon Books, 1976).
Albert Ellis, *How Not to Make Yourself Miserable About Anything, Yes Anything!* (Secaucus, NJ: Lyle Stuart, 1988).
Albert Ellis and Robert Harper, *A New Guide to Rational Living* (Los Angeles, CA: Wilshire Books, 1976).

CHAPTER 7
RELAXATION

'The body registers stress long before the conscious mind does. Muscular tension is your body's way of letting you know you are under stress.'
Martha Davis, Elizabeth Eshelman and
Matthew McKay,
Relaxation & Stress Reduction Workbook, 1982.

As you saw with Bill Witherspoon's early ancestor Harry, when you experience stress, your nervous system over-works. Whether dodging dinosaurs or the Johnny Pains of this world, your biochemical changes under stress are the same: your pulse and respiration rates increase while your blood pressure climbs and your muscles tense. A variety of chemicals such as adrenaline and cortisone are released throughout your body. In pre-industrial revolution days when we were active on our feet, our lifestyle afforded us natural relief from the biochemical changes that occur during our 'flight-flight' response to stress. Our more sedentary life today puts us at much greater risk for chronic stress and associated illnesses.

Whereas the previously described self-management techniques which rely on modifying attitudes appear to be the most appropriate for modifying our emotional stress reactions which we are generally aware of, relaxation techniques have long been suggested in the stress management literature for use to directly modify the body's physiological response to stress.

The variety of relaxation techniques described in this chapter can be used for at least three distinct purposes. Relaxation can be used as 'preventative medicine' in order to postpone, delay or prevent the onset of the extreme physical and psychological stress reactions described earlier. Relaxation can also be used during high periods of stress at the beginning and end of the day to reduce your physical arousal level and discomfort level and to give you extra fuel in the tank for the next day. As well, you can use some of these relaxation techniques to help to prepare for and cope in the face of specific teaching stressors during the day.

I have introduced relaxation procedures to many teachers who are aware that they are experiencing excessive physical strain. They complain that before entering their own class where they anticipate a large amount of student disruption, they experience acute chest pains and nausea. I recently saw a school librarian who was self-conscious of her excessive physiological arousal when senior level students were working (and playing) in the library. She described how her voice audibly weakened, her face and throat flushed and her temples pounded. The reason that she was too self-conscious was that her physical stress reactions became themselves stressful. She would think to herself at these times, 'Oh no, the students can see I'm really uptight and losing control. This is terrible. They'll never respect me.'

Teachers I have worked with who experience severe physical stress reactions profit greatly from the practice of different relaxation techniques. They use relaxation at the end of the day to calm them down. Equally importantly, they use relaxation before they enter a stressful situation and while they are in the situation in order to maintain self-control.

Just as attitude change is not everyone's cup of tea so, too, do people react differently to the suggestion of incorporating some type of relaxation in their lives. People who are most negative are those who believe its use is not consistent with their 'macho' image or who feel guilty about devoting some part of their own time to themselves. The research indicates that, for some people, relaxation can be effective in treating specific disorders such as anxiety, depression, insomnia, headaches, backaches and high blood pressure. We know relaxation done effectively reduces perspiration, pulse rate, respiration and blood pressure. Under these circumstances, my view is 'Don't knock it if you haven't tried it'.

Seven of the more popular relaxation techniques are: muscle relaxation; controlled breathing; meditation; guided imagery training; self-hypnosis; autogenics; biofeedback. These are described below, concluding with a brief reference to other more informal relaxation techniques which teachers report using use to successfully relieve their stress.

MUSCLE RELAXATION

'Relaxation simply means doing nothing with your muscles.'
Edward A. Charlesworth and Ronald G. Nathan,
Stress Management: A Comprehensive Guide to
Wellness, 1984.

Progressive relaxation

Progressive relaxation is a muscle relaxation technique developed by a Chicago physician, Dr Edmund Jacobson, in the 1920s to help people take the anxiety out of their lives which he attributed to the increased competitive pressures of his times. His research revealed that when people where simply instructed to 'relax', most people still manifested significant electrical activity in their muscle fibres, indicating that they were not fully relaxed. He discovered that by tensing a muscle before relaxing it, the muscle would return to a more deeply relaxed state than it would by simply relaxing it. By teaching people to tense and relax major muscle groups, he was able to teach people how to more fully relax themselves. His technique is based on the simple principle that it is impossible to be physically tense if you are relaxed.

Progressive relaxation has you focused on the eventual removal of tension from four major muscle groups: hands, forearms and biceps; head, face, throat and shoulders including forehead, cheeks, eyes, nose, jaw, lips, tongue and neck; chest, stomach and back; thighs, buttocks, calves and feet. By becoming aware of the difference between how a muscle feels when it is tense and when it is relaxed, you will become more attuned to detecting and removing muscle tension from different parts of your body.

In learning this procedure, it is recommended that you practise at the same time each day for at least fifteen minutes and that you do not practise within one hour of eating. Using this schedule, you will develop initial mastery of progressive relaxation within one week.

In learning this technique, you will initially have to follow a set of instructions concerning the order in which you progressively relax your muscles and how to go about actually relaxing a muscle. There are a variety of commercially available cassettes which provide such instructions which you may wish to purchase (see references at the end of this chapter). Other options include familiarising yourself with the instructions which I will shortly provide, making your own cassette recording using these instructions or having someone else reading the instructions aloud to you.

To begin progressive relaxation you need to find a quiet place where you will not be interrupted by the telephone, children, television, etc. You may wish to hang a 'do not disturb' sign on your door and take the telephone off the receiver. You can learn this technique lying on the floor or on a comfortable bed or sitting in a chair. You should wear comfortable clothing, loosen your belt, remove glasses/contact lenses, tie and shoes.

Instructions for progressive relaxation

In the instructions which follow, you will notice that you begin with relaxing your head followed progressively by your shoulders and arms, body and legs. In order to learn how to relax, you will follow a four-step instructional sequence.

1. Separately tense your individual muscle groups.
2. Hold the tension about five seconds.
3. Slowly release the tension.
4. Notice the difference between feeling tense and feeling relaxed.

Word-by-word relaxation

Head 'Wrinkle up your forehead keeping the rest of your body relaxed. Feel the tension. Your forehead is tight... now relax. Feel the difference between being tense and relaxed... Squint your eyes tight and feel the tension around your eyes... now, relax and let go... Open your mouth as wide as you can feeling the tension in your jaw, tense... now, gently close your mouth... notice the difference between tension and relaxation... Close your mouth and push your tongue against the roof of your mouth... notice the tension... relax and let go... Keeping the rest of your face and body relaxed, clench your jaws tightly... feel the tension in your jaw muscles... and relax... let go... notice the difference between tension and relaxation... Think about your head, your forehead, eyes, jaws and cheeks... notice your whole face becoming smooth and relaxed as tension slips away.'

Shoulders and arms 'Shrug your shoulders up and try to touch your ears... Feel the tension in your shoulders... Now relax, notice the difference... Now stretch your arms out and make a fist with your hands... Feel the tension in your hands and forearms... Now relax, and let go... Now, push your left hand down into what it is resting on... Feel the tension in your arm and shoulder... Now let go... Push your right hand down into what it is resting on, hard... feel the tension... Now let go and relax... Now bend your elbows and tense your upper arms as if you wanted to show off your muscles... feel the tension... Now relax... Feel the relaxation as it moves across your shoulders, your arms and hands... Feel also the relaxation in your face and neck.'

Body 'Now take a deep breath that totally fills your lungs... Notice the tension in your chest and around your ribs... Slowly breathe out and notice the deepening relaxation as you continue to breath out... Now arch your back up (or forward if you are sitting) paying attention to the tension, hold it tense... Now relax... Notice the difference ... Now tighten your stomach as if someone was going to hit you there... hold the tension... and relax... notice the tension filling your stomach... tension out as relaxation comes in... Now push your stomach out as far as it can go... hold the tension... and slowly relax your stomach muscles ... feel the waves of relaxation flow through your stomach... your back... your chest... neck... chin... face ... head... shoulders... arms... hands.' You will learn that you can relax any part of your body by letting go of the tension...

Legs 'Tighten your hips and legs by pressing down the heels of your feet into the surface they are resting... press hard, tense ... relax and let go... Notice the difference between tension and relaxation... Curl your toes downward and try to touch the bottom of your feet with your toes... feel the tension... now relax and let go... bend your toes as you let go of the tension... feel the tension being replaced with relaxation... Bend your toes back the other way towards your head... feel the tension, tense and hold ... now, relax and feel yourself letting go of the tension ... relax and feel the difference... Feel how good it feels to be relaxed ... continue to feel more and more relaxed as you breathe in and out.'

Once you have mastered the technique you will gradually be able to learn to focus on and relax specific muscles groups as you become aware of them during the day. With further practice, you can learn to let go of muscle tension without having to first tense the muscle. Your memory will have stored the sensation of how the muscle feels when it is relaxed and you can reinstate physical relaxation on your command using certain cue words such as 'relax'.

Cue-controlled scanning relaxation

A more advanced form of muscle relaxation is 'cue-controlled scanning relaxation'. It is a technique which you can use often during the day to rid yourself of unwanted tension. The basic procedure involves you scanning your different muscle groups, sort of X-raying your own body. Once you detect elevated levels of muscle tension, you relax that area. The reason the procedure is referred to as cue controlled is that you generally need some cues or reminders to scan. You can get so caught up with what's going on you simply forget to look for your tension. In school, some good cues would be the end of the class bell (if you have one), waiting to get something photocopied or just before you have a cup of coffee or tea during morning recess.

As scanning relaxation involves your use of controlled breathing, you may want to wait until after you have practised some of the breathing exercises which follow before beginning this muscle relaxation technique.

The basic technique involves you breathing in while scanning your major muscle groups (head and neck; shoulders and arms; chest, stomach and back; hips, legs and feet). As you breathe out, you relax that area and then move on to other areas of your body. While this sounds like it might take three-quarters of the day, with practice you can complete the scanning-relaxation process in a very short period of time.

An example of the self-instructions you can use to guide scanning relaxation of your face and neck is as follows:

'As you breathe in, scan the different areas of your face and neck... As you exhale, feel the tension flowing out. Feel your face and neck relax. Once again, scan your neck and face as you inhale, paying attention to your forehead, eyes, jaw and neck... As you exhale, feel your relaxation becoming deeper and deeper.'

A similar set of self-instructions can be employed for scanning and relaxing the other parts of your body.

CONTROLLED BREATHING

'By using our own physiological ways of breathing we can steady the system, stop panic from mounting, or deal with a very difficult situation in which our blood

> *pressure is likely to rise and make us hot, tense and uptight. By using the breathing related to the system "at peace", you can count on reducing the pressure and remaining cool and clear headed.'*
> *Audrey Livingston Booth*, Stressmanship, *1985.*

When you are under pressure, your breathing changes from what it is at rest. It tends to be shallow and fast and you use only the top part of your lungs. Increased breathing rate is a sign that you are preparing for a fight or flight. And if you are getting ready to put on a suit of armour and head off to the crusades, you would want your body to be at a high level of arousal. However, for the most part, shallow and fast breathing along with other aspects of a fully activated sympathetic nervous system only makes many stressful situations at school more difficult to handle. When you are experiencing high stress, you breathe inefficiently or, put another way, you lose regulation over your breathing. This is a problem because poor breathing makes you more stress-vulnerable and less able to take charge of the situation.

A number of negative consequences ensue when you fail to breathe using the full capacity of your lungs. If an unsufficient amount of air reaches the lungs, they can't provide sufficient oxygen to the blood which your heart pumps throughout your body. As the oxygen in the blood is exchanged for the waste products in the cells, poorly 'oxygenated' or 'purified' blood is unable to remove the waste products, so they keep circulating and, over time, poison the system. This can cause cholesterol levels to remain high and hamper the digestion of food. Poorly oxygenated blood appears purplish as opposed to bright red in colour— sometimes you can detect this in a person's poor complexion. Reduced oxygen in the blood can also contribute to an increase in anxiety, depression and fatigue.

Western civilisation has only recently become aware of how important it is to breathe correctly. In the East, breathing has been and continues to be an important part of the overall development of the individual. The practice of yoga in particular is designed to increase self-discipline through controlled breathing and other techniques. In our own society we are today adapting many Eastern breathing techniques to meet our current needs and developing our own. It is clear from research into stress management that when you learn to become aware of and take control of your breathing, you can control your body's and mind's reaction to stressful events at school.

Most of the breathing exercises described below can be done sitting or standing up straight.

Calm breathing

This technique will introduce you to a very easy form of controlled breathing. The aim of the activity is for you to begin to use more of your lung capacity, especially in your upper chest cavity.

Sit in a comfortable chair, allowing your shoulders to drop down naturally by your sides in order to allow for full lung expansion. Sit up straight in order to expand your lungs upwards. Looking straight ahead take five slow deep, gentle breaths. You are now ready to begin calm breathing.

Breathe in easily, counting to yourself 1–2–3 and then breathe out just as easily also to a count of 1–2–3. Rather than trying for deep breathing, in a very relaxed and gentle fashion allow your chest to expend outwards.

Because your relaxed breathing is not noticeable to others, you can use it in public places such as just before you want to say something at a staff meeting or when you are confronting an unruly student. You can also use it whenever you feel yourself getting uptight, or preventatively, such as when you are driving to school in the morning.

Diaphragmatic breathing

Most of us are 'chest' breathers. Except when we are sleeping or fully relaxed we take in air using our chest muscles. Try breathing from your chest and you'll see what I mean.

Your diaphragm is a muscle located towards the bottom of your lungs; it separates your chest from your abdomen. To locate your diaphragm, place your hands flat across your stomach. When you breathe from your diaphragm, your hands will expand outwards. When you expel air from your lungs, your stomach collapses and your hands come together as you breathe out.

Practise diaphragmatic breathing, moving your stomach muscles and diaphragm outwards as you inhale, and allowing these muscles to contract and relax as you exhale. Try to keep your shoulders and top of your lungs as still as possible. Practise this technique so that you can clearly separate 'chest' from 'diaphragmatic' breathing.

Deep breathing

Deep breathing is the most natural form of breathing and the following yoga exercise has the purpose of teaching you how to breathe filling all parts of your lungs: lower, middle and upper.

Picture both of your lungs as balloons running most of the length of your chest cavity. In this technique, you fill your lungs fully, starting with the lower part which you fill using your diaphragm and stomach muscles, filling your middle section as your ribs and chest move forward and finishing with the upper part which you fill lifting your chest and pulling in your abdomen. To 'top up' your lungs fully, raise your shoulders and collarbone. When you observe yourself deep breathing, you should see one continuous wave motion beginning with your diaphragm and ending at the top of your lungs. The steps to deep breathing are as follows.

1 Breathe through your nose.
2 Inhale slowly filling your lower section of your lungs.
3 Fill the middle part of your lungs.
4 Fill your upper part of your lungs.
5 Hold your breath for a count of three.
6 Exhale slowly allowing your abdomen to contract slowly.

The 5–3–5 technique

This controlled, deep breathing relaxation technique can be used either when sitting or lying down. To use this technique most effectively, you should employ deep breathing beginning with your diaphragm and ending with filling the top of your lungs.

Use the following instructions: 'To begin with, rapidly exhale all the air from your lungs. Next, slowly to a count of five, inhale...one...two...three...four...five... Hold your breath of air for a slow count of three...one...two... three... Now slowly, very slowly, exhale the air to a slow count of five...one...two...three...four...five... You have just completed one repetition. To continue to relax, breathe in slowly again to count of five, hold for a count of three, and again exhale to a slow count of five.' After you begin the exercise with an exhale to a count of five, all repetitions consist of counts of 5–3–5.

The cleansing breath

This short yoga exercise can be to help purify your lungs and to revigorate your body.

Inhale a deep breath of air using the deep breathing procedure described above. Hold this breath for a count of three and then exhale a small amount of the air with strong force through a small round hole you have made between your lips. Stop, then exhale a bit more air. Continue this procedure until you have exhaled all of the air.

The following three exercises are taken verbatim from Dr Audrey Livingston Booth's excellent book *Stressmanship* (London: Severn House, 1985, pp. 113–114). Their appeal is that they producing an immediate relief from stress.

Head clearer

'This can be done in a chair and is a very useful tension reducer before a meeting at which you want a particularly clear head, in the middle of a hurassing day, or when you feel irritations are beginning to pile up. You now know that this is the way to raise your heart rate, your blood pressure and your cholesterol count, so this is the point at which you must take action to dampen them down.

Flop back in your chair. Take a first deep breath in and now breathe out fully as if you were a balloon deflating completely. Go down with the deflating balloon. Allow your lungs to refill without any effort on your part. You are concerned with deflating yourself and driving out all of the tension with the exhaled air. As you repeat this cycle you will feel yourself becoming more floppy with each deflating breath. As more of yourself goes limp and the tension and irritation leave you, you will find the head getting clearer and clearer. After two munites take a deep energising breath, feel alert, and breathe away quietly and normally. Now go to your meeting with a clear head and a refreshed mind, happily unhampered by tension.'

Shoulder release

'Do this during a break during the day such as a tea break. You will not have realised that your shoulders are tense until you stop and attempt to loosen them. You can in fact do this sitting down but it is better to stand to give free movement to your arms.

Stand. First stretch high with both arms and then with each separately. Now stand with feet just a little apart to give you a good firm base and raise your arms in front of you to shoulder level. Then loosely and lazily swing them down and behind you and then back again. Do not put any effort into this as you are loosening shoulder joints and reducing tension. Effort only increases tension. So slowly and easily let them flop down and back, forward and up, repeating these swings rhythmically ten times. Finish by moving the shoulder joints in a vertical circle, five times forward and five times backward for each shoulder, and they will be much less tense and much easier to live with.'

Rag doll

'This technique is the important rag doll-like flop that switches off the stress response completely. You will recall that the stress response alerts the sympathetic nervous system which is the activating system that makes everything else in the body go faster. This technique calls up the opposite system, the para-sympathetic, often called the "rest" and "digest" system. As the two cannot operate together at the same time, the stress response, sensing the resting state of the body, realises that there is no emergency and switches itself off. So, this is a very useful stress reducer at lunch time or at the end of the day before facing the journey home.

Sit on an armless chair. Do ten deep, slow diaphragmatic breaths and with every outgoing breath breathe out forcefully, deflating like a balloon, and begin to flop forward at the head and neck. Gradually flop further forward with each breath out letting the shoulders and arms fall further and further forward until you are hanging limply from the waist like a rag doll. Hang there for a minute or two and then come up very, very slowly. Rest your head back on the chair and then breathe slowly, gently and easily with your hands resting limply and lightly on your lap. Sit quite still like this for as long as you can manage, though four minutes is quite long enough to reduce the pulse, heart and blood pressure rates. When you are ready to take the threads of work again, take the deep energising breath and you will feel alert and free from tension.'

The squeeze technique

The squeeze techinique is an abbreviated deep breathing relaxation technique designed to reduce physical agitation as well as give you a burst of added energy.

Take a slow deep breath filling your lungs as much as possible. Now stiffen your stomach muscles as if someone is about to hit you and hold your breath for a count of three. Now exhale forcefully.

If you use this technique several times in succession you can bring down your anxiety and tension levels before having to perform some stressful task at school.

The quieting response

The quieting response was developed by Dr Charles F. Stroebel and his colleagues as an instant response to stress. It takes approximately six seconds to perform and therefore is suitable for use on the spot. Here is how to use it.

When you notice your stress level increasing (e.g., muscle tension, changes in breathing, headache, anxiety) do this.

1 Imagine yourself smiling inwardly especially with your eyes.
2 Think to yourself 'Alert mind, calm body'.
3 Take a slow, deep breath of air.
4 While exhaling, relax your muscles beginning with your face and shoulders and then feel the relaxation spreading downward to your toes.

Dr Stroebel recommends regular practice of the quieting response. It then has a good chance of becoming an automatic reflex which is triggered by increases in your stress level.

MEDITATION

'Stuffing your interior world with thoughts, feelings and images regarding your daily life is not just a disease of modern times. The problem is age-old. Ways have to be found to turn off your mind's obsessive search for solutions to pain and threat. For thousands of years members of almost all cultures have sought inner peace and harmony through one form or another of meditation.'
Martha Davis, Elizabeth Eshelman and
Matthew McKay,
The Relaxation & Stress Reduction Workbook, 1982.

I must admit I was initially sceptical about meditation, believing it synonomous with Eastern religion and requiring hours of chanting and self-sacrifice for some intangible end of spiritual peace and harmony. I can now see more clearly that meditation offers significant benefits as a stress-reducing technique for those people committed to its use.

Meditation is becoming more widely accepted within Western society and can be practised with or without a religious emphasis. Herbert Benson, M.D., a Harvard University professor and author of *The Relaxation Response*, is perhaps the person most responsible for giving the most popular form of meditation, Transcendental Meditation, scientific legitimacy. After conducting a range of experiments at Harvard's Thorndike Laboratory and Boston's Beth Israel Hospital, where he studied the changes in physiological activity in people who meditate, he concluded meditation brings about decreased oxygen consumption, decreased carbon dioxide elimination, decreased rate of breathing and lowers high blood pressure in certain patients. He also found decreases in the levels of lactic acid in meditators, a substance known to be associated with anxiety and tension. Other researchers have repeatedly found that meditation results in an increase in intensity and frequency of alpha brain waves which are known to be present in people in states of deep relaxation.

Over the years, meditation has offered the promise of 'altered states of consciousness' and the resulting feelings which have been described as ecstatic, clairvoyant, beautiful, totally relaxing and pleasure. To my knowledge there have been no studies to date which have examined whether meditation actually works to reduce stress. From my own reading and from the few teachers I know who practise meditation regularly, I believe it offers some promise.

Teaching yourself to meditate requires an initial committment of about twenty minutes twice daily for a month with a gradual shortening of time required after that. It is obviously a technique which requires that your lifestyle and commitment allow for such a degree of involvement.

In his book, Benson distills from a variety of age-old meditation techniques four basic elements.

1 *A quiet environment* Ideally, you should choose a quiet, calm environment with as few distractions as possible. A quiet room is suitable as is a place of worship. The quiet environment contributes to the effectiveness of the repeated word or phrase by making it easier to eliminate distracting thoughts.

2 *A mental device* To shift the mind from logical, externally oriented thought, there should be a constant stimulus: a sound, word or phrase repeated silently or aloud; or fixed gazing at an object. Since one of the major difficulties in the elicitation of the Relaxation Response is 'mind wandering', the repetition of the word or phrase is a way to help break

the train of distracting thoughts. Your eyes are usually closed if you are using a repeated word or sound; of course, your eyes are open if you are gazing. Attention to the normal rhythm of breathing is also useful and enhances the repetition of the word.

3 *A passive attitude* When distracting thoughts occur, they are to be disregarded and attention redirected to the repetition or gazing; you should not worry about how well you are performing the technique, because this may well prevent the Relaxation Response from occurring. Adopt a 'let it happen' attitude. The passive attitude is perhaps the most important element in eliciting the Relaxation Response. Distracting thoughts will occur. Do not worry about them.

4 *A comfortable position* A comfortable position is important so that there is no undue muscular tension. Some methods call for a sitting position. A few practitioners use the cross-legged 'lotus' position of the yogi. If you are lying down, there is a tendency to fall asleep. As noted previously, the various postures of kneeling, swaying, or sitting in a cross-legged position are believed to have evolved to prevent falling asleep. You should be comfortable and relaxed.

There are a variety of meditation exercises which are designed to increase your control of your mind in order to bring about deeper and deeper meditative states. Instructions for the most common form of meditation, mantra meditation, are provided below (from Davis, Eshelman and McKay. *The Relaxation and stress Reduction Workbook*, 1982, p 47).

1 A mantra is a syllable, word or name that is repeated many times as you free your mind of thoughts. 'Mantra' is Indo-European in origin: 'man' means to think and 'tra' means 'to liberate'. Some teachers of this form of meditation insist that each individual should have his or her own special mantra, with a specific meaning and vibration. Others state that two consecutive nonsense syllables selected at random are as effective as special mantras. Still other teachers recommend the use of any word or phrase that the individual is drawn to, such as 'peace,' 'calm', 'relaxed', 'quiet', or 'harmony'. Two typical Eastern mantras are 'OM' (I am)

and 'SO-HAM' (I am he) or 'SA-HAM' (I am she). Choose a mantra that feels right for you.

2 Centre yourself in your quiet place, paying special attention to relaxing your chest and throat.

3 Chant your mantra aloud. Avoid chanting too loudly (which strains your voice) or too vigorously (which causes hyperventilation and dizziness). When it isn't possible to chant aloud, do it without sound. When your mind strays, refocus it on your chanting. Let your mantra find its own rhythm as the sound of your voice fills you and makes you relax.

4 After five minutes of chanting your mantra aloud, shift to whispering it. As you do, relax deeper and deeper, flowing with the rhythm of the sound.

5 Chant fifteen minutes a day, five to seven days a week for two weeks, at which time you may want to increase the length of the sessions to thirty minutes. Within the first week if things are going well, you may find yourself aware only of your chanting for brief periods of time. Try this exercise for about a month before deciding whether to continue or cease it.

6 After you are comfortable chanting, you may want to try writing your mantra as slowly as possible over and over again with your unaccustomed hand. Remember to sit up straight and just experience your hand writing the mantra.

7 When you are at ease with the mantra and the breath meditations, combine them. Breathe spontaneously. Observe yourself inhale, exhale, and pause for a while without influencing your rhythm. When you feel it is flowing naturally, listen to your mantra in it.

There seems to be some agreement that the rapid deep relaxation which can be achieved through meditation results from the focusing on one thing (mantra) at a time.

If you are interested in learning to meditate, I suggest obtaining some of the commercially available books on meditation listed in reference list at the end of this chapter and visiting one of the centres for Transcendental Meditation located in the capital city of your state.

GUIDED IMAGERY

'Now close your eyes, sit back and relax. Eyes closed, sitting back relaxing. Now visualise yourself standing by the shore of a large lake, looking across an expanse of blue water and beyond to the far shore. Immediately in front of you stretches a small beach, and behind you a grassy meadow. The sun is bright and warm. The air is fresh and clean. The sky is pale blue with great billowy clouds drifting by. The wind is blowing gently, just enough to make the trees sway and make gentle ripples in the grass... You're in your suit now, walking towards the water, feeling the soft, lush grass under your feet... Now you can feel the warm sand underfoot ... The water's warm, almost like a bath... You take a deep breath and glide a few feet forward down into the water. You surface and feel the water run down your back... You can feel the warm sun on your skin.'

J.J. Horan,
'Coping with Inescapable Discomfort', 1976.

Just as negative and irrational thoughts play havoc with your stress level, so too can the images which flow through your mind. Replays of past failures or previews of possible forthcoming disasters can also increase your levels of muscle tension and autonomic system arousal.

There are several stress-management techniques which involve you using your imagination to create new, pleasant images which not only prevent the other stress-creating images and thoughts from maintaining your stress but also in themselves bring feelings of relaxation and pleasantness.

One way you can pull yourself out of a stress-downer is to change the scenes in your mind. By learning how to use your creative imagination, you can literally turn off your stress. While such techniques do not appear to have enduring stress-reduction effects, they certainly distract you from what's going on, give you a temporary high, and, hopefully, leave you a good enough feeling to do something different (e.g., hobby, exercise) which will further help the cause.

The key to using guided imagery is to develop at least one, if not many, personally relaxing scenes which you can use for relaxation such as the beach scene above. Make sure you visualise the scene as clearly and vividly as possible. The scene should involve all of your senses. Make believe you can 'see' the grass, 'hear' the water lapping up against the shore, 'feel' the sand beneath your feet, 'taste' the salt of the perspiration running down your brow and 'smell' the scent of nearby flowers.

Some people have difficulty creating a pleasant scene in their imagination. It can take some time and with practice you do get better. As well, sometimes your thoughts of the day can interfere with your forming a nice picture. If that's the case, wait until they pass, or shout 'no' loudly to yourself which can effectively shake them out.

You may wish to guide yourself through guided imagery exercises yourself using the directions below as a sample. Alternatively, you may elect to tape record the instructions or have them read by a friend. In all cases, the directions should be read slowly.

While you are experiencing the pleasant images, be sure to use your progressive relaxation and breathing techniques to reduce areas of tension in your body.

The basic technique for employing guided imagery is forming a clear image of a pleasant scene including images from as many senses as possible. Possible suggestions for images include walking up a mountain path, alone on a tropical island, spending time with a 'desirable' partner, watching the sun set, driving in a car with the top down.

To begin guided imagery training get as comfortable as possible and then close your eyes and breathe slowly and rhythmically while you concentrate on your breathing. Then form a clear image listening to a tape or from your own mind.

An example of guiding instructions for forming an image of walking up a mountain path would be something like the following:

'Imagine yourself at the bottom of a mountain path. As you look upward you can see how the path meanders upwards. It is a bright and sunny day and you are conscious of both the shadow and sunlight shining along the path. You can feel a warm breeze blow softly across your face. In the distance you can hear the sound of a fresh mountain stream. You stoop down to pick up some brightly coloured wild mountain daisies. You rub one up against your face and can just taste a slight bitterness as you nibble one. You feel unburdened, relaxed and free of all the hassles of work. It's great to be among nature.'

You can choose to shift to other images or stay with one. In finishing each session, you should, before opening your eyes, tell yourself that when you open your eyes you will be alert and relaxed. Then slowly to a count of three, open your eyes.

SELF-HYPNOSIS

'Hypnosis is the altered state of consciousness that results from focusing attention on a set of suggestions and allowing oneself to be receptive to those suggestions, thereby allowing free reign to one's powers of imagination.'

K. Woolfolk and F. Richardson,
Stress, Sanity and Survival, 1978.

For many people, the word 'hypnosis' conjures up all sorts of strange associations such as a hypnotist subconciously programming them to act like a chicken at their next party or an elderly bearded doctor with an Austrian accent swinging a watch in front of them eyes saying quietly, 'You are getting sleepy, very sleepy'. And indeed there are entertainers and actors who exploit the public imagination with their wild claims of mind control.

Notwithstanding these strains to credibility, there are a large number of mental health practitioners who employ hypnosis to treat successfully a variety of problems including insomnia, chronic pain, headaches, nervous tics and tremors, chronic muscle tension and fatigue, and anxiety.

You may be interested in knowing that before the discovery of ether in 1846, hypnosis or mesmerism had achieved prominence for painless surgery. With the advent of ether, hypnosis appeared to lose favour in the medical establishment until the publication in 1895 of Hyppolite Bernheim's book *Suggestive Therapeutic* which rekindled the practice of hypnosis by the medical and psychiatric professions. Freud in particular employed hypnosis in the treatment of anxiety.

As you would anticipate, there are a variety of hypnosis techniques which the experienced practitioner uses. A few of these have been adapted for use by the individual as 'self-hypnosis'. A popular one which I will not be describing involves you accessing your subconscious mind through the use of a pendulum which swings in certain directions, allowing you to discern what your subconscious wishes and desires really are.

The technique which seems to have most relevance for modifying stress is a self-induction procedure called *eye fixation*. This technique is a fast, safe and easy process which you can employ to achieve relaxation. No, you can't accidentally program yourself to go into your principal's office and leave chicken droppings on his desk, much as you may like to. The hypnotic state, or trance if you will, you put yourself in will not be new to you. Frequently when you are lost in thought or daydreaming you enter a different state of mind-body which we could call hypnosis without formal induction. Eye fixation brings you to that state fairly rapidly when used effectively and practised. If used in combination with auto-suggestions, you may also notice self-improvements in the suggested direction.

This technique requires you to do the following.

1 Select a location where there is minimal noise and human traffic.

2 Sit in a comfortable position much as you would in meditation.

3 Stare at a stationary object.

4 Take several deep breaths releasing the air with a 'sigh'.

5 While looking at the object, tell yourself that your eyelids are getting heavier and heavier, too heavy to hold up.

6 Using a pre-selected word such as 'relax now' or your

Relaxation

favourite colour, say the word when your eyes begin to
close and repeat it after they are fully closed. (In time, the
word itself can come to induce relaxation.)

7 Repeat the suggestions that your eyes are getting heavier
every minute or so until relaxation begins.

8 Once your eyes have closed, relax yourself with deep
breathing and by tightening and relaxing your muscles following the sequence employed in progressive relaxation.

9 While relaxing, repeat a special word such as 'peace', 'love'
or 'happiness'.

10 When you want to come to complete alertness, you can
awaken yourself by thinking 'I am now going to wake up',
pausing and counting to three.

Once you are in a relaxed state with your eyes closed you
may wish to give yourself some simple suggestions, known
as auto-suggestions, which may under certain circumstances
have an effect on you when not in the hypnotic state. (My
view is that auto-suggestion can be effective for certain
people who are open to the idea and by nature easy to
persuade.) Examples of auto-suggestions might be the following.
    'I can be calmer when I speak to the principal.'
    'I can work steadily tonight as I feel more relaxed.'
    'Whenever I feel nervous, I can say to myself "I can do
it!"'
    'I can control my anger. I am the master of my own fate.'
    'The next time I see Johnny Pain, I can tell him politely,
nicely but firmly who is the boss.'
    Additional suggestions for increasing the effectiveness of
auto-suggestions include the following.

1 Suggestions should be repeated often.
2 Expect small, rather than large, changes.
3 Express suggestions in the positive.
4 The more you believe in the power of hypnosis, the more
likely it to have a positive benefit.
5 During self-hypnosis, visualise yourself as being relaxed.

Once again, if you are interested in the current techniques

165

of self-hypnosis, consult some of the books listed in the references at the end of this chapter.

AUTOGENICS

'Autogenic training helps you to control stress by training the autonomic nerous system to be more relaxed when you are not faced with a real need to fight or run... It can be thought of as helping reprogram the subconscious mind to create to state of internal calm.'
Edward Charlesworth and Ronald G. Nathan,
Stress Management: A Comprehensive Guide to Wellness, 1984.

Autogenic Training (AT) is an approach to stress management which has wide popularity in parts of Western Europe and in Great Britain. It was developed by a Berlin psychiatrist, Johannes H. Schultz, who wrote a book, *Autogenic Training*, published in 1932, about a new system of healing which combined aspects of auto-suggestion and yoga techniques.

According to Schultz, under stress your body chemistry becomes unbalanced and along with it your physical, mental and emotional states. Given that your stress system frequently gets turned on unnecessarily—especially the activation of the autonomic nervous system for flight-fight—it is no wonder that the amount of stress suffered has increased.

Essentially, AT is a system which teaches you how to over-ride or turn off your autonomic nervous system activity and return your system to a state of relaxation and balance. In a nutshell, AT exercises are designed to produce a state of general relaxation and normalisation of the body aimed at reversing the fight-flight response.

In using AT, you will have to employ a passive attitude of concentration which involves focusing on a relaxing phrase that will help to activate passively the automatic response you desire. You need to experience whatever physical, mental or emotional responses arise as a result of the AT exercises without having any expectations—just let them happen.

AT activities are designed to induce in your limbs and body a state of warmth and heaviness which is physiologically incompatible with feelings of tension and fatigue. Verbal instruction (e.g., 'My right arm is warm and heavy') are seen to lead to a relaxing of the voluntary muscles of your limbs and peripheral vasodillation where blood flows from the trunk and head to the extremities.

The sequence of AT instruction begins with you either sitting or lying down in a comfortable position. Assuming an attitude of passive concentration, you begin to breathe deeply, regularly and rhythmically, helping your heart rate assume a calm and regular beat. Once a relaxed state has been achieved, you concentrate fully and passively on your right hand and arm and say to yourself, 'My right arm and hand are heavy and warm'. Say this four or five times to yourself. It is important to study the feelings of warmth and heaviness in your right arm and hand. You then progressively turn your attention to your left arm and hand, both arms and hands, your legs, and then all limbs. For each part of your body, you should say to yourself three or four times 'My ____ (names of parts) are warm and heavy'. As you progress, notice how the warmth and heaviness spreads throughout your body. You may also wish to include your forehead with the self-instructions 'My forehead is cool'. To conclude the exercises, imagine yourself back in your room feeling relaxed and pleasant and counting from one to three and taking a deep breath at each number.

AT may take from four to ten months to learn if you use the exercises regularly once or twice a day for 30–40 minutes. In a similar fashion to meditation, AT requires such a large time committment that you really have to decide it is a top priority and want to make it a part of your lifestyle.

BIOFEEDBACK

Biological feedback involves you controlling your biological activity through your thought processes. Biofeedback equipment usually consist of electrical devices that transform biological activity (e.g., heart rate, skin temperature, brain waves, blood pressure) to electrical currents which can be detected, measured and recorded and brought to your awareness. The equipment is attached to your body to measure specific muscle groups, finger temperature, brain waves, etc. Using techniques which have just been presented, such as relaxation and meditation, you are able to moderate your bodily activity through receiving feedback on your efforts via the biofeedback equipment.

Biofeedback can be an extremely useful stress-management adjunct when you are concerned with learning to take finer control over an aspect of your physical functioning such as hyperventilation, blood pressure, muscular tension or anxiety where previous methods have failed. The biofeedback equipment provides you with external information about your internal functioning and, specifically, about your efforts at self-regulation. It can be very helpful in the treatment of a variety of stress-related disorders.

As you can imagine, biofeedback equipment is very expensive. It is generally available in hospitals and clinics.

Additional informal stress-management techniques

The following five activities should be kept in mind as antidotes to stress.

Massage Having a masseuse or friend massage tense and tight muscles can bring you immediate relief. A number of good books and videos are available on this topic.

Bath Soaking in a warm bath with bath salts or scented oils can afford great relief of physical tension. If you bathe for approximately thirty minutes and then go straight off to bed and relax for another thirty minutes, you'll have a potent anti-stress remedy.

Time alone I'm a great believer in time away from the madding crowd. When you are stressed up to your eyeballs with school and, perhaps, even your loved ones at home, give yourself permission to go away. It may be for only fifteen minutes or several hours. Go for it. You've earned it and you'll come back fresher.

Music People vary a bit on this one but for some an hour

or more of listening to your favourite music can be very relaxing. You might want to take a music break at morning break or while you're sitting down grading papers.

Hobbies If you have abandoned an earlier hobby or have never really developed one, now mighty be the time to pick one up. Whether it be physically active like volleyball, or more sedentary like cooking, sewing or french polishing, the reinforcing properties associated with your hobbies can provide you with needed relief from stress.

'Hey, Billy Boy,' called Mary across the school parking lot.

'You look terrible. A bit of the old stress, I'd say.'

'How come you're so cheery?' panted Bill as he ran off to class to be early.

'I'm relaxed, cool as a tomato.'

'You have a good night, did you?'

'Cut it out. Had a bath, relaxed a bit and saw my favourite movie on video for the fifth time.'

'What's that?' said Bill, wishing Mary would somehow evaporate.

'*The Texas Chainsaw Massacre.* Great stuff.'

'I'll bet,' replied Bill, wondering what Mary was carrying in her extra-sized school bag.

'See you at recess, ol' Billie Boy.'

ACTIONS SPEAK LOUDER THAN WORDS

Continue to monitor your daily stress level.

See if you can apply a Stress Script or RET Self-Management Form to a particular stressor which you have encountered this past week.

Search through the array of relaxation procedures just presented. Select one or more that you think suits you and begin to try them out.

RECOMMENDED READING

Relaxation

Russell Frank Atkinson, *The Book of Relaxation* (Brookvale, NSW: Simon & Schuster, 1988).

Iris Barrow and Helen Place, *Relax and Come Alive* (Auckland, NZ: Heinemann, 1986).

Herbert Benson, *The Relaxation Response* (London: Collins, 1976).

Herbert Benson, *Beyond the Relaxation Response* (New York: Berkeley Books, 1985).

Deborah Bright, *Creative Relaxation* (New York: Ballantine Books, 1986).

Joseph Cautela and June Groden, *Relaxation: A Comprehensive Manual for Adults, Children, and Children with Special Needs* (Champaign, Ill.: Research Press 1978).

Leon Chaitow, *Your Complete Stress-Proofing Program* (Wellingborough: Thorsons, 1985).

John D. Curtis and Richard A. Delert, *How to Relax: A Holistic Approach to Stress Management* (Mountain View, CA: Mayfield Publishing, 1981).

Martha Davis, Elizabeth Robins Eshelman and Mathew McKay, *The Relaxation and Stress Reduction Workbook* (Oakland, CA: New Harbinger Publications, 1982).

Editors of American Health Magazine, *The Relaxed Body Book* (New York: Doubleday, 1986).

James Hewitt, *The Complete Relaxation Book* (London: Rider, 1982).

Sandra Horn, *Relaxation* (Wellingborough: Thorsons Publication, 1986).

Edmund Jacobson, *Progressive Relaxation* (Chicago: University of Chicago Press, 1974).

Leslie Kenton, *Stress and Relaxation* (London: Century Hutchinson, 1986).

Jane Madders, *Stress and Relaxation: Self-Help for Everyone* (London: Macdonald Optima, 1988).

Lyn Marshall, *Lyn Marshall's Instant Stress Cure* (London: Century Hutchinson, 1988).

Laura Mitchell, *Simple Relaxation* (London: John Murray, 1988).

Louis Proto, *Total Relaxation in Five Steps* (New York: Penguin, 1989).

Israel Regardie, *The Lazy Man's Guide to Relaxation* (Phoenix, Arizona: 1985).

Jonathan C. Smith, *Relaxation Dynamics* (Champaign, Ill.: Research Press, 1985).

Eric Trimmer, *The 10-Day Relaxation Plan* (London: Piatkus, 1984).

Meditation

William Bloom, *Meditation in a Changing World* (Glastonbury, Somerset: Gothic Image Publications, 1987).
Simon Court, *The Meditator's Manual* (Wellingborough, Northhamptonshire: The Aquarian Press, 1984).
Roy Eugene Davis, *An Easy Guide to Meditation* (Lakemont, Georgia: CSA Press, 1988).
Ian Gawler, *Peace of Mind* (Melbourne: Hill of Content, 1987).
James Hewitt, *Teach Yourself Meditation* (Seven Oaks, Kent: Hodder Stoughton, 1978).
Naomi Humphrey, *Meditation the Inner way* (Wellingborough, Northhamptonshire: The Aquarian Press, 1987).
Steve Kravette, *Complete Meditation* (Westchester PA: Whitford Press, 1982).
Lawrence LeShan, *How to Mediate* (Wellingborough, Northhamptonshire: The Aquarian Press, 1989).
Ainslie Meares, *A Better Life. The Guide to Meditation* (Elwood, Vic.: Greenhouse Publications, 1989).
Lucy Oliver, *Meditation and the Creative Imperative* (London: Dryad Press, 1987).
Erica Smith and Nicholas Wilks, *Meditation* (London: Optima, 1988).
Paul Wilson, *The Calm Technique* (Elwood, Vic.: Greenhouse, 1985).

Transcendental Meditation

Alan Bloomfield and others, *TM* (London: Urwin, 1976).
Denise Deniston and others, *The TM Book* (Fairfield, Iowa: Fairfield Press, 1986).
Mahesh Maharishi Yogi, *The Science of Being and the Art of Living* (New York: Signet, 1968).
Robert Roth, *Transcendental Meditation* (New York: Primus, 1987).
Peter Russell, *The TM Technique* (London: Routledge and Kegan, 1976).

Imagery and visualisation

Barbara Ardinger, *Seeing Solutions* (New York: Signet, 1989).
Melita Denning and Osborne Phillips, *The Llewellyn Practical Guide to Creative Visualisation* (St. Paul, Minn.: Llewellyn Publications, 1983).
Gerald Epstein, *Healing Visualisations: Creating Health Through Imagery* (New York: Bantam, 1989).
Patrick Fanning, *Visualisation for Change* (Oakland, CA: New Harbinger Publications, 1988).

William Fezzler, *Creative Imagery* (New York: Fireside, 1989).
Shakti Gawain, *Creative Visualisation* (New York: Bantam, 1982).
Emily Bradley Lyons, *How to Use Your Power of Visualisation* (Red Bluff, CA: Lyons Visualisation Series, 1980).
Ronald Shone, *Creative Visualisation* (Wellingborough: Thorsons Publications, 1984).

Self-hypnosis

Frank S. Caprio, *Better Health with Self-Hypnosis* (New York: Parker Publishing, 1985).
Rachel Copelan, *How to Hypnotise Yourself and Others* (New York: Bell, 1984).
Arthur Jackson, *Stress Control through Self-Hypnosis* (Sydney: Doubleday, 1989).
Duncan McColl, *The Magic of Mind Power* (Bath: Gateway Books, 1987).
Melvyn Powers, *A Practical Guide to Self-Hypnosis* (North Hollywood, CA: Wilshire Publishing, 1961).
R. N. Shrout, *Self-Improvement through Self-Hypnosis* (Wellingborough: Thorsens, 1985).
Roger A. Straus, *Creative Self-Hypnosis* (New York: Prentice-Hall, 1989).
James M. Yates and Elizabeth S. Wallace, *The Complete Book of Self-Hypnosis* (New York: Ivy Books, 1984).
Pam Young, *Personal Change through Self-Hypnosis* (North Ryde: Angus and Robertson, 1986).

Audio-cassettes

Marc Allen, *Stress Reduction and Creative Meditations* (Whatever Publishing).
Edward Charlesworth, *Relaxation and Stress Management Training Autogenics Training* (Stress Management Research).
Fail Feldman, *Relaxation Methods for Coping* (Speaking of Health Series)
Ken Mellor, *Creative Release Meditation* (International Master Practitioner Series).
Matthew McCay and Patrick Fanning, *Progressive Relaxation and Breathing* (New Harbinger Publications).
Charles Stroebel, *Quieting Response Training-An Introduction* (BMA).
Charles Stroebel, *Quieting Response Training-Relaxing Skeletal Muscles* (BMA).

CHAPTER 8
LIFESTYLE MANAGEMENT

'If your body is out of tune, it burns unnecessary fuel, and it runs roughly, which increases its wear and tear. It does not run efficiently or economically, and it is more likely to break down eventually... Similarly, if your body is "out of tune", meaning unfit, it will not run efficiently, and its struggle to keep up with your stress load will also lead to increased wear and tear. You become more likely to "break down" in the exhaustion stage of the General Adaptation Syndrome.'

Bob Montgomery and Lynette Evans,
You and Stress, 1984.

There is definite consensus that lifestyle moderates the influence of stress. My own research, referred to earlier, with a group of over 500 teachers showed this relationship. In considering the amount of physical and emotional stress experienced as well as general life stress, even after taking into account the number of stressors within teaching and in the rest of life, a bad lifestyle was associated with high stress. And conversely, a good lifestyle was associated with lower physical-emotional and general life stress.

In the stress management literature, lifestyle is not the 'lifestyle of the rich and famous'. Rather, lifestyle is an umbrella term for diet/nutrition, exercise and recreation/rest. Simply put, if you have a good diet, exercise moderately and regularly, and get away from your sources of stress in some form of recreation, you will soften the effects of stress.

You will find most of the material in this chapter familiar. You'll have either heard about it from parents, friends or in-service courses or read about it in newspapers or magazines. What is startling is not the specific guidelines for a healthy lifestyle, but rather the fact that you and just about everyone else reading this book (and writing this book!) fail to maintain a good lifestyle— especially when you are under stress. For many different reasons, including the popularity of the fast food industry and your own innate tendencies to do what's easy and not good for you, you can fall into unhealthy lifestyle ruts. It is quite common in the face of stress to act against your better judgement and in order to secure relief from stress eat a chocolate bar or get 'stuck into' alcohol. The fatiguing aspects of stress can also take away your energy and the motivation which is required to maintain a good lifestyle. You will tell this by observing if, when you are away from school stresses during summer holidays, you change from an unhealthy to healthy lifestyle.

What follows are the basic principles of lifestyle management in the areas of diet, exercise and recreation. If you believe that your lifestyle is pretty good in one or two of the areas, then just read the area which has relevance to you.

DIET

'Early in most people's education, a teacher stood in front of the class pointing to charts of fruit, vegetables, breads, meats, milk and other nutritious item. The teacher talked about the importance of the food groups and recommended the number of servings that should be eaten every day. That same teacher probably failed to eat breakfast, and gobbled a sandwich and a cup of coffee for lunch.'
Sheldon F. Greenberg, **Stress and the Teaching Profession,** *1984.*

There are two ways aspects of your daily nutritional intake which can effect your stress. The first, *inadequate diet,* refers to the absence of certain nutrients your body requires for healthy functioning especially when faced with demands associated with high stress. Second, *excessive diet*, involves including in your diet unhealthy foods and drinks such as excessive caffeine, alcohol, sweets, fatty foods, and foods high in sodium (salt) content. A third aspect of your diet is not what you include in it, but rather has you skipping meals and, generally speaking, having an *irregular or inconsistent dietary intake*. Let's briefly look at some examples of the effects of a poor diet on your ability to tolerate stress.

When you are under stress, your need for essential nutrients increases, for example, you need more calcium and B-Vitamins. A diet low in milk and leafy vegetables can lead to a chronic calcium deficiency. When your muscles produce a high level of lactic acid, which they tend to when they are tense, there isn't enough calcium in the body to counteract the effects of the lactic acid. As a consequence, you may feel more fatigued, anxious and irritable than if you ate a balanced diet.

Excess coffee can also exacerbate the effects of stress. Caffeine stimulates the release of stress-producing hormones (e.g., adrenaline) which results in an initial burst of energy. Such energy bursts have the effect of draining your system and, in the case of caffeine, causing low blood sugar levels.

It is estimated that 60 per cent of people have systems which are sensitive to changing sugar levels. Eating foods high in sugar while under stress has the effect of stimulating your pancreas to produce insulin which after a while depresses your blood sugar level to a level lower than before you consumed the sugar. This results in a variety of physical and emotional stress symptoms including drowsiness, anxiety and irritability.

Under these physiologically and emotionally stressed conditions, you can easily start the cycle again with another cup of coffee, chocolate bar, etc. The effects? A constant state of emotional and physiological irregularity which itself can be an additional source of stress.

The negative effects of too much sugar

'Refined sugar taken in excess is a quick source of energy, but can have several negative side effects. First, it can lead to tooth decay—itself stressful. Second, it can lead to insulin-blood sugar swings (reactice hypoglycemia), stimulating manic depressive swings on a smaller scale. Third, many sugary products, such as candy, cookies and soft drinks, are virtually devoid of vitamins and minerals. Therefore, the body must "borrow" vitamins, especially B vitamins, from other food sources to complete the metabolism process. This can lead to a B-complex deficiency in the body. When a high-sugar, unbalanced diet is combined with a long, elevated stress period, a vitamin B deficiency can develop, aggravating the stress symptoms already present through heightened anxiety, irritability and general nervousness.'

W. *Schafer*, Stress Management for Wellness, *1987.*

Balanced diet

In order for you to stay reasonably healthy, your body needs 40–60 nutrients including ten essential amino acids, twenty different minerals and thirty vitamins. These nutrients are available in a good balanced diet containing the following elements.

1 *Proteins* Proteins provide the antibodies to fight disease and are essential to the make-up of your muscles, bones, blood and bodily organs. As a society we tend to consume far too much protein relative to our bodily requirements. Proteins which store approximately four calories per gram should make up between 15–20 per cent of your caloric intake. Protein is found in most food, especially, meat, fish and poultry.

2 *Fats* Fats come in two forms, animal and vegetable. As they are the basic building blocks to your immune system

and are involved in energy storage, you should make sure that fats (mainly polyunsaturated) make up between 30 and 35 per cent of your caloric intake. Fats store approximately nine calories per gram.

3 *Carbohydrates* The important ones are the complex carbohydrates (e.g., found in starches, grains, fruit, vegetables); avoid the simple carbohydrates ('empty calories') found in refined sugar, flour and alcohol. Complex carbohydrates are the easiest source of energy for your body to assimilate. Carbohydrates, which only store four calories per gram, should make up about 50 per cent of your total calories.

4 *Fibre* Fibre, commonly called 'roughage' is a vital and still under-rated part of your diet. The cell material of plant foods, fibre is not digested and passes unchanged through the bowels. There are many benefits of eating fibre including slowing down your eating, which can help reduce the quantity of food you consume. In the stomach, high fibre food takes longer to process, leaving you with a sense of being 'full' for a longer period of time. Eating lots of fibre also will result in more calories being lost in your stool of undigested food. It has been reported that fifty grams of fibre can carry out 100 undigested calories in every bowel movement. Fibre also slows down the rate of absorption of sugar into your bloodstream which can be of enormous benefit for people with diabetes. Fibre is found in all plants, wholegrain breads and special high fibre biscuits. It is recommended that your fibre comes from a variety of foods.

In order to obtain the necessary nutrients found in the above elements, you need to include in your diet all five of the following basic food groups.

Vegetable and fruit group (citrus fruits, leafy green vegetables, potatoes).

Bread and cereal group (breakfast cereal, bread, foods made from cereals and bread).

Milk and dairy food group (600 ml children, teenagers, pregnant and nursing mothers; 300 ml for adults; 250 ml can be replaced by 1 × 200 ml container yogurt or a 3 cm/35 g cube firm cheese).

Meat group (beef, mutton, lamb, veal, pork, poultry, rabbit,

fish, eggs, organ meats, dried peas, beans and nuts).
Butter and table margarine group (30 g butter daily on bread and in cooking).
In the average week, your healthy diet should contain approximately 33 per cent vegetables and fruit, 33 per cent bread, cereal and grain products, 16 per cent dairy products and 16 per cent meat, poultry and fish.

In order to get a more objective picture of how healthy your diet really is, complete the following food diary for four days. For each day, record the amount of each different food and drink you consume in each of the categories. At the end of the four days, make an estimate of the percentage consumed over the four days of each category. (The four percentages should add up to 100.) Then compare the individual percentages with the above recommended percentages to see which food groups you need to moderate.

Food Diary

	Day one	Day two	Day three	Day four	%
Vegetables/fruit					
Bread/cereals					
Dairy products					
Meat/poultry/fish (include eggs)					

Total: 100%

Stress-related dietary recommendations

In addition, a number of more specific recommendations related to diet and stress can be made.
Eat a variety of food Select foods each day from the major food groups.

Maintain your ideal body weight   Consult a weight chart which shows what you should weigh given your sex and height. Here's a stressful thought. If you are 25 per cent over your ideal weight, you are two and a half more times likely to have a heart attack. For most of us, your weight should be not much more than it was when you were 20–25 years of age.

Avoid too much fat, saturated fats and cholesterol   This recommendation is especially important if you have high blood pressure, smoke, or have a family history of heart disease. The fats you should first remove from your diet are the saturated ones found in fatty meats, butter, hydrogenated margarines, whole milk and ice-cream. Non-fat, low cholesterol food includes lean meat, fish, poultry, dried beans and peas. Limit your intake of eggs, organ meats (e.g., liver), and shortenings. Trim fats from meat, remove the skin from chicken and avoid frying your food.

Insure adequate fibre   Whole foods deliver fibre to your system which aids digestion, reduces chronic constipation and other gastrointestinal disorders. Whole foods which contain complex carbohydrates include raw or lightly cooked vegetables, fruits, wholegrain cereals, bread and biscuits, brown rice, nuts, beans, peas, seeds and nuts.

Avoid too much sugar   It is estimated that on average Australians consume more than 130 pounds of sugar per head each year. To avoid excess sugar: use less of all sugars, including white, brown and raw sugars, honey and syrups; eat fewer foods containing sugar such as sweets, soft drinks, ice cream, cakes and chocolates; select fresh fruits rather than canned fruits in a sugar syrup; read food labels for clues on sugar content, being on the lookout for ingredients such as sucrose, glucose, maltose, dextrose, lactose, fructose, or where syrups are listed first.

Avoid too much sodium   While an 'unsupervised' daily diet can include up to fifty grams of sodium, the recommended level of sodium consumption is around five grams. Table salt contains 40 per cent sodium. Other foods to be on the lookout for are sandwich meats, sauces, pickled foods, sauces and food cooked with monosodium glutamate (MSG), and even many medications (e.g., antacids). To avoid too much sodium: learn to enjoy unsalted flavours of foods; cook with only small amounts of added salt; add little or no salt at the table; limit your intake of salty foods; read food labels carefully to determine the amounts of sodium in processed foods and snack items.

Keep alcohol consumption to a minimum We all know the negative effects of alcohol on our well being, social relationships and driving. And 'hangovers' are, perhaps, the worst antidote for coping with a stressful situation at school the next day. If you drink, especially during the school week, limit yourself to one to two drinks per night. On weekends, you should drink in moderation.

Vitamins

'Some doctors have been carving out a profitable niche for themselves in the field of nutrition. Some of these doctors place undue emphasis on how complicated their subject is. These doctors sell not only their time and advice, but a host of expensive food supplements, backed up with a battery of somewhat silly tests done on the urine, bits of hair and so on. Often these are done as frequently as every week by the doctor's nurse.

Unsuspecting patients can become hooked on both the doctor and his or her supplements, at great expense, with little medically proven benefit. While such practitioners are few in number, they do command a loyal following. I would suggest that, before people invest their money in this type of treatment, they seek a second medical opinion to find out if it is truly necessary. Cases of severe dietary deficiency warranting radical and expensive treatments are extremely rare on this continent.

In my own practice, I find that most people do not need large doses of any one vitamin. I prefer them to get the bulk of their diet requirements from a proper, balanced diet. However, due to the depletion of zinc and vitamin C from the body under stress, and the apparent wisdom of taking vitamins C and E to help protect against cancer of the bowel, I usually recom-

*mend the daily use of a standard combination of these,
such as a "stress" formulated tablet with zinc.'*
Dr Peter Hanson, The Joy of Stress, 1986.

The evidence on whether vitamin and mineral supplementation can help you function better under stress is equivocal. Some 'experts' argue that when you are under stress you require more of all vitamins and minerals and that deficiencies in the B-vitamins, Vitamin C and calcium/magnesium are linked to stress-related symptoms such as insomnia, irritability and depression. Some nutritionists take the line that a balanced diet supplies all the nutrients you need while others say that today's supermarket foods are nutritionally inadequate.

Adele Davis in her excellent book *Let's Get Well* offers one of the most common regimen of supplements to combat stress. It includes a high protein diet supplemented by 500 milligrams of Vitamin C, 100 milligrams pantothenic acid, 2 milligrams each of vitamins B2 and B6. An all-purpose multi-vitamin supplement can do no harm and may provide needed nutritional support.

The following foods can increase your intake of natural vitamins and minerals: brewer's yeast, cod liver oil, raw wheat germ, wheat germ oil, rose hips, bone meal, kelp, lecithin and whey powder.

If you have been feeling stressed and rundown and considering a high-intensity vitamin program, consult your physician. *Self-prescribed vitamin programs should be avoided.*

Losing weight

*'There is only one way to lose control weight and that is
the physiologically balanced way of burning up food by
oxygen to produce energy.'*
Audrey Livingston Booth, Stressmanship, 1985.

Without going into the many 'ins and outs' of dieting, there are a few basics to keep in mind. To lose one pound of body fat, you must take in 3500 calories less than you expend. To know how *slowly* you will lose weight without some form of exercise, make an estimate of how many calories you need to maintain your current weight. Subtract your calorie intake on a diet from that weight and what's left over is your calorie loss per day. If your weight maintenance level is 1600 calories and you consume 1100 calories per day, you should by the end of the week lose one pound.

There are two basic components to any successful weight reduction program: calorie reduction and exercise (discussed in next section). Cutting back on high calorie foods and starting up an exercise program will get you heading in the right direction. Here are some specific suggestions.

1 Don't go on a crash diet. Try to lose weight slowly by recognising your lifestyle.

2 Set small, achievable goals for yourself. The one I use is the 'one pound (or half a kilo) a week plan'. When I have to lose some weight, I plan on losing at least one pound a week. That minimises the pain, increases my chances of success, allows me to have some 'non-diet' food and, if I fail to lose a pound, I can discipline myself to lose two pounds (one kilo) the following week.

3 Weight yourself once a week.

4 Change your diet to reduce calories and increase your intake of fruit and vegetables.

5 Keep alcohol intake to once a week (if you have to).

6 Eat smaller portions of food.

7 Eat slowly.

8 Don't eat when you're anxious, angry or tired. Find another competing activity.

9 Eat regularly. Don't starve yourself. Have low caloric snacks planned for periods between meals.

10 Monitor weekly progress and reward yourself for achieving your goals.

Let's now examine an equally important way of making sure you are in shape to combat stress at school and in the rest of your life: exercise.

EXERCISE

'The human body was designed to be exercised. That is why research studies show the following: that long-shoremen with lifting and carrying jobs live longer than fellow workers with desk jobs; that among 17 000 graduates of Harvard over a thirty-four year period, those who vigorously exercised several times each week had fewer heart attacks and a longer life span than those who did not exercise; and that middle-aged men who began to regularly walk, run or swim lowered their cholesterol, blood pressure, weight, anxiety, and depression.'
W. Schafer, **Stress Management for Wellness**, *1987.*

Of all the many stress management techniques I have so far reviewed as well as the ones which will appear in subsequent chapters, the one which seems to be to offer the greatest promise in preventing and reducing physiological distress symptoms is physical exercise. I know it's not for everyone, and by that I mean because of age or other circumstances you find it not feasible to exercise. I would hope, however, that before coming to that conclusion you search in yourself and examine your environment to see if there isn't room for exercise. It seems to be that if you experience a great deal of stress (e.g., fatigue, physical ailments, emotional ups and downs) then exercise offers you great promise for symptom relief.

Vigorous physical exertion is the natural outlet for your body when it is in the 'flight-fight' state of arousal. It provides a way of releasing a great deal of the muscle tension and general physical arousal accumulated in response to stress. After exercise, your body returns to normal equilibrium and you feel relaxed and refreshed. Exercise seems to clear your thinking, providing you with new insights into the problems which you might find stressful. Its beneficial effects on your body weight and physical well being lead to an enhanced self-image. And an increased self-image does wonders for your ability to cope with the variety of hassles you encounter at school. Recent research shows that exercise can augment the effects of vitamins in fighting off disease.

'Physiologists have repeatedly shown that a regular exercise program will improve endurance, reduce total peripheral resistance in blood circulation, lower systolic and diastolic blood pressure, increase the inner size of arteries, increase the number of capillaries, lower blood lipids, and improve lung capacity and muscular strength. This all adds up to an increase in endurance and a greater resistance to fatigue.'
  Edward A. Charlesworth and Ronald G. Nathan,
  Stress Management, 1984.

Many people including yours truly do not take to exercise naturally. We have to exert a fair amount of will power to get started and to continue. This is especially the case if we get injured or get sick. We find it hard to get started again. Why? It's what Pogo referred to when he wrote: 'We have met the enemy and it is us'. Something inside us, call it need for comfort if you like, creates an oppositional force to exercise. That force we can reduce by starting; it does get easier.

Exercise has an additional benefit to stress management. It will also reduce your risk of heart disease as well as, as previously discussed, help you manage your weight.

No, I'm not suggesting that you immediately start to jog around town or power walk every morning. I am encouraging you to move from a completely sedentary lifestyle to one where you start exercising. You can start off with simple walking for twenty minutes or so combined with a little muscle stretching and conditioning. A program of graduated exercises will help prevent muscular atrophy due to inactivity and will help eliminate your fatigue.

'Doc, I don't need much endurance. I work at a desk all day, and I watch television at night. I don't exert myself any more than I have to, and I have no requirements for exerting myself. Who needs large reserves? Who needs endurance?'

'You do. Everyone does. Surely you know the usual symptoms caused by inactivity as well as I do. Yawning at your desk, that drowsy feeling all day, falling asleep after a heavy meal, fatigue from even mild exertions like climbing stairs, running for a bus, mowing the lawn or shoveling snow. You can become a "social cripple", "too tired" to play with the kids, "too tired" to go out to dinner with your wife, "too tired" to do anything except sit at your desk or watch television, and maybe you're even getting tired of doing that. And the final clincher, "I guess I'm getting old". You're getting old all right, and a lot sooner than you should.'

Kenneth Cooper, Aerobics, *1977.*

Aims of exercise

When you exercise, your aim is to gain physical fitness which can be broken down into three areas. *Cardiorespiratory endurance* involves using your large muscles by engaging in certain activities such as walking, swimming or jogging for long periods of time (20–30 minutes). This type of endurance relies heavily on your heart and lungs. *Flexibility* involves having an extended range of motion about a joint such as when you bend to touch your toes. *Muscular function* refers to strength, power and endurance of your muscles.

Guidelines for exercise

1 Your exercise program should be designed to develop all parts of your body.

2 Particular attention should placed on building up your weaker areas.

3 For adults, cardiorespiratory endurance is considered the most important fitness component. The material on aerobic exercise is particularly designed to improve cardiorespiratory fitness.

4 Include exercises specifically designed to strengthen stomach muscles.

5 Pick activities which are fun and practical for you.

6 Exercise on alternative days, for example, Monday, Wednesday and Friday. As you progress, you may choose to add a session on the weekend.

7 Get into an exercise program gradually and take it easy. This is especially important if you are past thirty-five. Your body ain't what it used to be when it was twenty. So, for example, if you are deciding to take up jogging, start with a short distance and a slower pace.

8 Keep cool. Don't overdress.

9 Warm up. Use a variety of warm up exercises (e.g., arm circling, toe touching, jumping jacks) for at least five minutes before getting into muscle conditioning and aerobic exercises.

10 Drink plenty of water. Water will help your body remove the waste products generated by your exercise. Drink a glass of water before starting off jogging in the morning.

11 Allow a five-minute cool-down period. End your exercise with five minutes of slow walking. Rotate your head around your neck and swing your arms gently.

Aerobic exercise

The most popular form of exercise to increase cardiovascular efficiency has been popularised by Dr Kenneth Cooper and his work on aerobics. Aerobics are basically activities in which you use oxygen to produce energy. They involve sustained, rhythmic activity of the large muscle groups, especially the legs. Aerobic activities use lots of oxygen through increasing your heart and respiratory rates. This in turn leads to a relaxation of the small, peripheral blood vessels which allows more oxygenated blood to reach your muscles. Common aerobics activities include walking, running, swimming, bicycling, swimming and dancing.

The key to aerobic exercise is insuring that your heartrate reaches its 'aerobic range' for at least twenty minutes. Your 'aerobic range' involves you working at 70–85 per cent of your maximum heart rate. Your maximum heartrate can be estimated as follows: 220 minus your age = minimum heart rate. For example, if you are forty years old, 220 − 40 = 180 heart beats/minute. Your target 'aerobic range' is 70–85 per cent of your maximum heart rate. Using the above example: .70 × 180 = 126 beats per minute; .85 × 180 = 153 per minute. Therefore, your 'aerobic range' would be between 126 and 153 heart beats per minute. If you are beginning your exercise program, it is good to exercise in the lower part of your 'aerobic range' so that you will be able to exercise comfortably for between twenty and thirty minutes.

There are definite benefits of aerobic exercise which can help you modify stress level. Physical stress-related benefits include release of muscle tension; burning off adrenaline; production of endomorphs (body's natural pain killer and mood elevator); reduction of cholesterol, triglycerides, blood sugar, body fat, blood pressure; post-exercise quieting of your sympathetic nervous system and reduction of adrenaline output; more energy; and faster recovery from acute stress. Psychological stress-related benefits include: release of pent-up emotions; enhanced self-image and self-esteem; greater sense of personal control; clearer thinking and better concentration; feelings of well being and comfort.

Muscle conditioning

Calisthenic and isotonic exercises can increase your flexibility and muscle strength, power and endurance. Exercises centre on your major muscle groups including abdomen, trunk, thighs/hips/ buttocks/lower back and arms/shoulders/chest. Strength exercises include weight lifting, knee bends, push-ups and side leg raises. Flexibility exercises include toe touching, body stretching, single leg raises, calf and achilles tendon stretches, side bends and head rotations.

In summary, a good exercise program should contain four parts: warm up, muscle conditioning, aerobic exercise and cool down. If you are interested in starting to exercise regularly, read some of the many fine exercise books now on the market.

Some more tips for exercising effectively

1 *Exercise with neighbours, friends, spouse, children or the family dog.*
2 *Change exercise routines to provide variety.*
3 *Light competition might be an incentive.*
4 *Exercise to music.*
5 *For people who have trouble sleeping, exercise before going to bed.*
6 *Establish a reward system, allowing a prize of some sort for successful accomplishment. This aids in the breaking up of the boredom.*
7 *Maintain records on the exercise program and keep track of accomplishments.*
8 *Be positive. A day missed is not a calamity.*
9 *If one exercise routine does not work, others should be tried.*
10 *Gym equipment is unnecessary. Exercise does not have to be expensive.*
11 *Goals should be established and ranked in their order of importance.*
12 *Exercise should not occur within one hour of eating a meal.*
13 *Your ability to perform exercise can vary from day to day. This should be recognized and more frequent breaks should be taken on those days exercise requires more strain.*
14 *It is important to be as fit as possible for a person's age. It is not important for all people to be as fit as a 20-year-old athlete.*

**M. S. Halper and I. Neiger,
Physical Fitness, 1980.**

RECREATION

'So, if you think you have a job that's a source of distress to you, that does not offer much relaxation, amusement or refreshment, then you will have to accept your personal responsibility to look after yourself, by making sure you do have sufficient recreation in your life.'

Bob Montgomery and Lynette Evans,
You and Stress, *1984.*

The third area of your lifestyle which can buffer you from stress is recreation. You would think that recreation would come naturally and that everyone would know how to recreate. Surprisingly, many of us are extremely poor re-creators. We tend to limit ourselves to a very few inactive activities such as watching television or going to the pub. As I'm sure you're aware, educators concerned with preparing our youth to cope with the fewer number of jobs and work hours projected to characterise our work in the twenty-first century are targeting recreation as a topic which needs to be introduced in the school curriculum. Recreation as a self-management skill offers the promise not only of stress-reduction but is also an area of personal endeavour apart from your job which can bring you satisfaction in the future.

Recreation as an activity would appear to have five defining attributes. Any activity which *relaxes, amuses, refreshes* and satisfies your *need for social involvement* and *need to be alone* can be considered a form of recreation. I think of recreation as 'time out' from stress where you are able to relax your mind and body. You get away in time and space from those stressors within and outside school which you experience as stressful. What you do when you are away from the madding crowd can and should vary considerably. At times, you may wish to simply curl up with a good book, take a long bath or go for a long walk. These more solitary recreational activities are generally motivated out of your need to be alone, away from people, so that you can collect and take charge of yourself, rather than react to serve the desires of others.

Recreation may also involve others such as friends or family. Time with friends offers companionship and support as well as amusement and stimulation. Friendships offer a great deal. Unfortunately, when you are under stress, you can ignore your friends, thereby losing out on one of the main resources for stress-reduction. Friendships need to be worked on.

Another type of activity which can relax and refresh you surrounds your hobbies. Too many of us, when we get heavily involved in our work and have family commitments, put our hobbies and interests on the back burner. We give up playing squash, bush walking, walking at all, taking photographs, fixing old cars, collecting and renovating antiques and so on. Aside from distracting us from work, hobbies also offer the additional good feelings which go along with the intrinsic satisfaction of doing something well which you have chosen to do.

So laughing, playing, going on a short walk, taking a brief holiday, getting involved in a hobby, playing sport, taking a class or just relaxing can cut your stress.

Why not have a little check-up on your recreational habits to see what you are and are not doing and then move on to expanding your recreational options? (Adapted from B. Montgomery & L. Evans, *You and Stress*, Melbourne: Thomas Nelson, 1984).

How to develop a good recreational lifestyle

Step 1: Examine your present recreational activities
For the next month, make a written record of all the recreational activities you engage in both inside and outside of school. Make a note of exactly what you were doing, who you were doing it with, how much time you spent doing it, and how much enjoyment you received from the activity. You may want to use a diary, calendar or note pad for such an activity.

Step 2: Evaluate your present recreational activities
For some, this step will take very little time as their recreation

is very limited in time and scope. If you have recorded different recreational activities, consider each one in terms of what it achieves for you. Use the five criteria of recreation (relaxation, amusement, re-energising, relationships, time alone). Try to draw some conclusions as to the nature of your recreational pursuits. See if you are failing to engage in certain activities which might help satisfy more of your recreational requirements.

Step 3: Select new recreational activities
In identifying gaps in your recreational program, you will be oriented towards activities which would be a good addition to your lifestyle. For example, you may see there is an absence of any self-development hobby or interest and elect to take one up. Or you may realise that you are exercising far less than you thought and want to expand your exercise program. Or you may notice that the time you spend with friends is out of proportion with the priority friendships hold for you.

Step 4: Get organised
Before charging into a new recreational activity, get yourself organised. Decide when you are going to do it. Get a hold of any material or equipment you might need. Investigate different options about where to go for a short holiday.

Step 5: Put it into action
You've heard the expression 'paralysis through analysis'? Don't over-analyse what you are going to do, just get a bit organised and get into it. Sure, you might not like it and have to modify it accordingly. The main thing is to make the committment to trying out some new activity for a while— giving yourself a full chance to judge whether its for you. You may have to try many different activities to come up with a few that really suit you and that you enjoy.

Barriers to recreation

There are a few little devils which can prevent you from trying out new things. One is your own attitude about taking time out for yourself. You may be so used to doing things for others that the thought of doing something for yourself only increases your guilt and stress. Remind your-self that everyone is entitled for some time in their own day-to-day life for themselves. As well, by taking the time, you will have more to give to others and provide it more generously.

Another barrier is simply time. You believe there is no time. As you'll see shortly, one of the keys to finding more time is by learning to monitor, plan and manage it better. By scheduling events in your hectic life — especially during your peak periods — you will find time to recreate.

Finally, you may want to recreate and think you deserve it and will perform better once having had it, but you might feel anxious about asking your significant other (if you are in a relationship) to support you by assuming some of the household responsibilities. The section on assertion in the following chapter will offer you some insights to standing up for and asserting your basic rights in a pleasant way.

Mary was just finishing her grocery shopping when out of the corner of her eye she spied Bill resting up against the lamp post, perspiring madly. He was carrying what seemed to be a golf club and was drinking some green-looking liquid from a plastic bottle he had just unhooked from his belt. Mary hoped if she ignored him, 'it' would go away. He didn't.

'Hey Mary, let me have a look at your groceries,' yelled Bill as he swiped Mary's bag away.

'What are you doing? Give me back my groceries. What's happened to you? If the kids — or Gunn — see the way you look, Billie Boy, you'll never hear the end of it. And I'm moving offices well away from you!'

'No wonder you have such high blood pressure and are so crabby at school. Look at this. Whole milk, two quarts of strawberry icecream, two dozen Mars Bars–'.

'Hey, you were the one who gave me the chocolate. What's got into you?'

'I'm getting healthy, that's what. I'm out for a jog and off to drive a few golf balls. And I'm having a few sips of 100 per cent pure rain water. I'm tuning up my body; you know, getting fit. Not like you, my tubby little tuba. Here's your groceries. I'd say you'd be a walking cholesterol time bomb.'

Before Mary could get out another word, off sped Bill in the general direction of the golf course. Feeling a bit off centre, she balanced her groceries on her knee, opened a Mars Bar...and then another. As she wandered off, she wondered whether Bill was going to settle down before Monday's after-school staff meeting.

ACTIONS SPEAK LOUDER THAN WORDS

1 *Develop a plan for good nutrition* Write down a list of five things you could do to improve your daily diet including minimising stress-increasing foods. Select two that would be easiest for you to implement and do so for one week. Gradually make other changes to your nutritional plan and add other improvements to the list.

2 *Develop a plan for exercise* List a variety of types of exercises (e.g., walking, jogging, tennis, stretching, bowling) which would be possible for you to engage in. Try to schedule at least three sessions of exercise per week.

3 *Develop a recreational plan* From a list of solitary recreational activities and ones involving friends and family, select one activity from each category which would be the easiest to do and most pleasurable. Schedule each activity over the next month. Slowly schedule other recreational activities.

RECOMMENDED READING

Leon Chaitow, *The New Slimming and Health Book* (Wellingborough, North Hamptonshire: Thorsons, 1989).
S. Boyd Eaton Marjorie Shostak and Melvin Konner, *The Stone-Age Health Program: Diet and Exercise as Nature Intended* (North Ryde NSW: Angus and Robertson, 1988).
Garry Egger, *Commonsense Health* (Sydney: Allen and Unwin, 1986).
Ruth Englis, *Your Health and Your Figure* (Canberra: Commonwealth Department of Community Services and Health, Australian Government Publishing Service, 1989).
Robert M. Griler and Kathy Mattews, *Medical Makeover: The*

Revolutionary No-Willpower 8 Week Program for Lifetime Health (North Ryde NSW: Angus and Robertson, 1988).
Bob Montgomery and Laurel Morris, *Your Good Health* (Port Melbourne, Vic: Lothian, 1990).
Laurence Morehouse and Leonard Gross, *Total Fitness* (London: May flower, 1986).
Catherine Saxelby, *Nutrition for Life* (Frenchs Forest, NSW: Reed Books, 1986).
Rosemary Stanton, *Complete Book of Food and Nutrition* (Brookvale, NSW: Simon and Schuster, 1989).

CHAPTER 9
TIME MANAGEMENT

'The Grand Magi asked Zadig, "What, of all things in the world, is the longest and the shortest, the swiftest and the slowest, the most divisible and the most extended, the most neglected and the most regretted, without which nothing can be done, which devours all that is little and enlivens all that is great?"
Zadig answered "Time".
Nothing is longer since it is the measure of eternity.
Nothing is shorter since it is insufficient for the accomplishment of our projects.
Nothing is more slow to him that expects; nothing more rapid to him that enjoys.
In greatness, it extends to infinity; in smallness, it is infinitely divisible.
All men neglect it; all regret the loss of it; nothing can be done without it.
It consigns to oblivion whatever is unworthy of being transmitted to posterity, and it immortalises such actions as are truly great."'
Voltaire, Zadig: A Mystery of Fate.

You might be one of the many teachers I have spoken to who believes that time management is an appropriate skill for people who work in business or the government, but not for teachers. After all, where is the available free time for you to manage? Teaching is different from other jobs where you have the freedom to plan your day to maximise the achievement of your goals. If you are a teacher, you know what you have to do, where and when you have to do it. This is especially true if you are a primary teacher. If you teach at upper levels, you will have available a number of 'free' periods throughout the week. However, my experience has been that even though you may perceive that you have little control over your time, you may well still want to know of ways to find more time.

In this chapter I will discuss some of the techniques which have helped teachers use their time more efficiently. They do not work for every one. You will need to experiment with different ones and select the ones which work for you. A discussion of time management skills will be followed by a consideration of the causes of and solutions to procrastination. There is a very high correlation between poor time management skills and the extent to which you procrastinate. Learning some basic time management skills plus learning how to overcome procrastination will find you more time.

I have found that making certain changes in habits can give increased control over time. In beginning to make changes, it is important that you are realistic about the amount of time you will be able to find. That is, change can be slow. Do not expect rapid changes overnight. This is because no matter what you do, teaching will always be very demanding of your time. 'Free time' will always be a scarce commodity no matter how efficient you become.

One final point before beginning. As I indicated in Chapter 3, teachers vary in their belief about how much control they have over their lives. 'Externals' believe that they are always at the beck and call of others. They see themselves as always serving and giving and having no control over the decision of where and when to respond to the needs of students and the requests of teachers, parents and colleagues. 'Externals' feel helpless to do anything about the time they are putting into their job and, as a consequence, feel somewhat despondent and pessimistic.

Embracing a totally different perspective, 'internal' teachers believe that they can exercise some control over the time they spend doing things related to their jobs and, in particular, in managing how much they give to others and in which tasks they complete and which they do not. Teachers with a high degree of personal responsibility look for ways of cutting down distractions which interfere with the tasks they have to complete both during teaching time and beyond the classroom.

So consider the extent to which you believe deep down you can actually make changes over things and people at school who essentially rob you of your available time. In order to be successful in making the positive changes in your time management habits, it will be important to be confident that you can change others; you can change the ways you do things. Do not wait until next term hoping that things will let up. They frequently will not. Now is the time to start to plan and make changes. And as you see your efforts resulting in you obtaining even five minutes extra a day to use as you wish, your sense of personal control will also increase.

TIME AND WORKLOAD PRESSURES

One of the obstacles which everyone has in the face of too much work to do and not enough time to do it is emotional stress. And while it is normal and helpful for you to feel concerned, frustrated, disappointed or irritated about all the many things you have to do both inside and outside of school, including attending meetings, high anxiety, intense anger or feelings of despair and helplessness will actually make it harder for you to get on with making the best of a bad situation.

Now it is for many different reasons objectively bad when you cannot get everything done at work and at home at a standard you consider acceptable. However, you still have a choice about how stressed you will be in the face of excessive work and home demands.

The answer is *not* saying 'I don't care'. That's throwing away the baby with the bathwater. Working on making your attitudes more realistic and not putting yourself down can help keep your stress in check.

Consider Bill Witherspoon. At times, he does have too much to do and an insufficient time to do it all. He has family commitments which prevent him from doing as much

planning and preparation as he would like to do. His showing up late to school is largely due to sleeping in because of
his dog tiredness. He can do something about his emotional
stress by not giving in to negative and stress-creating thinking.

A rational attitude towards accomplishing things at work
has you continuing to want to succeed at your work and
keeping very high professional standards for fulfilling your
commitments. Rational attitudes, however, also have you
being realistic, knowing that you 'can't please all the people
all the time'. You can only do what for you is humanly
possible. When you fall short of your own or other's expectations, do not come down hard on yourself. You have
nothing to 'prove' to anyone. Your value as a person and a
teacher cannot be judged in terms of whether you get
everything done. Sure, getting everything done on time is a
sign of hard work and efficiency. It may also be a sign that a
teacher is on the road to a mental breakdown! Maybe.

One final point on the management of the frustration of
battling to get everything done. Work hard on managing
your own discomfort which is associated with putting in
long and tedious hours. Watch out for the attitudes of 'I
can't stand this' and 'I shouldn't have to work so hard'. As
I've explained in the last section of Chapter 6, when dealing
with frustrating work tasks, tell yourself you *can* stand
things you don't like doing. And your work is the way it is
because that's the way it is. No use saying it shouldn't be.
The trick is to not let it get to you too much. Then you can
work on ways of getting all that you can get done with a
minimum of emotional distress and a maximum of efficiency.
Let's now look at some methods which can help you manage
your time more economically.

EFFECTIVE TIME MANAGEMENT

In this section, I present some activities which will give you
greater insight into how efficiently you use your time. Also
included are techniques for improving your time utilisation.

Daily time use

One useful activity is to observe what you do during the day and note how important the activity is in helping you achieve what you need to accomplish. I suggest you complete the following time log for a typical week at school. You can choose to include your weekends as well. Be sure to include things you do after your last class is over and until you call it quits for the night. You might think that it will be pointless to write in what you do during your classes. On the contrary, briefly noting what you covered in each class can be useful for you in determining whether what you are doing in class is sufficient to help you to achieve the outcomes you have set for your students.

For each activity, indicate on the five-point scale how important the activity is for you to achieve your work goals (1 = not important, 5 = very important) and how effectively you use your time during that thirty-minute period also using a five-point scale (1 = not effectively, 5 = very effectively). Make a note of the nature of any interruptions during each thirty-minute work period (e.g., student disruptions, colleagues coming in to talk, meeting called during time you had set aside for preparation). Also, make a note of what you do when you are not working including any recreational activities.

Daily Time Analysis Form

Time	Activity	Importance	Effective	Interruptions
7.00 am	_____	1 2 3 4 5	1 2 3 4 5	_____
7.30	_____	1 2 3 4 5	1 2 3 4 5	_____
	_____	1 2 3 4 5	1 2 3 4 5	_____
8.00	_____	1 2 3 4 5	1 2 3 4 5	_____
	_____	1 2 3 4 5	1 2 3 4 5	_____

8.30	_____	1 2 3 4 5	1 2 3 4 5	_____
	_____	1 2 3 4 5	1 2 3 4 5	_____
9.00	_____	1 2 3 4 5	1 2 3 4 5	_____
	_____	1 2 3 4 5	1 2 3 4 5	_____
9.30	_____	1 2 3 4 5	1 2 3 4 5	_____
.				
.				
10.00 etc	_____	1 2 3 4 5	1 2 3 4 5	_____

The data from your daily time analysis forms will provide you with an objective basis on which to evaluate your time management efficiency.

In looking at the above data, a useful exercise is to write down what it was you had hoped to accomplish by the end of the week. Make a list of the specific objectives you wanted to achieve across the following areas: teaching (coverage of specific content, skills), corrections, class preparation, exam preparation, individualising work programs, parent meetings, committee work, pastoral care and any other area you are involved in at school.

Now see if the activities which you engaged in and the amount of time you spent on the activities enabled you to achieve your goals. Did you spend too much time on certain work activities both inside and outside the classroom which served low priority objectives? For example, if one of your goals for the week was to prepare a new unit of material, did you find yourself spending too much time doing other things such as talking to students?

Also, make some judgements about how effectively you spend your time. When are your 'peak' periods? That is, is there any consistent pattern as to the time and place where you are able to accomplish what you set out to do?

The management of distractions are also a vital skill in managing your time. During those periods of time when you are *not* teaching and are trying to accomplish a work task, what interruptions do you experience? See if you can make some generalisations between those distractions you can control and those you have difficulty managing. If you are sitting at your desk trying to get some work done during a free period, lunch or after school, what distracts you from achieving what you're setting out to do? If you have set aside some time at home to work, similarly, are there interruptions which prevent you from getting started or getting the job done.

Hopefully, considering the way in which you use your time will have alerted you to whether what you are doing with your time is directed at achieving your high priority work activities. You should have a sense as to whether the hours you are spending outside of teaching are goal-directed. As well, you will have a greater understanding of those distractions which because they delay you getting completing tasks actually serve to waste your time.

Planning

Murphy's Laws
1 Nothing is as simple as it seems.
2 Everything takes longer than it should.
3 If anything can go wrong, it will.

My experience has been that during certain periods of the school year you can manage your time more effectively by using a weekly and daily plan. I will present the basic outline of how to do both. You can then modify either one to suit what it is you have to do and your particular style of planning.

Weekly plan

Objectives (Write down what you want to accomplish by the end of the week):

1 _____

2 _____

3 _____

4 _____

5 _____

Activities (Write down what you have to do to achieve your objectives, the priority of each activity, 1 = top, 2 = middle, 3 = low, the time you believe the activity will take and the day you will do it).

		Time	
Activity	*Priority*	*Needed*	*Day*

There are a few rules of thumb in completing a weekly planner. Make sure that the different activities lead to the stated objectives. This requires that you have been reasonably careful in analysing all the different things you have to do to accomplish each objective.

Complete your weekly planner on the Saturday or Sunday before going to school. Do not leave completion of the planner until Monday as doing the actual plan will interfere with completing those activities you have set out to accomplish.

Also, I do not have to tell you that your weekly planner has to be *flexible*. One of the most predictable things about schools are their unpredictability. You never really know when you will have to attend an unscheduled meeting, spend extra time disciplining a student or even having a meeting with your school's psychologist or counsellor about one or more students. So be prepared to depart from your planned activities. In those situations, you will have to drop off the lower priority activities for the week if you cannot make up the time.

Daily planning

Parkinson's Law
'Work expands to fill the time available for its accomplishment.'

As with many teachers, I find that when I have many important things to accomplish on a day, a daily plan can help organise me and make sure that I maximise the use of my time and that I do not forget the important things I have to do. Before I go home from work, I will usually complete a daily planner for the next day which includes all the things I have to do the following day, their priority and how much time I predict the activity will take. I also try to schedule when I am going to perform the activity. The following format may need to be modified to suit your circumstances.

On the form below, first write down what you have to do, its priority and how much time you estimate you will need. You may want to begin with writing in your teaching commitments. If some of your teaching involves students working independently, seeing a video, etc., you can schedule certain activities during in-class time. The activities should probably be ones which do not require sustained concentration and, perhaps, should be the more clerical, routine ones. Then in the Daily Activity Schedule below write in those top priority activities. Schedule as many activities as time allows. However, leave room for unscheduled, brief interruptions. Once you have completed the activity, write 'yes' in the completed column in the first part of the form.

Activity to be done today	Priority	Time Needed	Completed Yes/No
_____			
_____			
_____			
_____			
_____			
_____			
_____			

Daily activity schedule

am	pm
8.00 _____	2.00 _____
8.15 _____	2.15 _____
8.30 _____	2.30 _____
8.45 _____	2.45 _____
9.00 _____	3.00 _____
9.15 _____	3.15 _____
(and so on)	(and so on

Other early morning or evening activities: _____

One of the keys to managing your time during those periods when you have too much to do and not enough time to do it is planning the use of your time. If you wait for free moments or when you feel like doing what has to be done, you will get less done and, therefore, will experience more stress.

Setting priorities

Organising routine

*1 Identify all the work to be done and sort it into three
   groups: A-highest priority; B-important; C-routine
   or trivial.*
*2 Take the B items and divide them, putting about
   20% in the A group and the remainder in the C
   group.*
*3 Now take the larger C group and divide it into two
   groups, perhaps 30% to 40% in C1 and the remainder
   in C2.*
4 Take the C2 items and put them away.
*5 Place all C1 items in a folder; when a folder becomes
   too thick, work on some of them.*
*6 Review the C1 folder one or two times each day to be
   sure items with a deadline are finished on schedule.*

Charles E. Kozoll,
Time Management for Educators, 1982.

Another key to successful time management is being able to
determine the priority of the different activities you are
supposed —in principle—to do. I think I am on safe
ground when I say that if you wrote down everything you
could be doing at work across all your different role functions that there is simply not enough time to get all the
activities done. For example, if time permitted, you could
schedule weekly meetings with each one of your students to
discuss their progress in your subject and revise your teaching program to suit the needs of each individual student.
Sounds nice, doesn't it? Unfortunately, there are many
planned and unforeseen things which you have to do which
will mean that you simply cannot devote as much time as
you should to individualising instruction, no matter how
noble the activity is.

So during peak time-workload periods—and even during

other times of the year—it is a good idea to start to make judgements about the different priorities of the activities you perform. Priorities can be determined by how essential the activity is to the accomplishment of an objective. And objectives themselves can also vary in priority. Consider the following two objectives and an activity which goes along with the achievement of each objective.

Objective: familiarising myself with the latest curriculum programs in maths with an eye to modifying what I use next year.

Activity: locate and read McGraw-Hill's latest maths program.

Objective: reduce the degree of student misbehaviour in my classroom.

Activity: meeting with misbehaving students; supervising detentions.

I think you can see that in terms of your goals for this year the above objectives may have different priorities and the enabling activities may also differ in their priority.

Another way to consider priorities is in terms of who it is that you are providing services for. The priorities of things you do requested by the principal will probably be different from the priority of things you do requested by parents, colleagues and students. Top priority activities need to be done; low priority activities get done if time permits.

The time you have to do something is also important in judging priorities. If you are in charge of making a booking for a school camp you are to run in eight months' time, making the booking may be a low priority during the early part of the school year and a top priority around the time that bookings need to be made to ensure that a bus is available.

To simplify the process of deciding whether something actually has to be done today, a colleague of mine, Professor Hedley Beare, asks himself and the person who might be making a request which involves him offering his time: 'If I do not do the activity, will the manner in which the person or organisation operates be significantly disadvantaged?' In other words, will the show go on if I do not honour the request today? If no one is significantly negatively affected, then the task becomes a low priority.

Identifying and eliminating time wasters

From your Daily Time Analysis Form, you will gain a clearer idea of the types of interferences which can prevent you from completing your work tasks efficiently. Common interferences during a school day include the following.

1 Staff room is noisy.

2 Someone who is sick at home requires attention before and after school.

3 Your principal asks you to assist in an additional student activity for the remainder of term.

4 A meeting is called after school during the time you had planned to do some corrections.

5 A parent arrives at school requesting to have a meeting with you.

6 A colleague asks to talk to you about a problem while you are planning tomorrow's lesson.

Add to the list those things which interfere with you getting done what you have to.

One of the important skills in managing your time better is learning to say 'no'. There are two areas where this skill is important. One is in saying 'no' to doing everything everyone, including you, expects you to do—especially to low priority items. I have known too many highly competent teachers who have driven themselves to distress because they believe they should be a 'super teacher' and do everything which is expected of them, high or low priority. The 'super teacher' attitude will grind you down over time through the exhaustion it brings. It is possible to be a 'great teacher' without doing everything there is to do. One of the keys to bringing down your stress is giving yourself permission to say 'no' when you are faced with low priority activities.

The other area in which saying 'no' can help you manage your time better and reduce your stress is in responding to low priority and unreasonable requests from others. As indicated in the chapter on relationships saying 'no' to unreasonable requests will reduce the stress of giving in to requests which deep down you believe are unfair. I am, of course, aware that saying 'no' or 'can you come back a bit later, I've got to get this done' can be a diplomatically tricky judgement. You certainly do not want to earn the reputation as being self-centred and not a team player. However, you can get yourself into trouble if you accept unreasonable requests simply because of your underlying need to be liked and approved of by others and your intolerance of being criticised.

When you refuse a request or prevent an interruption using one of the assertive techniques to be discussed, someone may rightly or wrongly think you are a bit self-centred. Most will not, a few will. You then have to ask yourself what is more important, getting what you want done and feeling less stressed, or pleasing the other person. If you make up your mind to be more assertive in refusing requests because of your attempt to manage your time better, it is frequently a good idea to inform your colleagues ahead of time so that they understand your motivation for pursuing what you want to do.

Controlled concentration and the 'battered mind syndrome'

Charles Kozoll, a director of the Office of Continuing Education and Public Service at the University of Illinois, has described a method which you can use to blow a mental whistle on time-distracting conditions including your own exhaustion. He has written about busy educators who often suffer from a condition known as the 'battered mind syndrome', characterised by the following.

1 Many thoughts at one time.

2 Worry about what remains to be done.

3 Loss of focus as new concerns divert from the task at hand.

4 Expectation of being interrupted and, as a result, failure to become deeply involved in work.

Essentially, what Kozoll is saying is that you can waste time by working on tasks where you're not concentrating fully. And if you are not concentrating fully, not only does it take you much longer to finish the task, but you actually use less of your 'brain power' so the end result is often quite ordinary.

Kozoll offers the following six-step process for enhancing your concentration. He recommends initially using the method for five minutes and then increasing your time up to approximately thirty minutes.

1 *Select a task, time and place where your energy is high and there is less chance of interruption* Start off by identifying one or two short tasks which you now do well, such as sending a note home to parents or filling in your weekly work program. After you get the hang of it, select other tasks which you find more difficult to do well or complete.

2 *Develop a frame* A frame is a simple message to yourself which clarifies the importance of centring on the task, such as 'Now concentrate, what do I have to do?'.

3 *Relax for a moment* Using a simple breathing or muscle-relaxing technique before beginning will help focus your mind on the task and stop your mind from wandering.

4 *Develop a mental picture* Visualise doing the task and what the final product will look like.

5 *Take a few deep breaths* This step will help you lock in just as athletes do before a competitive event.

6 *Establish 'flow' with a directing message* In order to establish persistence towards task completion, you should say something to yourself like: 'I'm going to finish this plan of work during my free period'. 'As soon as the students leave, I'm going to grade all these papers.'

Controlling your concentration will result in a heightened intensity and arousal which will enhance your ability to complete the task in as short as time as possible.

Time-saving techniques for meetings

1 *Call meetings only when there is a specific objective to be achieved.*

2 *When you have several meetings to schedule, try to schedule them back-to-back to avoid breaking up your day.*

3 *Find a quiet place to hold the meeting.*

4 *Choose participants with care. Invite only those who are responsible for the issues at hand.*

5 *Have the secretary divert calls and visitors when you hold meetings in your office.*

6 *Prepare and distribute an agenda.*

7 *List topics or questions to be covered.*

8 *Assign topics or questions to individual participants.*

9 *Schedule time to discuss each item on the agenda.*

10 *Start the meeting on time.*

11 *Stick to the schedule to keep the meeting from being sidetracked.*

12 *Assign one person to keep a record for assignments, deadlines and decisions made.*

13 *Curtail pointless arguments and long-winded reports by asking individuals to summarize their findings or viewpoints.*

14 *Formulate questions that ask for specific information, instead of generalisations.*

15 *If a topic gets bogged down, assign one person to study it further and report back to you at a later date.*

16 *Schedule the next meeting if one is necessary before participants leave this meeting.*

17 *Conclude the meeting with a summary with what has been decided.*

18 *End the meeting on time.*

19 *When meetings go off-target, request that the conversation be refocused on the objectives set for the meeting.*

Janet Attard,
53 Ready-to-Use Time Management Checklists and Worksheets, *1984.*

OVERCOMING PROCRASTINATION

Procrastination is a very strange behaviour because you know that you want very much to succeed yet you are sabotaging your own chances of success by needlessly delaying. No one is forcing you to delay; no one is standing over you with a whip threatening you. True, you may be stressed out or there may be too many distractions or you may simply not feel like doing the task. What is aggravating about procrastination is that ultimately we all know that we are responsible for not doing things which are in our best interests to do.

I often get asked as to whether procrastination is always a bad thing. Not always. Sometimes, if you delay making a decision because you do not have all the facts, you will be acting in your own interest. By postponing a decision until you have had an opportunity to examine options and secure more information, you can maximise the likelihood you are making the right decision. Just as indecisiveness, a major form of procrastination, is self-defeating, so too is over-decisiveness which involves you making a decision prematurely. You may do this because you believe others expect you to make a quick decision, you have a high need for approval, or because you can't tolerate the ambiguity of not knowing which way to go. While some procrastination is good, most of the time you procrastinate when you see the disadvantages of delaying and you still put off what you have to do.

Many people use the anxiety associated with missing deadlines to do what they have to do. While the deadline for completing some task or activity is far away, many procrastinators occupy themselves with more enjoyable activities. As D-Day arrives, they sweat and work up until the last minute to do what has to be done. Once again, I am frequently asked if this is a good or bad thing. It certainly is common. Just about everyone I know manages to lift their efficiency as deadlines approach. Up to a point, anxiety does help motivate us. However, it is also apparent that many people who procrastinate leave their run a little bit late. They get the job done, but the quality suffers. As well, the extreme stress they put themselves under by not starting their job earlier can distract them from performing at the top of their ability.

Everyone procrastinates. No exceptions. Some procrastinate more than others. In this section, you will examine areas where you procrastinate, some of the causes, and some techniques for overcoming this nasty and annoying human tendency.

Self-assessment of procrastination

Shortly, you will have an opportunity to identify specific tasks and activities you put off doing. If you would like a general indication as to the extent of your procrastination in comparison with the general population, complete the following brief procrastination inventory.

Procrastination Inventory

Directions: Indicate the extent to which you engage in the following behaviours. Circle 1 for 'almost never'; circle 2 for 'sometimes'; circle 3 for 'often'; circle 4 for 'almost always'.

	Almost never	Some-times	Often	Almost always
1 I put off until tomorrow what I should be doing today	1	2	3	4
2 I procrastinate at doing important tasks	1	2	3	4
3 I put off doing or saying things which might make me feel uncomfortable	1	2	3	4
4 I seem to leave doing things until the last minute	1	2	3	4
5 I can't be bothered doing boring and tedious work	1	2	3	4

Total score _____

The average score for the general population is eleven. If you score above thirteen, you are someone who procrastinates often relative to others.

Tasks you procrastinate at doing

The next few sections will concentrate on things you put off doing at work. In the chapter on Rational Effectiveness Training, I provided a list of a range of tasks which people at work commonly find frustrating, boring and unexciting (see page 137). From this list, and from your own experience, write down some of the boring or frustrating things you delay doing at work which lead to poor time management. Common tasks include corrections, report writing and record keeping.

List of boring and frustrating tasks

_____

_____

_____

_____

A secondary category of tasks which you might avoid doing are things which you are angry about having to do possibly because you have been given insufficient support or resources. You might be postponing doing them as a way of getting back at someone or the system.

List of 'unfair' tasks

_____

_____

_____

_____

A third category of activities which you might postpone doing are those about which, when you think of doing them, you experience tension and anxiety. For example, you might postpone talking to a colleague or superior about an aspect of their behaviour towards you which you would like them to change because of your anxiety about what they will think of you. Or you might put off handing in an important report or proposal because of anxiety about whether it will be good enough or what the principal will think of you if it is not.

List of situations where my work skills or myself are being evaluated

_____

_____

_____

_____

There may be some other activities you avoid doing which you might find difficult to put in any of these three categories. You might want to note them below.

Other activities

_____

_____

_____

_____

Now that you have identified things which you put off doing at work, the next step in learning to be more efficient with your use of time is to see if you can recognise the causes which underlie your procrastination.

Causes of procrastination

In thinking about why you do not accomplish things as readily as you would like, consider whether the causes of your procrastination are to do with things going on outside you (environmental) or result from aspects of you (attitudes-emotions) surrounding the task. In discussing a variety of different causes of procrastination, see if you can link up the causes with the different things you procrastinate at doing. There may be multiple causes for why you are not doing one particular thing. And the causes will vary across the different tasks you are procrastinating at.

Environmental causes

Frequently, the environment in which you are attempting to get some work done is not conducive to sustained effort. If one or more of the following environmental factors are making it harder for you to settle down and work, you can start to take immediate steps to change your environment.

1 *Distractions*   As discussed early, it is almost impossible to get work done if you are being interrupted.

2 *No privacy*   Having too many people around you or not having a place to go where you can be alone to do your work can prevent you from getting it done.

3 *Sloppy work area*   Without wishing to insult your intelligence, if your desk or work area is a mess, then it will be much harder for you to have a clear run at your work.

4 *Disorganisation*   People vary in terms of at what stage or level being disorganised leads to chaos. If you at that point, start to get things filed away.

5 *Missing important material*   There is nothing more wasteful of your time than not having what you need on hand to complete a job. Get in the habit of anticipating what you'll need before you start a task.

Attitude-emotional causes

As stressed in Chapters 3 and 4, your emotional reactions to situations strongly influence your ability to function adaptively in managing the situation. Your attitudes directly influence the intensity of your emotions and behavioural reactions. Together, emotions and attitudes can lead to procrastination. Let's look at six causes of procrastination that have more to do with what's going on inside of you than with the situation itself.

1 *Hostility* As I mentioned, sometimes you get so angry with having to do something or by the manner someone treated you, you think to yourself 'I'm going to fix their wagon. I won't do it!'. At these times, you have to ask yourself whether by not doing the task you are helping yourself achieve your goals. Many teenagers fail to oblige their parents or teachers because in their judgement they have been harshly done by. And they cannot see that their rebellion is hurting them more than it is hurting others.

2 *Self-downing* Some people who procrastinate develop a problem in addition to their procrastination. They get depressed about their procrastination because they tell themselves 'I'm a failure, hopeless, for not doing what I should be doing. I don't deserve anything from life because I am such a hopeless procrastinator.' Rather than simply seeing themselves as someone with a range of procrastinating behaviours, they irrationally conclude they are total procrastinators and totally hopeless. With this added problem, they find it doubly hard to motivate themselves to do what they've been postponing.

3 *Need for approval* Some people who procrastinate in refusing other people's unreasonable requests or who delay handing things in, avoid doing things because they are afraid of being criticised or rejected. People with this attitude frequently consider approval or avoidance of criticism more important and vital for their survival than getting the job done.

4 *Perfectionism* Some people avoid completing tasks and even getting started on tasks because they are afraid the final product will not be perfect enough. These 'self-raters' equate their self-worth with perfect task performance and get quite anxious and depressed about the thought of not performing perfectly.

5 *Low frustration tolerance* This is one of the two main

culprits which can prevent you from doing tasks at school you find boring and which take time. As discussed in Chapter 5, low frustration tolerance arises from you telling yourself that things *should* be easier and more fun and that you *can't stand it* when things are boring and take time.

6 *Short-term hedonism*   A close cousin to low frustration tolerance, short-term hedonism is an attitude which says that *I must have what I want, now!*' and 'It's *awful* to have to give up the enjoyments and pleasures of the moment and do boring and frustrating work'. Rather than working towards a balance between fun in the short term and putting in the effort to achieve longer-term goals, short-term hedonists are out of balance.

'Cures' for procrastination

Changing your environment is a step which can provide you with surprisingly immediate and large benefits in improving your task performance. If your work area at school or home is a bit of a disaster zone, stay back or up late and get it cleaned up and organised. Further, figure out some ways of controlling the outside distractions so that when you have to work, you are free to concentrate and make the best of your time.

If attitudes and emotions are interfering with you getting things done, I strongly recommend that you go back to the chapter on Rational Effectiveness Training and use the rational self-management model. By gaining practice in modifying your self-talk and emotions in the face of situations which you commonly avoid, you will develop emotional control which will do much to overcome your procrastinating tendencies.

Here are some 'rational' attitudes which can help you to counter procrastination-inducing atttitudes.

1 If people give you something unfairly to do, give them the right to be wrong. Give up your hostility and only delay doing things that will help you and never to get back at others.

2 Recognise that you are not totally hopeless because you

procrastinate, only someone with procrastinating behaviour. Accept yourself so that you can then work on your procrastination.

3 If you fear other people's negative evaluations, remember that while it's definitely nicer to have approval, you don't need approval. You can still be happy and successful without it.

4 If you are a perfectionist, try to see that it is sometimes good to perform less than perfectly in order to discover what you can and cannot do. We learn by trial and error.

5 Admit that it is difficult to do a difficult or boring task promptly and well, but that it is really never *too* hard, which is a magical term meaning harder than it should be.

6 Remind yourself that in order to obtain pleasant results, you have to do unpleasant things.

Finally, there are a number of techniques which you can use to overcome procrastination.

1 *Knock-out technique* The harder and more distasteful a task is, do it the more immediately.

2 *Small-sequential steps* When you procrastinate doing something, break down the task you are procrastinating at into smaller, manageable parts and set yourself a small part each day. Once you have finished one part, do the next part.

3 *Five-minute plan* Take a task you've been procrastinating at and work a minimum of five minutes a day. Once you've finished five minutes, you can add another five minutes and then another.

4 *Worst-first approach* Identify the most difficult part of the task and do it first.

5 *Remember-forgetting technique* Whenever you remember a task you've been procrastinating at, do it—at least some of it—immediately.

6 *Swiss cheese method* Do anything in connection with the task you want to accomplish. Gradually eat large chunks or holes in the task until it becomes easier to do.

7 *Self-reward* Reward yourself with something pleasant when you've finished the difficult or onerous task.

8 *Self-punishment* Penalise yourself by depriving yourself or forcing yourself to do something you do not like to do if you have not finished the task.

9 *Cost-benefit analysis* Make a list of all the good things which will happen if you stop procrastinating at an important task and go over the list regularly. Make a list of all the miserable results of your procrastination and review it before going to bed each night.

Roger Gunn was relieved to have the staff meeting over. Very relieved. He couldn't believe that Bill Witherspoon had actually volunteered for the position of head of science. He always seemed like such a wimp and irresponsible. Yet, he had noticed that lately he seemed better. He couldn't quite put his finger on it. More confident. Anyway, Roger was dreading going back to his office. He knew he had a stack of telephone messages to return and a curriculum meeting to prepare for. He wasn't even sure if he had all the papers he needed. 'The truth is, my office is a shambles. Maybe that's why I've been so irritable lately. I can't get anything done. I can't find anything! I know what I'll do. I'll call home. I'm going to have to work back late and get myself organised. And what about all these phone calls I've been putting off? What was that technique I read about in the *Women's Weekly* — the worst-first approach? That's what I'll do. I'll sort through these and do the worst one first. Let's see... Definitely this one.'

'Hello, Mrs Pain, how's little Johnny feeling? We were all so pleased that you came by and are supporting what we're doing — especially Mr Withers, er Mr Witherspoon. Next time, just give us a little call so that we can be ready for you.'

ACTIONS SPEAK LOUDER THAN WORDS

Make a list of all the things you have to do over the next week both at school and on a separate sheet at home. Place a 1 next to all the high priority activities, a 2 next to middle priority activities, and a 3 next to lower priority activities. Concentrate on the higher priority activities first. Then work your way down the list. For those things you do not get done, work on managing your emotional stress.

You may wish to include in the above exercise the use of the Weekly Planner and Daily Planner Forms. Start to get into the habit of planning what you are going to do in the coming week. Include both work, family and personal activities. Schedule time when you are going to accomplish the high priority activities in each of these areas. Inform people at work and at home that you are getting organised.

RECOMMENDED READING

Merrill E. Douglass and Donna N. Douglass, *Manage Your Time, Manage Your Work, Manage Yourself* (New York: Amacon, 1980).

Sally Garratt, *Manage Your Time* (London: Fontana, 1985).

Marion E. Haynes, *Make Every Minute Count: How to Manage Your Time Effectively* (London: Kogan Page, 1988).

Alan Lakien, *How to get Control of Your Time and Your Life* (New York: Signet, 1973).

R. Alec Mackenzie, *The Time Trap* (New York: McGraw-Hill, 1975).

Bradley C. McRae, *Practical Time Management* (Vancouver: Self-Counsel Press, 1988).

CHAPTER 10
CLASSROOM MANAGEMENT

'Discipline, class control, classroom management — by whatever name you call it, keeping order in the classroom is a teacher's greatest concern. You may not like that fact; you may wish it weren't true. But it is. That's a given in the daily life of teachers. Discipline is so crucial, so basic to everything else in the classroom, that most educators agree: it is the one thing that makes or breaks teachers... If students don't stay on task, they don't learn. At least they don't learn what they are supposed to. If they do whatever they want, the best plans, activities, and materials don't mean a thing. It needn't be the whole class that misbehaves. Three of four students, even one, can so disrupt a class that learning becomes impossible for even the best-behaved students.'

C.M. Charles,
Building Classroom Discipline from Models to Practice, *1981.*

As mentioned in Chapter 1, one of the main causes of the increase in teacher stress today is the increase in student misbehaviour. There is little question that over the past two decades student conduct has deteriorated. Students' attitudes towards the authority of teachers have changed. Whereas not too long ago you could reasonably expect that most students would follow class rules and obey, times have changed. No longer can you take for granted that students will respect you.

In the 1950s, the prevailing discipline model was authoritarian in nature. Teachers by right of their position in the school hierarchy were vested with power over students who were expected to conform to school rules and regulations. The aim of discipline was to make students conform to rules. In the 1980s and early part of the 1990s, the discipline model has shifted in emphasis largely due to the failure of the older power authority model to bring about the desired results. Currently, partly because of students' greater awareness of their rights and partly due to changing values of our society, school discipline has moved slowly to a more democratic 'justice for all' model with the goal of empowering students to acquire self-discipline. With the abolishment of the 'cane' arrived a more humanistic form of discipline approach which attempted to instill a set of values in students which would have the effect of motivating them to respect the rights of others.

While in some schools the strict, authoritarian teacher can still be found to maintain a reasonable amount of classroom control through harsh, intimidatory tactics, my observation is that they are a vanishing breed. Whereas once new teachers could use the John Wayne 'shoot-em-up' style of discipline as a model, today the Rambo counterpart would not for the most part survive. Students have become more assertive and aggressive in standing up for themselves and are for the most part, especially as they get older, no longer prepared to cooperate with harsh and demanding teachers. New discipline models are constantly being devised and revised to cope with the changing times. While some inroads have been made in articulating principles of discipline policy and cognate discipline procedures, I'm sure you'll agree that there is still a long way to go.

So if you are finding classroom disruptions a continuous distress, frankly, it is not surprising. And you have plenty of company. It is my belief that if the community was really made aware of how hard it can be to teach today with the constant and high degree of poorly behaving students in some schools, teachers would be much more supported than they are now. As the major television networks are designing miniature microphones to pick up on-the-field chatter at major sporting events — perhaps we should develop one for use in the classroom! (But you can't really win because you would cop the criticism if things were a bit out of control.)

It would be impossible for me to attempt to review the current state of the art in classroom management. There are just too many different variations on the same theme to cover in one chapter. The books recommended at the end of the chapter are ones that contain valuable information on which to build a foundation of an effective approach to discipline. In this chapter I discuss the difference between stress and distress in response to student misbehaviour. I then present some ideas on how to form sound discipline policies, which are necessary as a starting point to managing student conduct problems. A presentation of basic discipline skills along with an exposition of the importance of using logical consequences wherever possible rounds out the section.

STUDENT MISBEHAVIOUR

Student misbehaviour belongs right up there as one of the main contributors to teacher stress. No matter what their age, students can disrupt your class by talking out of turn, distracting others, damaging equipment, getting out of their seats without asking permission, fighting verbally and physically with others and by swearing at you (to name just a few of the most common offences). These activities not only both prevent you from getting on with your teaching and other students from learning but the constant demand on you to get them to cooperate and to settle down can really take it out of you physically and emotionally.

My experience has been, and my research has shown, that teachers vary in terms of how stressful they find student misbehaviour. Some teachers can handle it better than others. Just as there are individual differences in teachers' ability to manage and tolerate time and workload pressures, so too it is possible to see differences between teachers in how they cope with poorly behaved students.

What determines how well you can keep the stress in check has to do largely with your attitudes, coping skills and ability to relax under pressure. If you consider two teachers in the same school who have to teach the same students, the teacher who copes best is the one who manages to maintain emotional control most of the time, who knows how to relax and who has a discipline plan for managing misbehaviour. The more highly stressed teacher loses emotional control more readily, either does not know how to or fails to relax, and lacks a thought-out discipline plan.

You make me so angry!

The first step to managing emotional stress in this area is to take emotional responsibility for your feelings, especially your anger. Remembering back to Chapter 3 on personal responsibility you will recall that, while things which happen in your classroom start the emotional stress chain, your attitudes and self-talk about the misbehaviour and the students as well as yourself will determine the *intensity* of your emotional reactions as well as how long they last. Taking emotional responsibility means really accepting the fact that 'I upset myself about my students' miserable misbehaviour'. While this insight does not do a lot for helping you get upset to begin with, my experience is that it is quite helpful in reducing the time it takes to calm down after an upsetting incident.

While extreme anger is generally quite unproductive, let me again say that anger is a natural human emotion. This is especially the case when you are continuously frustrated by misbehaving students. And just as it would be incorrect for you to think that anger is an effective discipline strategy, so too it is harmful for you to think 'I shouldn't be angry'. From time to time, anyone who teaches experiences anger. The key is to recognise, not deny it, and not put yourself down because you are angry. Rather, the view I offer is one of learning to moderate and control it through using the rational attitudes and self-talk described earlier, relaxation skills and the discipline skills offered in this chapter.

Distress-creating attitudes and self-talk

Your attitudes and self-talk can help make mountains of molehills. Let me clearly illustrate this relationship with an example.

Consider a typical classroom 7E, with a typical disruptive student you've already met, Johnny Pain. He comes into class late, does not have all his books, hasn't done his homework, makes silly comments throughout the period, gets out of his seat to belt Alex who sits two seats in front of him, throws spitballs when his teacher turns his back and, when he can, reads *Playboy*. The situation is objectively demanding because Johnny's teacher has not only to get through the lesson with his other students but also has to figure out how to motivate and control Johnny. The degree of stress is, however, largely under the influence of the teacher's attitudes.

Two of Johnny's teachers might experience quite different degrees of stress and act quite differently. Harold Jones rationally thinks to himself: 'I would *prefer* Johnny to behave himself and for me to have control over his behaviour. It is a hassle for me to teach this class with Johnny in it. I don't like it but no doubt I can put up with it. I wonder how I am going to motivate Johnny or, at least, reduce his disruptive influence.' As a consequence of these rational attitudes towards Johnny, Harold Jones would feel somewhat uncomfortable, irritated and stressed about Johnny, but he wouldn't be raging and 'off the wall'. And equally importantly, he would have his wits about him and would be in a better position to solve his *practical problem* than if he was raging.

Mary Brunette, a teacher of similar age, intelligence, background and experience as Harold Jones, creates a different problem for herself about Johnny's behaviour. Not only does she have the practical problem, she also virtually manufactures (with some help from Johnny) distress as an *emotional problem* because of her distress-creating, attitudes. 'Johnny *should always* behave himself in my class and I *should* have control over my students all the time. This is really *awful* that he is behaving this way. *I can't stand it!* Johnny Pain is really a *rotten and hopeless* student who deserves to be punished!' The consequnce of these irrational attitudes for Mary B. is a high amount of stress everytime she walks into 7E. By *overly* upsetting herself about an objectively unpleasant and demanding situation, she will find it very difficult to solve her own and Johnny's problems. Chronic levels of this type of frustration often lead to health problems and teacher burnout.

Why are Mary's attitudes irrational? As I explained in the chapter on Rational Effectiveness Training, while it would certainly be desirable if Johnny acted better, there is no law of the universe which says he *must*. By *demanding* good behaviour (rather than desiring it), Mary is setting herself up for excessive stress whenever she is faced with misbehaviour in the class. She also exaggerates the problem by thinking 'This is awful' which really means that it is 100 per cent bad or worse! Obviously, an objective rating of Johnny's behaviour would put in the moderate range of life's catastrophes. Mary's idea that 'I can't stand! Johnny's behaviour' is irrational because even though she doesn't like it and she feels bad, she patently *can* stand it (it hasn't killed her, she's never fainted, her eyeballs haven't popped out). And finally, she is *overly* stressing herself by her thought that because Johnny is badly misbehaving, he is *totally* rotten and hopeless. By *globally rating* Johnny's value as a person from one aspect of his behaviour (conduct in class), Mary is irrationally equating Johnny's self-worth with his behaviour and, as a consequence, is more enraged that she need be.

Your answers to the Teacher Irrational Belief Scale presented in Chapter 2 will give you a clearer idea of which attitudes you bring with you to student misbehaviour which only make it worse. 'Authoritarian attitudes' will add excess and unnecessary anger to your emotional stress reactions when faced with poorly behaving students.

Excessive anxiety in the face of classroom disruptiveness is frequently motivated by 'self-downing' attitudes. If you experience at times extreme anxiety, poor self-confidence, low self-esteem and even depression as a consequence of your students' misbehaviour, you may well have either a high need for achievement and/or need for approval. Unsettled students or a class will be threatening to you because they reveal that you have not achieved your goals and hence are not perfect. As well, others might formulate negative opinions of you.

If you scored high in 'low frustration tolerance' you are likely to evaluate excessive classroom misbehaviour as being too hard and not something you can (or care) to deal with. Low frustration tolerance attitudes actually partly determine how much frustration you can tolerate. The greater your low frustration tolerance, the less able you will be able to endure the frustrations of facing unruly students.

If you find yourself getting very stressed about teaching your own version of Johnny Pain, rational attitudes and thinking skills can be vital emotional lifesavers. If you find yourself to be self-downing, then it is imperative if you want relief from stress that you do some clear thinking which separates your worth as a person from your achievements as a teacher, as well as separates your self-worth from the disapproval you might receive from students, teachers and senior administrators. For many and varied reasons, most people — not just stressed teachers — take to heart lack of success and criticism; that is, they take it personally. While you may feel like a total failure when some students in your class are disobedient, rude or disruptive, their bad behaviour is not sufficient evidence for you to conclude you are a hopeless teacher or hopeless as a person. A rational attitude towards a class which is not behaving up to your standards has you rejecting the idea that I *need* to be successful in disciplining this class and I *need* to be approved of and receive recognition for my achievements or else I rate as a failure. Such a summary is irrational. Replace it with the more rational idea: 'While it would be preferable to be successful in disciplining my students and to be recognised for my efforts, I do not *need* such success and recognition to be a worthwhile person'. Think about it. If you have been getting very anxious or down, you will be selectively focusing on the negative behaviour of your students and your inability to manage it and excluding the other important aspects of you as a teacher and a person.

As indicated, authoritarian attitudes about the way students *should* be can lead to excess stress. A rational approach towards undisciplined students has you maintaining your values of respect for authority, cooperation and self-discipline, but not *demanding* that students demonstrate these values. It would be wonderful if students would always behave respectfully, cooperatively and in a self-disciplined way, but there is no law of the universe which says they *must*. When you bring with you an absolute unbendable will that your students do as you expect, distress is the inevitable result. Students *will* behave in opposite ways. A rational approach has you sticking with your preferences and not your demands.

My own research has shown that highly stressed people, especially those who lack confidence, blow things out of proportion. This tendency, which is referred to as 'awfulising', means that you think to yourself something like 'It is 100 per cent bad I have to teach this class (or student)'. The exaggeration can be found in the 100 per cent. Rational thinking has you putting the awfulness of classroom behaviour in perspective with all the other bad things which could happen to you both inside and outside teaching. (Remember the catastrophe scale presented in the list of instant cures?) If you find yourself 'awfulising' about the Johnny Pains of this world, ask yourself to compare the badness of their behaviour with nuclear war, death or serious illness to you and your immediate family, disabling injuries or heart attack. You'll clearly see that while having poorly behaved students *is* clearly bad because it prevents you from achieving your goals—it may even be very bad—such behaviour is nevertheless not of the same order of catastrophe as these other really bad events.

One of the greatest stress-creating attitudes which resides in your head and creates distress is, as already indicated, 'I can't-stand-it-itis'. Briefly, when you are at your most stressed about an undisciplined student or class, you can fall into the trap of thinking to yourself: 'This feels *so* bad, I can't stand it this any longer!' This type of thinking is irrational because it is largely untrue. While it does feel very bad, you know objectively that the bad feeling isn't going to kill you; you'll survive as you have before. So when you are getting towards the end of your tether with your students, look out for your 'I can't-it-itis'. If you find it, ask yourself: 'Where is the evidence that I can't put up with this situation any longer?' and your objective answer will sound something like 'There is none. I don't like it. But I can put up with it.' This will help you manage your own stress more effectively.

Learning to change your thinking requires practice. Chapters 5 and 6 give you the opportunity to analyse your thinking and develop 'scripts' which you can develop ahead of time to help you manage your emotional stress reactions. The point I am making here is that when you find yourself getting too stressed about your students' classroom behaviour and especially when you cannot immediately change it, you can learn to manage your own emotional stress reactions through rational thinking, relaxation and other self-management skills. Even though at times students may try to victimise you, you do not have to play the role of victim. You can do something about yourself.

In this next section, I will present some ideas and skills which will alert you to ways of managing discipline problems differently. One of the innovators in the area of classroom discipline is William Rogers, author of *Discipline and Student Welfare: A Policy Approach* (with Brian Stewart and Felicity Jack), (Ministry of Education, Western Metropolitan Region, 1987), *Making a Discipline Plan* (Nelson, 1989), and *You Know the Fair Rule: Strategies for Making the Hard Job of Discipline in School Easier* (Australian Council for Educational Research, 1990). Rogers makes a major contribution in showing how discipline skills need to be embedded into an overall discipline and student welfare policy. As well, his work demonstrates clearly how you can manage a discipline situation and reduce your stress by internalising a plan of action and developing skills which you can draw on according to the severity of the student misbehaviour.

The material presented below is reproduced, with minor alterations, with William Rogers' kind permission.

RIGHTS, RESPONSIBILITIES AND RULES

One of the main aims of a school community is to insure that all its members develop certain *values* which help us to relate to each other in a positive and mutually beneficial way. Important values which promote healthy community relations include the following.

Worth and the dignity of the individual	Communication
Consideration and care	Confidence
Cooperation	Self-esteem
Pride	Self-direction
Respect	Self-responsibility
Trust	Social responsibility
Social relationships	Other acceptance

Rights and *responsibilities* are ways in which a school community expresses to its members these important values. Rights are in one sense expectations of how things ought to be if we are going to relate together in our community and encourage, teach and promote values. Important rights in a school community include:

a right to self-worth	a right to work
a right to be respected	a right to learn
safety rights	a right to communicate
movement rights	a right to participation

When we talk about rights, it is important that we express them in terms of their responsibilities and not as mere 'demands'. Rights and responsibilities naturally go together. Only by your responsibility can my rights be protected; only by my responsibility can your rights be protected. In order for my rights to be respected, I have a responsibility for acting in ways which protect your rights.

- If I have a right to self-worth, I have a responsibility to treat you with respect, consideration and acceptance.
- If I have a right to be heard, I have a responsibility to listen.
- If I have a right to safety, I have a responsibility to relate in a non-hurtful way.
- If I have a right to movement, I have to insure that I do so in a way that does not upset others.
- If I have a right to learn and work, I have a responsibility to behave in a way which helps others learn and work.
- If I have a right to develop social relationships, I have a responsibility to allow you to participate.

230

The way that rights are protected are through *rules*. A right to safety is protected by a rule for fighting. A right to develop social relationships is protected by a rule which allows for maximum social interaction and participation. Reasonable rules presume rights and responsibilities which in turn presume values.

When we break a rule, we in turn infringe a right and, therefore, we ought to face a consequence. The community owes it to itself and the individual to insure that rights are upheld and rules enforced.

Where feasible, rules ought to be stated as positive intents, not merely as negative limits, should be relevant to rights (e.g., safety, learning and movement), seen to be within the ambit of our rights and responsibilities as members of a school community, and penalties for breaking rules should be related logically to the consequences of violating someone's rights and teaching self-responsibility in the future. Logical consequences are consequences designed by teachers (and students, where appropriate) that enable students to see that their behaviour has certain outcomes (see below). These outcomes (consequences) are related to the disruptive-to-rights behaviour as far as possible.

The job of a rule is to: give protection to one's rights; highlight all community members' responsibilities to keep rules and maintain rights; demonstrate that a school, class, and students work and relate better by being cooperative. The following are examples of rules.

Conflict resolution rule (for younger children, 'Our fighting rule')

In our room if we can't get on with each other or cannot agree, we should try to talk it out. If we can't work it out, ask the teacher for help. We should not fight in our room. If you fight you will be separated immediately. You may be asked to stay back and explain your behaviour. You may be asked to apologise.

Communication rule

In our room, when we communicate (or talk) with others we

should talk quietly so others can get on with their work. When we ask a question of the teacher, we put up our hands without calling out. This gives everyone a fair go. If we keep calling out we will be reminded of our fair rule. We may be asked to stay back and explain our behaviour. If we need the teacher's help while we are working, we should wait until they can see our hands up. We should not call out across the room.

Safety/security rule

In our room, we all need to take care of our equipment and use it safely. Accidents can happen so we all need to be careful. If we use equipment in an unsafe way it will be taken from us and we will be asked to fix anything we break. We will not be allowed to use any equipment unless we use it safely and correctly.

Movement rule

This rule is difficult to specify because of teachers' wide differences regarding acceptable movement. The rule, how-ever, should specify the amount and kind of movement acceptable in our room. In our room when we get up out of our seat and move around, we need to (optional choices): ask the teacher first, do so quietly, only when you need to, do so without upsetting other students. If we move around noisily, or without good reason, we may be asked to stay back and explain our behaviour. (If the children can get out of their seat with permission, say so in your rule.) Added to the movement rule may be the 'coming in' and 'going out' movement rule.

Learning rule

It's hard to learn when other people are making too much noise. It's hard to learn if the teacher is unable to teach because of rudeness or noise, or children moving around. In our room we need to think of others who are trying to work as well. If we make it harder for others to work by making too much noise, or by interfering with others' work, we may be asked to move away and work by ourselves. If we damage other students' work, we will need to fix it up.

Values, rights, responsibilities and rules constitute a basis for promoting good self-discipline and mental health and for preventing discipline and social-emotional problems.

RULES AND ENFORCEMENT

'Positive' rule making, which is one of the main ways to insure that the rights and responsibilities of members of a school community are protected, has the following characteristics.

- Rules, where practical, should extend across a whole class and school.
- The actual rules ought to be few in number (in some classrooms the rules centre around several rule factors such as a movement rule, a safety rule, a communication rule, a conflict-resolution rule, a learning rule).
- It is better for rules to be stated positively. ('Students ought to be at class on time' is better than 'Do not be late for class'.)
- Rules are better if they are clear and specific. A student needs to be able to tell when its broken. ('Be considerate to one another' is a great philosophy but is not a rule. 'When we disagree with each other we talk it out rather than fighting' is more specific).
- Rules ought to be reasonable, fair and cover what is required concerning specific behaviour.
- Rules need to be enforceable and benefit one's rights.
- A rule should be displayed and reviewed from time to time.
- A rule should be related to logical consequences of behaviour.

Logical consequences

The more logically related a consequence is to a rule, the more likely a student will see sense in the rule's enforcement. Students can be encouraged to see that *all* behaviour has consequences. Examples of *natural consequences*: if you do not want to play by the rules chances are others will not want to play with you; if you fall over you will get hurt.

Logical consequences are consequences designed by teachers (and students, where appropriate) that enable students to see that their behaviour has cetain outcomes. These outcomes (consequences) are related to the 'disruptive-to-rights' behaviour as much as possible.

Logical consequences teach responsibility for one's actions. As the objective of a student welfare and discipline policy is to foster self-discipline and self-control, it is essential that students be encouraged to see that their behaviour results in specific positive and negative outcomes. They need to be made aware that it is their own choice of behaviour in a situation which determines the outcome. Because students may come from home backgrounds or have temperaments which predispose them towards neglect of the rights and welfare of others and to act in self-centred ways, a teacher is the main agent to enforce fair rules and protect the rights of individual members of the school community.

As an authority figure, you will call to your students' attention the logical connection between their behaviour and its consequences. Where students violate the rules which in turn violate the rights of other members of the community, logical consequences follow which are designed to teach students to respect the rights of others by acting responsibly. Logical consequences can simply be taught employing an 'if-then' rationale.

'If you vandalise, you replace or correct.'

'If you are rude, you apologise.'

'If you are careless or sloppy with your work, you have to repeat it in your own time if you want to pass.'

In order for logical consequences to be effective, students need to have a clear appreciation of the connection between their behaviour and its consequences. In this way, you can direct your concerns towards students' present or future behaviour. This is not mere punishment.

Fundamentally, logical consequences communicate to students that the following apply.

- Their behaviour is their own responsibility and the result of their own choice (even bad, foolish, immature choices; part of the teaching task is to help students make better choices).
- The 'reparation' (the 'then' part of 'if—then') is also their

234

choice and not merely punishment given out by the teacher.

- If the class knows the logical consequences of violating the rights of others by breaking rules, there is in place a clear discipline route which motivates the student to self-control.

Students see the justice and sensibility of facing up to logical consequences even though they might not like them. Giving 'lines' or copying from a dictionary are arbitrary, unfair and pointless actions which fail to teach a useful lesson and frequently invite hostility and alienation. If writing is going to be used relative to behaviour, it ought to be writing *about* behaviour. For example, students ought to be encouraged to examine what they did, why they did it, and what else they could have done.

The value of this approach

When a school develops its policy direction along a discussion of values, rights, responsibilities, rules and consequences, the actual rules are seen by all in a more positive, constructive and goal-oriented way. So often students see rules as tools of control by authority figures. To involve students when possible in the discussion and formulation of positive rule making in the context of values, rights and responsibilities, you both minimise the 'arbitrary sanction' view and maximise involvement, responsibility and the achievement of the goals of self-esteem, emotional and behavioural responsibility and self-discipline.

DISCIPLINE

In a large proportion of cases, students learn to respect the rights of other members of the school community and act responsibly as a consequence of the rules and their enforcement through the use of logical consequences.

Unfortunately, some children will still fail to respect the rights of others and act in anti-social, disruptive and disobedient ways. It is useful for you to have at your fingertips on these occasions a discipline plan and specific skills so that you can decide how you want to respond rather than merely reacting in the heat of the moment. If you do not plan your response, you'll most often fall back on your own feelings.

Goals of discipline

Current educational thought holds that discipline should serve goals other than control or punishment. While control is very important, it should not be obtained at the expense of the rights of students even when they have violated the rights of others. Moreover, discipline techniques should be viewed in terms of maximising positive outcomes in students. In particular, a discipline approach should result in students acquiring a great degree of self-discipline and self-control and should help build up and not tear down students' self-esteem.

So when you discipline, you need to ask yourself, 'What do I do day after day to help students towards these ends?' 'What means do I use which are most likely to achieve these outcomes in students?'

Why students misbehave

Rudolph Dreikurs has made us aware that students' appropriate and inappropriate behaviour is largely *goal directed*. Some students fulfil their needs to belong in a group through attention-seeking, aggressive and hostile ways. It is very important that teachers are aware of the goal of students' attention-seeking, power-struggling, revengeful and giving-up behaviours. Being aware that being disruptive may be *purposeful* behaviour will help you to plan effective steps and be less reactive. The four basic motivations for student misbehaviour are as follows.

Attention seeking This can range from merely tapping to out-of-seat behaviour. Such behaviour may reveal students' need for attention from significant adults or peers, whether in a negative (e.g., class clowning, smart comments, calling out) or praiseworthy fashion.

Power and defiance Some students seek to demonstrate that they can get their way by defying and demonstrating their power. Getting one's own way, being the boss, and extreme attention-getting behaviour often serves the goal of power. Students believe that this is the way that they can belong and act from the belief that 'I must have my way'.

Revenge This 'victim' role is difficult to handle because the student firmly believes that 'others have been unfair, unjust and have hurt me; I have a right to hurt back'. Group belongingness is achieved, according to Dreikurs, by damaging, hurtful and malicious behaviour.

Inadequate/helpless/isolated goal behaviour This behaviour is also very difficult to deal with simply because of its entrenched 'I don't care' attitude. This form of learned helplessness arises from the firm belief that one cannot gain any group acceptance. It is not shyness, but students' deep-seated belief in their incapacity, low self-esteem and power-lessness. Because such students tend to be non-disruptive in the sense of infringing on the rights of others, they can often be ignored or given up on.

'Firm and kind' discipline

The key to effective discipline involves you communicating to your students a set of rules which are reasonable and which they can see as being in their own best interest as well as the welfare of others in the school community. At older ages, you may wish to invite student participation in the decision-making process— especially during the first days of a new school year or term.

When confronted with a student or group of students who are breaking rules, it is vitally important that you are emotionally controlled. Managing your rage or anxiety will not only help keep your mind clear in order to decide upon the right discipline skill (see below) but also by being controlled you are less likely to employ 'indulgent' emotions. Typical statements which can accompany the enforcement of a rule which reflect indulgent emotions include the following.

'Gee, you're as thick as a brick.'
'Honestly, you are stupid!'.
'You never listen, are you deaf?'
'When will you ever learn?'

'Where were you when the brains were handed out?

Indulgent emotions are tempting to use when you're very frustrated but are unhelpful for students' self-esteem. In addition, emotionally laden statements are likely to provoke resentment and a power struggle in the student, rather than a change in their attitude and behaviour.

By using some of the assertiveness techniques described in the next chapter when you are faced with unruly students, and by focusing on students' wrong actions rather than the whole student, you will dramatically increase the effectiveness of your discipline techniques. Work on accepting the student as a fallible human being who is making a mistake, rather than someone who deserves to be blamed, condemned and punished.

I encourage some teachers not to attempt to discipline in a situation if they are angry. Calming yourself down first will help you calm your students down.

Lee Canter has developed an approach to student misbehaviour called 'assertive discipline' which has been adopted with good results in many schools in Australia. Canter's approach involves teachers taking positive actions towards insuring their own rights to teach as well as protecting the rights of students to learn. He identifies three different discipline styles which bring about different results. In his book *Assertive Discipline* he illustrates the contrasting styles using as an example a third-grade teacher with a number of children who frequently push and shove in order to be first in line. This results in constant fighting and yelling before the class goes outside.

Non-assertive style

The teacher walks up to children and states: 'I don't know what's wrong with you children. You're pushing and shoving again. You children need to learn how to line up like good boys and girls. Now I want you all to try to do so.'

Hostile style

The teacher walks up to the children who were pushing and grabs them and roughly yanks them to the back of the line.

Once they are at the end of the line she angrily states: 'You push and shove others, I'll push and shove you!'.

Assertive style

The teacher firmly tells the children, 'Stop pushing and shoving'. To back up her words, she makes all the children who were pushing and shoving go to the back of the line.

If you are someone who finds it difficult to be assertive with people including your students, the next chapter covers in more detail the nature of both verbal and non-verbal assertive behaviour.

The following list of discipline skills are consistent with Canter's approach which involves you taking definite steps to maintain the necessary control of your classroom in order to achieve your goals.

DISCIPLINE STEPS

'Take your wind out of their sails.'
                    Rudolph Dreikurs,
            expert on child management.

A good rule of thumb for selecting a specific technique for handling student misbehaviour is to use the least intrusive and the strongest technique as possible for dealing with a rule infraction. Do not kill mosquitoes with a sledge hammer.

Here are some techniques which you can use to handle different types of misbehaviour.

Ignore plus attend to positive behaviour in others

The procedure is useful for low intensity, low level attention-seeking behaviour. Rather than telling a student who is disrupting your class to be quiet, turn away from the student and reinforce other students who are listening by talking to them directly. Sometimes you might want to say, 'I really appreciate how well you are following our communication rule'. Because you do not give into the disrupting student's goal of attention, you do not reinforce the student's belief that belongingness equals wearing the teacher down. You also give the student a chance to choose 'hands up' behaviour.

Deflective statements

Rather than buying into a student's power struggle and conflict with you ('I'm not going to do this and you can't make me'), use a deflective statement such as 'I can see you're angry, we'll talk about it later'.

Deflective statements provide face-saving, heat-reducing routines away from the face-to-face 'I won't back down' stand.

Diversionary questions and statements

Before a minor conflict blows up, you can often stem it by diverting the student. When a student looks frustrated, you could say: 'Paul, I wonder if you could go over and get those blocks for me'; 'Michael, I need a hand for a minute, the office wants this, do you mind?' 'Ruth, could you come here for a moment... I wonder if you could sit next to Nora and give her a hand.'

Directive statements

These statements reflect your responsibility to insure that the rights of others are protected. 'Please stop talking now, David.' 'This is quiet reading time, please open your book and begin reading'; 'Eric, give me the scissors now. Scissors are not for playing.' Directive statements are offered without indulgent emotions.

Rule restatements

A simple reminder of the rule will help trigger students' own self-control skills. Rule restatements require, of course, that you have clear rules, positively stated, with an understanding of the rights which back up the rules. Keep the sentence to a minimum and get quickly to the class routine. 'Paul, you know the fair rule for communication'; 'David, this is against our fair rule for movement. Please return to your seat.'

Giving choices

Giving students choices is a good way of teaching self-control. Exercising choices over one's behaviour is central to teaching self-control. 'You can do your work now or after class'; 'Well, if that behaviour continues, I'll have to ask you to... Your choice'; 'Paul, you know the fair learning rule; if you continue to bother others around you, you'll have to be by yourself away from the group.'

Assertive 'I-messages' regarding feelings

Sometimes students will modify their own behaviour if, instead of blaming them for how you feel, you communicate without blame how their behaviour is influencing you. 'Paul, I am very angry about your swearing. Please stop it now. We'll talk about it later.' 'Diane, I get very annoyed when I have to re-explain the work to you because you haven't been listening.'

Defusing statements

Defusing statements are short, pithy, sometimes humorous sentences that take the heat out of a conflict or challenge.
Student: 'You're a big, fat slug.'
Teacher: 'Actually, I'm a moderately-sized P.E.R.S.O.N'.
(Then move off and concentrate on the rest of the class.)

'How' and 'What' questions

William Glasser argues that we waste time by asking 'Why' questions. For example, you ask, 'Why did you talk?' and student answers, 'Oh, Johnny Pain made me talk'. 'What are you doing?' questions focus on the child's behaviour such as 'What are you going to do about your behaviour?' and 'What is your plan so that you don't break the rule again?'. 'How' questions such as 'How does calling out help you to keep the class rule?' focuses students' attention on the relationship between their behaviour in protecting the rights of others.

Carry out consequences later

Sometimes it is unwise to spend too much dealing with the disruptive behaviour of a student in class. If a student's behaviour is unacceptable because it breaks a class rule, you might want to turn to the student and say, 'You have continued to break the class rule. Please see me after class so we can discuss ways you can improve your behaviour in the future.'

Time out

Time out means different things to different people. Time out is a treatment of last resort when all other avenues for maintaining the student in the classroom have failed. It should only be reserved for serious infractions including refusing to stop fighting, constant interruptions, persistent verbal abuse and continuous disturbance of other students' learning.

Time out is a short-hand expression for the full name of the procedure 'time out from reinforcement'. The procedure involves removing the student from the immediate vicinity of other students. With younger primary students, time out can occur in the classroom when the misbehaving child is physically removed away from the other classmates. With older students, a time out room or area outside of the classroom within the school is identified.

To use time out effectively, make sure students understand that their disruptive behaviour is violating the rights of others and that the consequence of their behaviour is that they temporarily lose the right to participate with others in class. Students need to be made aware that their offending behaviour is their responsibility. The time-out area should be non-reinforcing. There should be no interesting toys or materials to occupy students' interest nor should students' have the opportunity of having discussions with other students or members of staff. The average time students should spend in the time out area is 15–20 minutes. This is generally sufficient for them to calm down and consider the conditions upon which they will be allowed to be re-admitted to class.

Time out is not to be seen as punishment. It is the logical

consequence of students' violating the rights of others and breaking what are generally seen to be fair rules. Time out allows students to make choices about whether they wish to behave within acceptable limits and stay in class or to lose the privilege. When you use time out, remember that your aim is not to blame and condemn the student nor to crush to self-esteem. Rather it is necessary means to a justifiable ends.

Johnny Pain looked squarely at Mary Brunette. 'This will be fun,' thought Johnny, 'I'll really get stuck into her. I'll just paint the back of Helen's shirt with a heart and flowers.'

'Johnny, come here for a minute. I want you to help me cut out some faces from this **Playboy** somebody left behind in class.'

'Just a minute Miss.'

Maintaining her cool Mary walked over to Johnny. 'Johnny, I would really like your help now. Perhaps, you could say what you want to Helen in person rather than behind her back — if you know what I mean.' To cap it off, Mary gave Johnny a mischievous wink.

Johnny was doubly furious. Lost his **Playboy** and got beaten at his own game. 'Okay, Miss Hairy.'

The class gasped, knowing how Mary typically reacted at these times.

Once again, Mary made up her mind that she was going to stay calm. 'I know you think I've got nice hair, Johnny. Thank you. Now, here's the scissors. Cut out as many different ... hairstyles as you can find.'

'Sure ... Miss Brunette.'

After class, Bill caught up to Mary who was killing herself laughing.

'What's so funny? I thought you just had Johnny P. in your class. Usually you're ready to blow a gasket.'

'Hey, no more. I've had it with letting them get to me. It's all got to do with attitude. You know, kids are kids. Johnny's a difficult customer. I don't like it, but that's the way he is. Tough. Let me give you a few pointers on how to set up a discipline plan. And remember, if it doesn't always work, no catastrophe.'

Bill could only shake his head. 'Who said a leopard can't change its spots?', thought Bill. 'But Mary, somehow, she could have fooled me.'

ACTIONS SPEAK LOUDER THAN WORDS

Write down a list of those instances of student misbehaviour you find particularly stressful. Complete either a Stress Script (Chapter 4) or Rational Self-Management Form (Chapter 5) as a way of gaining more control over emotional stress.

Next, develop a step-by-step plan for handling a re-occurrence of the offending behaviour. What are the various steps you can take starting with its first occurrence and if and when it starts to escalate?

Another useful exercise is to identify a student who really gets up your nose. See if you can come up with positive and negative characteristics of the student both inside school and outside of school. If you have trouble consult with other staff members. If you come up with total negatives and not one positive, you'll know you've got real trouble. Otherwise, consider the student's negative classroom behaviour in the context of their other assets and negatives. Is he or she totally rotten through and through?

RECOMMENDED READING

David N. Aspy and Flora N. Roebuck, *Kids Don't Learn from People They Don't Like* (Amherst: Mass.: Human Resource Development Press, 1977).

Maurice Balsom, *Understanding Classroom Behaviour* (Hawthorn, Vic.: Australian Council for Educational Research, 1982).

Lee Canter, *Assertive Discipline* (Santa Monica, CA: Canter and Associates, 1976).

C. M. Charles, *Building Classroom Discipline* (New York: Longman, 1989).

P. L. Cheeseman and P. E. Watts, *Positive Behaviour Management* (London: Croon Helm, 1985).

Clare Cherry, *Please Don't Sit On the Kids* (Belmont, CA: David S. Lake, 1983).

Edmund T. Emmer and others, *Classroom Management for Secondary School Teachers* (Engelwood Cliffs, N.J.: Prentice–Hall, 1984).

William Glasser, *Schools Without Failure* (New York: Harper Row, 1969).

Thomas Gordon, *Teacher Effectiveness Training* (New York: McKay, 1974).

Robert Laslett and Colin Smith, *Effective Classroom Management* (London: Croon Helm, 1984).

A. J. MCKinnon and J. Kiraly, Jr., *Pupil Behaviour, Self-Control and Social Skills in the Classroom* (Springfield, Ill.: Thomas, 1984).

Mick McManus, *Troublesome Behaviour in the Classroom* (London: Routledge, 1989).

William Rogers, *Making a Discipline Plan* (Sydney, NSW: 1989).

William Rogers, *You Know the Fair Rule* (Melbourne, Vic.: Australian Council for Educational Research, 1990).

The Getting Started Group, *Six of the Best: A Practical Guide for Developing Co-Operative Classroom Behaviour* (Melbourne, Vic.: Robert Andersen and Ass., 1986).

Charles H. Wolfgang and Carl D. Glickman, *Solving Discipline Problems* (Newton, Mass.: Allyn and Bacon, 1986).

CHAPTER 11
RELATIONSHIP SKILLS

'If a person continues to see only giants, it means he is still looking at the world through the eyes of a child.'
                                                          Anais Nin.

The relationships you have with your colleagues, with senior administrators at school and with your students can have a significant bearing on your stress in at least two ways. First, if one or more of your significant relationships is characterised by conflict and negativity, such relationships can be a significant source of stress for you. I personally know of a number of teachers who have either requested transfers from their school or actually retired from teaching because of interpersonal problems with their principals. Second, your relationships with your colleagues and, especially, with friends can serve as a buffer to stress. Receiving support from your principal mediates stress. And through the development of support networks at school (discussed in Chapter 12), you not only receive emotional and practical support at times when you are especially stressed but groups of colleagues have a far greater chance of changing aspects of working conditions which are objectively stressful.

In this chapter, I discuss ways in which you as an individual teacher can go about managing your own stress reactions to difficult interpersonal situations as well as ways of improving your relationships. I review with you relationship skills including how to make and keep friends, basic communication skills which can help you manage interpersonal difficulties, anger management and conflict resolution skills and assertion skills.

RELATIONSHIP DIFFICULTIES

One of the more stressful activating events for people in all jobs is when they come in contact with what I call a 'DC', which stands for 'difficult customer'. A difficult customer is anyone at work (e.g, administrator, colleague, parent or student) who engages in what seems to be unfair, inconsiderate or unprofessional behaviour. Essentially, they give you what to don't want (hassles, criticism, negativity, slackness) and do not provide you what you want (fairness, consideration, respect, encouragement). As I have already indicated in the section in Chapter 6 on dealing with difficult people, the list of people and their unfair actions encountered at school could be rather long. For the purposes of the following discussion, make your own shortlist of difficult people.

One distinction I have found useful in learning to cope with difficult people is between *relationship dissatisfaction* and *relationship disturbance*. Relationship dissatisfaction occurs when someone with whom you have worked with over a long period of time has not given you what you want or given you what you don't want. Relationship dissatisfaction is a common occurrence in schools as it is in any organisation. When people have worked together for a long time incompatabilities are likely and do not mean that there is anything substantially wrong.

Let's take the example of Mary Brunette, head of the art department, and the head of physical education, Don Racer. Over the years, there have been many disagreements between the two over the priority of the art and sports programs. Mary has argued for school resources being used in her area as a way of encouraging the creative students as well as a means of encouraging the non-academically-abled. Don has strongly believed that the strength of a school can be traced to its physical education program and record in competition. Indeed, Don is of the belief that the greatest 'character-builder' for a young person derives from the discipline acquired through physical conditioning. Mary and Don have also what you might call 'incompatible personalities'. Mary finds Don's 'gung-ho' athleticism unappealing while Don finds Mary's outgoing and bohemian style unfeminine. Don stirs Mary up about her feminism while Mary derives some satisfaction from stirring Don up about his 'jock' style of dress.

In this situation, Mary and Don experience low satisfaction in their work relationship. Along with the dissatisfaction, both parties also experience some negative emotions such as annoyance, displeasure and concern. However, because neither Mary or Don are *overly* upsetting themselves about not getting what they want from each other in their work as well as the differences in their behavioural style, their relationship dissatisfaction is not interfering with their ability to work with each other and isn't leading to significant job stress.

On the other hand, *relationship disturbance* occurs when one or both people in a work relationship become intensely upset (anxious, enraged, depressed) about problems which exist in the relationship and engage in extreme behaviour towards the other which generally leads to an escalation of the difficulties. In the case of Mary and Don, if Mary became very upset about Don's enthusiastic support of athletics at the expense of the art program, or if Don became very angry about Mary's negativism about the sports program, then their relationship would be characterised by distress and would represent a relationship disturbance.

It is important to realise that you have a choice as to how you react and how much stress you experience when faced with relationship dissatisfaction and incompatability. It doesn't matter who you have the dissatisfaction with. No matter how onerous and negative the other person's behaviour is, you have the choice about how upset you will become. That is because no one—no matter who they are or what they are doing—directly controls your emotional stress reactions. As strongly suggested in the chapters on personal responsibility, stress-reducing attitudes and Rational Effective Training, it is your own interpretation and evaluation of their behaviour which determines how stressed you will become. Of course, the worse they behave, the harder it will be for you to remain rational and level headed. However, it is in your interest to do so.

Here are a few summary pointers on how to de-stress yourself when faced with someone who is acting contrary to what you expect and who has, perhaps, done so for some time.

To keep your anger under check, keep reminding yourself that some people simply are difficult customers. They behave in unpleasant ways towards many different people whenever they don't get what they want and when someone takes a stand against them. It's their style. I'm not saying for one moment that you should like their behaviour or even accept it. As I'll discuss shortly, by all means, in an assertive way, try to modify their behaviour. However, if they continue to act in difficult ways, keep your expectations realistic. People are the way they are because that's the way they are. It would be nice if they were different, but all the evidence suggests that they are not. Also, keep in the back of your mind that even though they have difficult aspects of their personality, they are not totally bad. Try to view their bad behaviour in the context of some of the good things you know about them.

Another mental strategy to use to handle people when they are acting unprofessionally, disrespectfully or unfairly is not to take their behaviour personally. I've learned over the years that sometimes people will get very upset with me for things I have or haven't done. I've got in the habit of saying to myself, 'Just because they are being critical of me doesn't make me totally hopeless'. The issue here is one of tolerating another person's criticism or disapproval without putting myself down. I've also learned to try to be objective in listening to their position and admitting when I have been unfair or wrong.

So when faced with a difficult customer at work, realise that relationship dissatisfaction is common, but that relationship disturbance and distress is not inevitable. Try to view your more difficult relationships objectively and try not to blow their significant out of proportion.

If your interpersonal problems are with a principal or senior administrator, ask yourself whether it is in your best interest to continue to pour fuel on the fire or whether a reduction in hostilities is desirable. For the most part, administrators will be too busy to continue to harbour a grudge against you if you do not give them reason to do so. They simply don't care that much. Their negativity towards you often stems from you having abraded one or more of their prejudices (e.g., arriving late, having a poorly behaved class on an outing). In time, once the issue passes or if you change your behaviour so that you are no longer being viewed as in conflict with their values, the heat in the relationship will ease.

Occasionally, you may find yourself working for a genuinely difficult customer. A-dyed-in-the-wool 'DC' is someone who has a permanent personality problem and, as a result, is able to hold indefinite grudges against people over the most trivial and un-reasonable occurrences. Or sometimes the personality clash may simply have to do with the fact that you're a male and your head is a female, or vice versa. Under these circumstances, you will have to work especially hard at maintaining a realistic attitude minimising the negatives and maximising the positives. In these situations, it is important that you realise that you can still be happy — though not as happy — and satisfied in your work even though you are working for a 'DC'. It is not uncommon to find that, over time, a difficult principal or senior member of staff can really become significantly stressful. If you cannot seem to redress the balance, see if you can find a way in discussions with them of getting them off your back even if it means agreeing with things you might not necessarily agree with (see 'fogging technique' in the assertion section of this chapter). And if that doesn't work either, you may have to see about changing your teaching situation.

The next section will deal with some basic ideas on improving your circle of friends.

MAKING AND KEEPING FRIENDS

Rules in making friends

1 Become genuinely interested in other people.

2 Smile.

3 Remember that a man's name is to him the sweetest and most important sound in the English language.

4 Be a good listener. Encourage others to talk about themselves.

5 Talk in terms of the other person's interest.

6 Make the other person feel important — and do so sincerely.

Dale Carnegie,
How To Win Friends and Influence People, 1936.

It's easy to get caught up in meeting the demands of school and at home and not put in the effort that is required to make and keep friends. But friends are important. They satisfy your human desire for social affiliation and afford you the opportunity to give to and receive from another person rewards and satisfactions that are different from those you give to and take from work and your family. No matter how shy or extroverted you are, do not underestimate the importance of close friendships. Without going into the ins and outs of what a close friendship means to you, I think you'll agree that your life is fuller when you have one or more good friends.

If you find yourself interested in getting to know someone better but find yourself at a behavioural standstill, you need to ask yourself why. There are at least six common obstacles which might prevent you from making or keeping friends. Ask yourself the following six questions.

1 Are friendships for me a top priority?

2 Does 'shyness' prevent me from initiating social contact?

3 Do I know what to do to meet and keep a friend?

4 Do I try to impress others in the way I act, talk or dress?

5 Do I hold strong expectations about the way others' should and will behave?

6 Do I blame others for how I feel?

If you answer 'yes' to any of these questions, you will have identified an obstacle which you need to overcome if your goal is to expand your friendships. Here are some ways to overcome these obstacles.

Make friends a high priority in your life On a scale of 1 to 10 where ten is highest commitment to making friends and one is a very low committment, what is the degree of your commitment to making and keeping friends? If your commitment is less than eight, it is not high enough. You see, if you are out of the habit or have never had the habit of making friends, you need high motivation to develop new social behaviours necessary to make friends. A commitment of less than eight will not provide you with the thrust necessary to change your behaviour; make it more social.

As well as having a high commitment, you must translate that commitment to 'shared time'. It may well that you spend sufficient quality time at school with someone to make it more than a professional working relationship. Some friendships, especially those you have with people outside of school, need to be cultivated. You need to spend time with someone to maintain a friendship. The way you do this can vary enormously. You may decide to call a friend on a fairly regular basis. Some people make and send cassette tapes to maintain a friendship with someone who lives out of town. You may decide to go away once a year on a special expedition just reserved for the two of you. Whatever form it takes, your friendship must be fed by intermittant 'quality time'.

Work on becoming less shy If you are shy join the club. Upwards of 40 per cent of people at your work are shy and between 10 and 15 per cent are 'painfully' shy. So shyness is common.

Now, the question is, what can you do to reduce your shyness in order to try to develop a new friendship? While I have serious doubts as to whether a leopard can change its spots, I do think you can modify aspects of your behaviour in social situations to enable you to approach people and for them to consider you more approachable.

Let me relate a story told to me by the founder of rational-emotive therapy, Albert Ellis, about how he overcame his shyness. When Ellis was a young man, he (using his words) was rather 'lusty', and, as a consequence, wanted to go out with females. Unfortunately, he was extremely shy and never had the confidence to ask females out on a date. One summer he decided that enough was enough and that he was going to take responsibility for solving his own problems. Living across from the Brooklyn Botanical Gardens, Ellis decided to wander over and approach females who were on their own and ask them out on a date. He invited over one hundred females and by the end of the summer he had totally cured himself of his social anxiety and shyness. This is especially remarkable because of all the females he asked out, all but one said 'no'. And the one who said 'yes' did not show up!

The moral of the above story is that to overcome shyness you need to do things you don't feel like doing, which in the case of meeting new people is initiating and maintaining contacts. You will learn that the discomfort you feel when thinking about approaching someone else will evaporate when you have done it a few times. And you know the fear you have in the pit of your stomach which can immobilise you? You know, the one which says, 'What if he/she doesn't want to know me, won't like me, won't want me to get to know them?' By working on making contact, you will find that you will not get knocked back. You will also see that if it turns out that the other person really doesn't respond positively to your contact, that it's not the end of the world. It simply shows that whatever 'chemistry' is necessary for a friendship to evolve isn't there. Sometimes you'll discover that the person you wished to spend time with isn't right for you.

Develop your social skills   If you find you do not know what to do or say when starting a conversation or getting beyond the superficialities of casual work relationships, it is never too late to learn. A beginning point is noticing how others initiate, maintain and end simple conversations. Once you've got that under your belt, it's time to initiate more advanced skills.

One way to advance a relationship is to identify a common interest you have with the other person apart from teaching and see if the two of you would like to explore it after school hours. For example, you might find someone who shares an interest in fishing, playing cards, cooking, reading, etc. By spending recreational time together, you

will have formed a sound basis for developing the friendship.
Be yourself I know this sounds a bit trite; advice you'd get
from reading popular magazines. How else can you be?
Sometimes, however, without you being aware of it, you
may try to impress people. We dress differently, drop names,
review our recent exploits, exaggerate the positive things
which have recently happened. There are some people who
react very negatively to someone who they find putting on
airs. They resent it because your 'notoriety' may make them
feel small, a bit of the 'tall poppy' syndrome. My advice is to
remember your good points (see Chapter 4 on self-esteem)
and let them shine through. Give people the opportunity to
accept and like who you are. And remember, how you come
across in your first impression will have a large bearing on
whether the person will want to pursue a relationship with
you. People can be very judgemental. They can quite irrationally take an initial impression of you based on a
limited encounter and use it to colour their total evaluation
of you as a person.
*Be guided by how people are and not what you think they
should be* Your own expectations can put a real weight on
any relationship. By that I mean that if you bring with you
strong expectations about how a person should act, then
when they act differently you will feel very let down and
less motivated to continue the relationsip. And they will feel
the weight of your disappointment.

When you think about it, it makes little sense to expect
that a person will act in any particular way; that is, until you
know quite a bit about them. For example, you might expect
that because a colleague says they will do something for you,
say, bring in a recipe, that they will. This is a reasonable
expectation to hold in general; unfortunately, what holds in
general does not necessarily hold for the individual. The
colleague who forgets to bring in the recipe may simply be
that way inclined—undisciplined and forgetful. You might
think to yourself, 'Well, if they were a real friend, the would
have remembered. I would have'. Then once again you
might withdraw your involvement with your colleague, even
though they meant no malice.

Be careful, too, not to expect too much out of a relationship too soon. While someone might seem enthusiastic in

being around you and you might feel very close to them, they may not be ready to reciprocate. Once again, your expectations will get in the way as sure as your disappointment.

Own your feelings As I've emphasised throughout this book, you exert a large amount of influence over your feelings via your attitudes and thinking. Try to get out of the habit of blaming other for your own feelings when they don't live up to your expectations.

Let's now examine three vital communication skills which can help you get along better with people you work with and which can come in handy when sorting out hassles with friends and colleagues.

COMMUNICATION SKILLS

'When a person is able to feel and communicate genuine acceptance of another, he possesses a capacity for being an effective helping agent. Acceptance of the other, just as he is, is an important factor in fostering a relationship in which the other person can grow, develop, make constructive changes, learn to solve problems, move in the direction of psychological health, become more productive and creative, and actualize his fullest potential.'
Thomas Gordon, Teacher Effectiveness Training, *1974.*

While some teachers are 'natural' communicators, others are not. This is because, as with most skills, you need an opportunity to learn the basics. During your life and throughout your teacher preparation course you may never have been shown good communication skills or practised or reinforced them. It is doubly important for you to have a reasonable grasp of these skills—they help you manage your relationships and also ensure you have good communication with your students. Research suggests that 80 per cent of the people who fail at work do so not because they are not any good at their job but because they cannot relate to others! Of course, bad communication is not only a problem for you personally, it leads to negative effects in other individuals and groups at school which can, in turn, influence the educational climate and efficiency.

Good communication skills in relationships are useful in achieving two goals. First, as just discussed, they are useful in making and keeping friends. Second, by having them on hand, you have an insurance policy to cover those ticklish conflict situations which arise not only with your colleagues but also with your friends. They'll help you to maintain your relationships during the tough times.

Good communication is vital when you encounter people who are acting disagreeably, negatively or obnoxiously and who are frustrating you in achieving what you want. In Chapter 5, which deals with rational self-management, some time was spent on illustrating ways of handling difficult people. In that discussion, the importance of moderating your emotional reactions to difficult people was emphasised as a prerequisite to responding effectively. The more angry and upset you become the harder it is to communicate effectively. This is because people tend to respond more to the emotional content of the communication than they do to what is being said. For example, while Mr Gunn may have a perfect right to pull Bill Witherspoon up for being late and request a change in his behaviour, his tone and volume of voice communicated more censure and scolding. His extreme emotional content of his communication over-rode the validity of his message.

It is important to be aware of the emotional aspects of the message you send along to another. It is important that your emotions are under reasonable control. You also need to pay special attention to your body language as over 60 per cent, and sometimes as much as 90 per cent, of your emotional impact on another is non-verbal. The following three skills combined with emotional self-management allow for clear and precise communication.

Skill no. 1: sharing your feelings

When someone does something which prevents you from achieving your goals or interferes with your rights in some way and, as a consequence, you experience extremely strong feelings, it is sometimes a good idea to express your feelings verbally rather than keeping them inside. This is not something many of us are accustomed to—especially if we are males. We tend to grit our teeth and growl at the other person. A better way to deal with your feelings at these times is to describe them to the other party. The X-Y-Z levelling formula which you can use to describe your feelings is: 'When you do "X", the effect on me is "Y", and I feel "Z"'.

X = other person's behaviour
Y = concrete description of how the behaviour affects you
Z = clear description of your feelings

So, for example, Bill could have said to Mr Gunn, away from earshot of his students: 'When you critcise me in front of the students the way you did, I have trouble settling them down and I feel quite annoyed'.

The extent to which you share and describe the strength of your true feelings will depend on who you are talking to. For persons you are close to, you can share precisely how you feel, whereas with a colleague at work you might choose to be a bit more general in your description of your feelings.

The following is a list of pointers in sharing your feelings effectively.

1 *Be specific* Describe exactly what is it you don't like about the other person's behaviour.

2 *Don't include your interpretations* Statements like 'You're just trying to make yourself feel important' go beyond the immediate situation and may or may not be accurate.

3 *Do not over-generalise* The statement 'You *always* criticise me in public' is probably not true.

4 *Do not smear the person's character* Omit statements such as 'You are such a hopeless, lazy character, it is no wonder you were late'. Character assassinations only inflame the situation.

5 *Do not moralise* Avoid statements which imply your

values are better than theirs such as 'You should be more reliable'.

6 *Do not threaten* Statements which communicate orders or threats — 'If you don't arrive on time, you won't be recommended for promotion' — only lead to resentment.

7 *Do not level for someone else* Rather than saying, 'Other people feel as resentful as do I' let others speak for themselves.

8 *Include the feeling part of the statement* By sharing how you feel, others will be more inclined to share how they feel.

9 *Communicate your honest feelings* Don't minimise how you feel by using weak phrases like 'a bit' upset. If you do not appear upset, people will not take the situation as seriously if they know your true feelings.

10 *Keep your levelling statements short and simple* Don't go over the top with long-winded statements. People do not cope very well with complex explanations when they are tense or upset.

11 *Level about good feelings* When you feel good about what someone has done, level your good feelings. For example, 'Being on time every day makes my job easier. I really appreciate it.'

There is another situation where sharing your feelings can have a positive benefit on someone else. Sometimes, you might be feeling upset about something at home or at work and without knowing it your upset influences the way you communicate with someone who has nothing to do with your bad feeling. In these situations, sharing the real reason for your growly or moody disposition will help the person to understand that they have not done anything wrong. No longer feeling responsible or under attack for causing you to be miserable, they will feel happy to support you in whatever way you allow.

Skill no. 2: listening

I am always amazed at how much effort can be put into

trying to get your point across and how little effort is spent on trying to understand what the other person is saying.

Listening is as much as a learned skill as sharing your feelings. It is an important skill because, if you are a good listener, through your body language you can communicate to the communicator that you respect them.

A good strategy in learning how to listen is to pretend you are a tape recorder and that you will be required to play back the message after the speaker has finished their message. You will need to pay attention to important details without trying to impose your own interpretations on what is being said. In listening, you are not trying to make a point or trying to make yourself understood. You are trying to understand what the person is saying in order to make them feel like they are understood.

Here are some pointers to being a good listener.

1 *Attend closely to the speaker* Attentive listening is best accomplished by paying close attention to what is being said.

2 *Show the person you are listening* Your body language is important here. Lean forward, give the person eye contact and keep a comfortable distance from them (approximately one metre).

3 *Shut your mouth* It is important that you do not interrupt what the other person is saying. Interruptions makes the other person think you do not value their opinions and often leads to them shutting up.

4 *Don't dominate the conversation* By talking too much, it will be difficult to hear what the other person is saying. Be sure to let others have their say.

5 *Backtrack* In order to make sure that you have accurately heard what the other person is saying and are not imposing your own evaluations or expectations, repeat word for word what the person has said. 'You said that when I come in late to class you have to cover for me and that you think such irresponsible people should not be teachers. Is that right?' While not agreeing with their statements, backtracking helps make the person feel valued.

Skill no. 3: validating

Validating is not to be confused with giving in. In validating, you simply show you accept what people say about their feelings as being true to them. Continuing with the example of Mr Gunn's confrontation with Bill, Bill could validate Mr Gunn's statement by saying: 'I can see how you would be frustrated and angry with having to cover class for me'. By validating you are not admitting you made the other person upset or that you see the problem the way the other person does. Validating simply means accepting what the other person has said about how they feel. Nothing more. The minimal validating statement is: 'I *understand* how you feel'. Here are some guidelines for validating effectively.

1 *Validate promptly*   Don't wait until you fully understand why the person feels the way they do before validating. You may never know!

2 *Don't defend your actions*   There will be many times when you haven't really meant to inconvenience someone or make them upset. So there is no need to defend yourself. Say: 'I can see you're upset. I didn't mean to create a problem for you.' It is also not advisable to bring up the person's past behaviour to justify your actions. Do not store up bad feelings from the past and trot them out at a time when someone is levelling with you. Deal with the present by validating their feelings.

3 *Do not tell the person to be logical*   In essence, you are telling the person they shouldn't feel so bad which generally only makes the person feel more upset.

4 *Avoid reassurance*   Reassuring people that everything will be okay has the same effect as telling them to be logical; it only serves to deny their feelings and makes them feel worse. People need to feel that they (and their feelings) are valued and understood and not that they shouldn't feel that way.

Now that I have covered some of the essential skills for forming and maintaining good relationships and for coping with your own bad feelings as well as another's, let's briefly deal with an essential skill which is necessary for living and working well with others: anger management and conflict resolution.

ANGER MANAGEMENT AND CONFLICT RESOLUTION

Some people more than others have a propensity for getting angry with others and either expressing it openly or keeping it bottled up inside. Completing the following Trait Anger questionnaire developed by Professor Charles Spielberger will give you some indication of how you stand relative to the rest of the general population in your degree of anger. (Permission to use scale obtained from Professor Charles Spielberger, director of Research in Behavioural Medicine and Community Psychology at the University of South Carolina.)

Trait Anger Scale

Directions: A number of statements which people use to describe themselves are given below. Read each statement and then circle the number which indicates how you *generally* feel.

	Almost never	Some-times	Often	Almost always
1 I am quick tempered	1	2	3	4
2 I have a fiery temper	1	2	3	4
3 I am a hotheaded person	1	2	3	4
4 I get angry when I'm slowed down by others' mistakes	1	2	3	4
5 I feel annoyed when I am not given recognition for good work	1	2	3	4
6 I fly off the handle	1	2	3	4
7 When I get mad, I say nasty things	1	2	3	4
8 It makes me furious when I am criticised in front of others	1	2	3	4
9 When I feel frustrated, I feel liking hitting someone	1	2	3	4

10 I feel infuriated when I
    do a good job and get a
    poor evaluation   1   2   3   4

                                    Total score _____

The average score on Trait Anger is approximately twenty. Scores above twenty-five are getting in the 'hot tempered' range.

Anger is a natural human emotion, a part of your biological equipment. It is an instinct, if you like, which at certain times needs to be harnassed before it does damage to you and others. I am not recommending for one moment that you suppress you anger and keep it bottled up inside. Sustained anger which you might not even be conscious of can pose a serious health risk to you.

In the chapter on rational self-management and in the opening section of this chapter, I describe the role of attitudes in the creation and reduction of anger. What follows are some additional ideas which can help you put a brake on your anger.

As a starting point, it is important to give yourself permission to be angry. Do not fall into the trap of thinking that, because extreme anger is bad, 'I should never be or show anger'. That will lead to unhealthy suppression. Recognise that it is human to be angry—even when you are harming yourself and others with it—and that you are not a failure or a bad person because you get angry. Your anger is like any other behaviour which you engage in that doesn't help you achieve your goal (e.g., smoking, over-eating). Because of its negative consequences it is generally bad, but it does not in any way mean that you are bad. Once you can accept yourself with your anger, then you can go about working hard to modify it.

There are ways in which you can over-ride your natural tendency towards anger. In the chapter on Rational Effectiveness Training, I explained that some of your anger comes from your own personal rules you hold towards others. In review, anger can stem from your demands that people *should* act fairly, considerately and professionally and in precisely the way you want them to behave and, if they don't, they are thoroughly bad and deserve to be blamed and punished for their inconsiderateness. You will recall that I argued anger management requires an acceptance of the other person's fallibilities and a recognition that just because a person may act unfairly, inconsiderately or abominably in one or more situations at work does not make that person a totally 100 per cent bad person deserving of damnation. By changing the expectations you have of others from demanding fairness and consideration to strongly preferring it, you can bring about a reduction in the intensity of your anger. You will no longer evaluate other people's inconsiderate and unfair behaviour as extremely as you do now. It's not that you will stop caring. You will still desire people to act kindly and professionally towards you and others and will try to get them to change when they do not. It's just that when they behave obnoxiously for many different reasons, including their own fallibility and what's happening in the rest of their lives, you will not blow it out of proportion. And your ability to tolerate people better will lessen the intensity and especially the duration of your anger. You will not stay upset as long as you used to and you will not get upset as often.

Another way to moderate and control rather than suppress your anger is through using any of the relaxation techniques I described earlier. One method I favour in managing anger is the Quieting Response described in Chapter 6. When you notice your anger level starting to increase do the following.

1 Imagine yourself smiling inwardly.

2 Think to yourself 'Alert mind, calm body'.

3 Take a slow, deep breath of air.

4 While exhaling, relax your muscles beginning with your face.

Principles of anger management

1 One of the most important things you must do to control your anger is to recognise the signs of arousal as soon as they occur. As soon as you become more and more sharply attuned to the signs of tension and upset inside you, you will achieve greater ability to short-circuit the anger process. Heightened anger makes you agitated and impulsive. As you learn to relax more easily, your ability to regulate anger will improve.

2 Anger can serve a very useful function. It can be an alerting signal for you that you are becoming upset and that effective action is called for, if a positive outcome is to result. Use your anger to work to your advantage. Remember, getting angry makes you agitated and impulsive; and impulsive, antagonistic acts get you into trouble. Stay task oriented and instruct yourself.

3 Sometimes becoming angry stems from doubting yourself, being unsure, or feeling threatened by someone else. It is always important to remember that you are a worthy person and that you have many good qualities.

4 Sometimes you get angry when you take things personally when there is no need to do that. But even when someone is being directly offensive to you, you can control and contain your anger by staying task oriented—stay focused on the task and stick to what must be done in the situation to get the outcome you want. When you begin taking insults personally, you get distracted from your task and get caught up in unnecessary combat. Don't let yourself get sidetracked or into a quarrel. Recognise what the other person is doing as a provocation, but stay task oriented and issue focused.

5 Sometimes you get angry simply because it is the one thing you have always done in a certain kind of situation. As you learn alternative ways of reacting to provocations that don't involve anger, you will be less inclined to react with anger.

6 Sometimes you get angry because things look like they are getting out of hand, and you want to take charge, so you get angry to control them. You will learn that when you self-instruct and manage your anger, you are in control of the situation. The best

way to take charge of the situation can be not to get angry when most people would expect or even want you to be upset.

7 *Sometimes you get annoyed, upset, and angry because you are problem-conscious rather than accomplishment-conscious. You forget or dismiss the good things you do, but you don't let yourself get away with the mistakes and failings. Remember to congratulate yourself when you have succeeded in managing your anger and let yourself feel good about it.*

8 *Learn to break down provocation experiences into chunks or stages. You will have a better handle on things, which is another way of putting you on top of the situation. Instruct yourself in advance on what to do in each stage of an anger-provoking situation.*

Ray Novaco, **Anger Control,** *1975.*

In summary, do these to manage your stress effectively.

1 Think about the negative consequences for you when you get very angry.

2 Become aware of you gradually becoming angry.

3 Use coping self-statements to keep your anger in check (see Chapters 5, 6).

4 Employ a relaxation skill which works for you.

5 When you do not get angry, pay close attention to the positive consequences.

Conflict resolution skills when applied to a conflict between two people have many things in common with anger management skills. They start with each person taking responsibility for their own anger without blaming the other, and either calming themselves down before their anger gets out of hand, or disengaging from the conflict surrounding a discussion and coming back to it when they have cooled down. If the other person is not prepared to take responsibility, it is even more important for you to follow the following strategy.

When it becomes apparent that a discussion between you and, say, another teacher or student is going to lead to anger and conflict, take time out from the discussion and focus on the fact that anger is getting in the way of solving the problem which means that cooler heads need to prevail before continuing. Say something like: 'Hold on a minute. I'm getting angry (or you look like you're getting angry) and I'd like to stop our discussion for a moment.' Once you've 'stopped the action', you have a number of options.

1 Continue the discussion, making an effort to stay focused on the topics and remaining cool.

2 Start the conversation again without letting either of you becoming sidetracked into other issues which can lead to conflict.

3 Re-schedule the discussion at a later time and use the intervening time period to cool down and work out a plan to handle the issue more constructively when you meet again.

As indicated in Chapter 1 there are aspects of the way the Department of Education and your own school organisation operates which can promote stress and conflict. If your school has undergone extensive changes including amalgamation and re-organisation, heightened conflict is likely. If extensive changes to your assessment and curriculum methods have been requested from the department, increased frustration and conflict is inevitable. If your school has unspecified discipline policies concerning misbehaving students, greater teacher-student conflict will normally result. If you are not consulted by administrators at school concerning issues which affect you (e.g., frees, curriculum days, excursions and camps), once again the amount of conflict across the school will be greater than if a more collaborative decision-making process was employed. And when you find yourself dealing with administrators who employ defensive and authoritarian management styles, it is quite likely that conflict between you and them will characterise your working relationship.

Sources of organisational conflict need to be identified by an appropriate school-based group which has a direct line to and representation from the school principal. Courses of action need to be proposed, implemented and evaluated to modify working conditions (see Chapter 13).

Guidelines for reducing organisational conflict

1 *The more bureaucratic and hierarchical the structure of the organisation, and the more centralised the decision making, the more conflict is likely. Collaborative decision making is obviously intended to counter these sources.*

2 *Aggressive or defensive management styles promote conflict. Encourage your managers or supervisors to adopt assertive interpersonal styles backed up by appropriate use of communication skills. If an individual manager or supervisor has difficulty doing this, he may benefit from some individual help, from your consultant or similar source.*

3 *Competitions that pit people in a workplace against each other, like many typical incentive schemes, promote conflict, reduce social support, and hinder co-operation. If you want to enhance motivation, use group-based incentive schemes that encourage co-operation within the group.*

4 *Vague, changing or unknown policies invite conflict. Announce policies and expectations clearly and stick to them consistently. If change becomes desirable, initiate it through the collaborative decision-making process.*

5 *Rapid changes, especially ones that are imposed on people, are unsettling and promote conflict. Your committee should aim for a rate of change that people can cope with, which may mean agreeing on priorities for change and starting with the more important, waiting until they are established before introducing the next.*

Bob Montgomery, Working Together, *1986.*

Now that you are 'full bottle' on basic friendship, communication and anger management skills, I will move on to describe how an assertive interpersonal style can help maintain good relationships and help you achieve your goals inside and outside of school.

ASSERTION

'Assertion rather than manipulation, submission or hostility — enriches life and ultimately leads to more satisfying personal relationships with people... Everyone is entitled to act assertively and to express honest thoughts, feelings and beliefs.'

Arthur J. Lange and Patricia Jakubowski,
Responsible Assertive Behaviour, *1976.*

Assertiveness is a type of interpersonal style which involves you honestly and directly expressing your ideas, feelings and desires to others. Assertion is based on the belief that you have certain rights including the right to establish and protect your rights as long as in doing so you do not violate the rights of others. Assertion involves among other things making reasonable requests of others and refusing unreasonable requests.

Have you ever thought about the rights of teachers? A lot has been written concerning protecting the rights of students, including their right to privacy, rights for equal opportunity of learning and the right to learning in the least restrictive educational environment. What about you? It seems to me that there are some basic rights which go along with the role of teaching which need articulating and protecting including the following.

1 The right to be respected by students, other teachers, administrators and parents.

2 The right to express your own feelings and opinions.

3 The right to say 'no' to unreasonable requests.

4 The right to be consulted about and participate in the making of decisions which affect your teaching.

5 The right to make your own mistakes (and to expect to bear the consequences).

6 The right to teach in an environment which promotes learning.

7 The right to equal opportunity regardless of sex, colour or creed.

No doubt you could come up with other rights which could be added to the list. These basic teacher rights are important because they protect you from exploitation and from conditions and situations at work which lead to job dissatisfaction and stress. As well, when your rights are upheld by others and by you, you will experience a happier and more fulfilled work life.

Besides *assertion*, there are two other interpersonal styles you can employ when someone at school behaves in ways which violate your rights. *Aggression* involves you standing up for your rights but doing so in a way which violates their rights and results in them feeling hurt, humiliated or embarrassed. *Submission* involves you not standing up for yourself, not expressing your own feelings and wishes and agreeing to requests no matter how unreasonable.

Let's briefly examine these three different ways of communicating in situations where your rights might be at risk. Common situations are when people make unreasonable requests of you or when someone is being aggressive towards you. In recognising that around 60 per cent of your message to another is conveyed by *how* you say it (your non-verbal behaviour), it is useful to examine the differences in interpersonal styles by examining both the verbal and non-verbal differences among assertion, aggression and submission. As well, there are characteristic differences in the self-talk among the three styles.

Assertive interpersonal style

Verbal behaviour: You state clearly and directly what you are honestly feeling, thinking and wanting and what you would like to occur. You stick to the facts and make your own choices.
Non-verbal behaviour: You employ a confident, warm yet firm tone of voice. You have good eye contact reflecting openness. Your pose and expression is relaxed and you use your hands naturally.
Self-talk: 'I would prefer that person not to act that way.

269

If they continue that way, I'll never get the job done or get what I want. I'd better let them know without being too critical and losing my cool that I dislike what they're doing and that I would like them to change their behaviour. If I don't stand up for myself now, no one will.'

Aggressive interpersonal style

Verbal behaviour: You use emotionally loaded accusatory words and statements and you demand you get what you want. Your statements convey your superiority and their inferiority. You blame and condemn them for what they have or haven't done. You threaten and make choices for others.

Non-verbal behaviour: You convey an air of superiority. Your tone of voice is sarcastic, tense, loud, icy and authoritarian. Your eyes are narrowed and cold. You stand with your hands on your hips, chest extended, fists and jaw clenched and you appear tense.

Self-talk: 'He shouldn't act so unfairly. I can't stand it. They should know better. I shouldn't have to put up with such inconsiderateness. What nerve! I'll show them. I'll get stuck into them so they'll know better next time.'

Submissive interpersonal style

Verbal behaviour: You never really say what you would like to say. You agree with what is being asked of you. You express yourself in a very rambling and disfluent style. You use apologetic words. Others make choices for you.

Non-verbal behaviour: You express yourself faint-heartedly. Your voice is quiet and shaky. You do not look the other person in the eye. You look downward, lean forward and stand well apart from the person you are addressing.

Self-talk: 'I don't like what she's done, but what can I do? I could say something, but she'd only get upset. Maybe it was my fault. Just thinking about saying anything just gets me too so uptight. I just couldn't cope. If I don't say anything, maybe she'll know I was upset and not do it again. Yes, that's what I'll do. Nothing.'

The impact you have on other teachers, administrators, students and parents will be greatly influenced by your interpersonal style. If you are assertive, others at school will feel more respected and valued by you and will be more willing to express themselves openly. Others will value you because they know where you stand. You often get what you want. You will feel confident and self-respecting.

If you tend to be aggressive, others will often give you what you want but they will not like or respect you. They will tend not to be loyal and will often feel inferior and hostile. Some people might try to get back at you. And you may feel uptight and anxious.

Submissive behaviour results in your students, colleagues and others feeling both superior and frustrated with you. Over a school year and beyond they will lose respect for you and will continue to violate your rights. You will feel unhappy because you will not get what you want. Because you will never be able to fully please everyone, you will feel inferior.

Sometimes it is easier to recognise things in other people than in yourself. Below are eight different situations at work. Rate whether each response to the situation is assertive, non-assertive or aggressive. The correct rating for each situation is listed at the end of the exercise.

1 *Situation*: The date is being set for the next meeting of the school committee of which you are a member. You are keen to attend but the proposed date accepted by everyone else means you cannot attend. When the chairman says: 'Is that okay for everyone, then?', you say:

Response: 'Well, all right, as it seems to be convenient to everyone else.'

Your rating _____

2 *Situation*: A colleague asks you for a lift home. It's inconvenient to you as you are late already and the drive will take you out of your way. You say:

271

Response: 'I'm about twenty minutes late so I won't be able to take you home. If it helps I can drop you off at the nearest bus stop.'

Your rating _____

3 *Situation*: A junior member of your teaching staff is about to have a meeting with a difficult student and his known-to-be difficult parents. You know the colleague is awkward in handling these situations. You say to him:

Response: 'You've got to stand up to them. Tell them what you expect from them. You *mustn't* let them off easy like the *last* time!'

Your rating _____

4 *Situation*: A colleague interrupts you when you are making an important phone call. You say:

Response: 'Just as soon as I finish this call, I'll be happy to answer your question.'

Your rating _____

5 *Situation*: A colleague hears you dealing with a difficult student. Afterwards, he praises the way you handled it. You say:

Response: 'Well, I only came in at the end'.

Your rating _____

6 *Situation*: A colleague of yours has volunteered your services to serve on a committee without consulting you. You say:

Response: 'What a nerve! Why didn't you ask me first? There's no way I can help out. I'm up to my eyes in it as it is. He'll have to work it out!'

Your rating _____

7 *Situation*: You walk in the staffroom after school and notice that Ian has just finished smoking a cigarette. Your staffroom is a non-smoking area. You say:

Response: 'Hey mate, this free-floating nicotine gets right up my nose. Can I ask you as a personal favour not to smoke in here.'

Your rating _____

8 *Situation*:   A colleague agreed to come to a special meeting after school but went right home. You ring her and say:

Response: 'Wendy, I understood you were coming to the meeting. I would have liked you to be there. What happened?'

Your rating _____

Answers:
1 non-assertive   2 assertive   3 aggressive   4 assertive
5 non-assertive   6 aggressive   7 assertive   8 assertive

How assertive are you?

Now that you've had a chance to consider what it means to be (and not to be) assertive, you'll have a chance to collect some objective evidence on yourself.

The Rathus Assertiveness Schedule was published in 1973 and is used as a guide for objectively judging how assertive you are relative to the general population. Containing thirty items, the Rathus looks at three types of interactions. 'Confrontation' refers to what you tend to do in social situations where your rights have been violated. 'Deficient social initiative' involves your ability to initiate social interactions with others, especially heterosexual interactions. 'Inhibited verbal expression' reflects your ability to express yourself in emotional situations. Your total score of the Rathus reflects your total assertiveness across these three areas. Rathus has suggested that if your score is less than zero, you may require assertiveness training. He also has indicated that if you score lower than minus twenty, then your unassertiveness may represent a big problem for you.

Rathus Assertiveness Schedule

Directions: Indicate how characteristic or descriptive each of the following statements are using the code below.

+3 very characteristic of me, extremely descriptive
+2 rather characteristic of me, quite descriptive
+1 somewhat characteristic of me, slightly descriptive

       −1 somewhat characteristic of me, slightly non-
       descriptive
       −2 rather uncharacteristic of me, quite nondescriptive
       −3 very uncharacteristic of me, extremely non-
       descriptive

____ 1 Most people seem to be more aggressive than I am (*)

____ 2 I have hesitated to make or accept dates because of my 'shyness'. (*)

____ 3 When the food at a restaurant is not done to my satisfaction, I complain about it to the waiter.

____ 4 I am careful to avoid hurting other people's feelings, even when I feel I have been injured. (*)

____ 5 If a salesman has gone to considerable trouble showing me merchandise which is not quite suitable, I have a difficult time in saying 'no'. (*)

____ 6 When I am asked to do something, I insist upon knowing why.

____ 7 There are times when I look for a good, vigorous argument.

____ 8 I strive to get ahead as well as most people in my position.

____ 9 To be honest, people often take advantage of me. (*)

___ 10 I enjoy starting conversations with new acquaintances and strangers.

___ 11 I often don't know what to say to persons of the opposite sex. (*)

___ 12 I will hesitate to make phone calls to business establishments and institutions. (*)

___ 13 I would rather apply for a job or for admission to a college by writing letters than by going through the personal interview. (*)

___ 14 I find it embarrassing to return merchandise. (*)

___ 15 If a close and respected relative were annoying me, I would smother my feelings rather than express my annoyance (*)

___ 16 I have avoided questions for fear of sounding stupid. (*)

___ 17 During an argument, I am sometimes afraid that I will get so upset that I will shake all over. (*)

___ 18 If a famed and respected lecturer makes a statement which I think is incorrect, I will have the audience hear my point of view.

____ 20 When I have done something important or worthwhile, I manage to let others know about it.

____ 21 I am open and frank about my feelings.

____ 22 If someone has been spreading false and bad stories about me, I see him (her) as soon as possible to 'have a talk' about it.

____ 23 I often have a hard time saying 'No.' (*)

____ 24 I tend to bottle up my emotions rather then make a scene. (*)

____ 25 I complain about poor service in a restaurant and elsewhere.

____ 26 When I am given a complaint, I sometimes just don't know what to say. (*)

____ 27 If a couple near me in a theatre or lecture were conversing loudly, I would ask them to be quiet or to take their conversation elsewhere.

____ 28 Anyone attempting to push ahead of me in a line is in for a good battle.

____ 29 I am quick to express an opinion.

____ 30 There are times when I just can't say anything. (*)

____ Total score (after reverse scoring questions with asterisk see below)

Before adding up your total score, you will notice that some of the questions have an asterisk (*) immediately following them. You need to locate each one and reverse your score for that item. So, for example, if you scored a +2 for question number 1, change the +2 to a −2. For all asterisked questions, change the sign of your answers: +3 becomes −3; a −2 becomes a +2. Do this only for the questions followed by an asterisk. Then add up each one of your answers to obtain your total score.

You might wonder why you or others fail to develop assertive interpersonal styles. I think our socialisation has a lot to do with it. Some people from an early age have been conditioned to do things for others, but not themselves. Some people have been taught not to lose their temper, to put others first and be ever-understanding. Others have been exposed to socialisation patterns which have encouraged a more aggressive pattern of behaviour including being tough, putting themselves first, not showing or sharing feelings and never asking for help.

Whatever the origins of unassertiveness, we know that it is possible through practice and encouragement from others to become less submissive and aggressive and to adopt a more assertive interpersonal style which can significantly improve the quality of your relationships.

Different kinds of assertion

A number of assertive behaviours are available, the choice depending on the nature of the offending behaviour which you wish to deal.

1 *Basic assertion* This kind of assertion involves you confidently using a firm tone of voice in standing up for your rights. Examples of basic assertive statements include: 'Excuse me, I haven't finished what I was saying, 'Please don't smoke here.' 'I haven't got any free time to join another committee.'

2 *Empathic assertion* If you acknowledge someone else's feelings or questions while at the same time disagreeing with them, you are being empathic. This is a more effective form of assertion because, by initially acknowledging their feelings the person is more likely to respond to you. For example: 'I can understand that you would like my students let out early so that they can have more practice for the school play, but they really need more time to spend on their maths if they are to pass the upcoming exam'. 'You may not realise it, but your talking is making it harder for other students to work. Please keep it down.'

3 *Escalating assertion* This type of assertion starts off with you making a simple request to someone else for a change in their behaviour. When the other fails to comply with your request and continues to violate your rights, you can escalate your assertion by become firmer and more forceful. For example: 'This is the second and last time I am going to ask you to talk quietly.' 'I'm fed up with always being the one to answer difficult parent questions.'

4 *Confrontative assertion* This type of assertion is generally employed when someone has agreed to do something but has not followed through on the agreement. You confront them with the objective facts of what they said they would do, what they did (or didn't do) and point out the contradiction. You may also add a request for them to change their behaviour. For example: 'You said you would leave the library in as good a shape as your class found it. When I arrived this morning, the area of the library you used was a mess. I would appreciate if you and your class could stop by and arrange the room as it was before you used it.' 'I was supposed to be invited to the meeting where the next term's science practical work was to be revised. Yet I notice the revisions all ready for typing. I want to review the changes before they get typed.'

5 *Levelling statements* As already discussed, levelling statements involve you using 'I-language' to express your negative emotions which are associated with someone elses behaviour. For example: 'When you do not obey class rules, I am not able to teach the material the way I would like and I get angry. I would like you to raise your hand before talking in class.'

6 *Persuasive assertion* This type of assertion is useful when you are in a group situation and you want to influence the position of the group without being aggressive. In using persuasive assertion, decide the issue which warrants an assertive stance. Then wait until about one-third of the group members have expressed their opinion before expressing yours. Finally, it is also recommended that you communicate your position tactfully by including something good which you have found in the other person's statement. For example: 'I agree with you about the decline in student motivation. But if we merely get tougher without finding out more of the reasons from students themselves why they are not working, students may perceive that we are being unreasonably harsh and may do even less work.'

Requesting a change in behaviour

1. *Describe the behaviour I see and/or hear in the other person. It is important that I use descriptive rather than attacking words.*
2. *Express the feelings I experience as a result of the other person's behaviour.*
3. *Ask for specific change in behaviour.*
4. *Spell out the positive consequences for the person for changing their behaviour and the negative consequences if they don't.*

Recommendations from the Institute for Rational-Emotive Therapy, New York.

Specific assertiveness techniques

In thinking about how to handle a situation assertively, it is handy to be able to bring to mind the following basic assertiveness techniques.

1 *I–language* Basic assertion can be used it situations where someone has trampled on your rights. For example: 'I get very angry that I was not consulted about how you disciplined one of my students.'

2 *Broken record* This easy-to-use technique is helpful in the face of someone making an unreasonable request. You simply, like a broken record, make the same point each time the person asks you to do something you don't want to do. For example, if a colleague repeatedly asks you to to supervise their after-school detention when you have already made plans, you can simply say after each request: 'Sorry, I've made other plans'.

To be really effective, you should use this technique without getting emotional. You need to make sure your non-verbals appear calm and composed.

3 *Fogging* Fogging is used as a way of dealing with criticism. Fogging allows you to cope with personal criticism in a way that protects your self-esteem. It allows you to receive the criticism without becoming defensive or anxious. In

fogging, you calmly acknowledge the possible truth in the criticism without confirming that it is right or wrong. By apparently accepting the criticism without being aggressive, you are able to maintain face. Here are ways in which Bill Witherspoon could have used fogging to deal with the criticism of Mr Gunn, the coordinator.

- Agree with any truth in the criticism. 'Yes, I was late.'
- Agree with the logic of the other person's argument. 'Yes, I can see why you think I am inconsiderate.'
- Allow for improvement. 'Yes, I could make bigger effort to get to class on time.'
- Empthy. 'Yes, I can see your point and understand you'd be feeling that way.'

In using fogging, offer no resistance or counter-argument. If you do this, the person will find it difficult to continue the criticism. Try to understand the point of view and acknowledge any part of the criticism that you agree with.

4 *Defusing* When someone is getting upset with you, you can assertively divert their train of communication by ignoring the content of someone's anger and putting off the discussion until he has calmed down. Say something like: 'I can see you're very upset. Let's discuss this later on this afternoon.'

5 *Assertive agreement* Another way to handle criticism is to respond by admitting that you made an error (if you did) and expressing the idea that you are generally not like that. For example: 'Yes, I did forget to attend the meeting, but I usually keep my promises'.

6 *Assertive delay* If you find yourself getting emotionally upset when having a discussion, rather than responding to a point of criticism emotionally, put off responding to a point of criticism emotionally, put off responding until a later time when you're calmer. For example: 'Yes, I hear what you're saying. Let me think it over and get back to you.'

Hints for making requests assertively

1 Don't apologise profusely.
2 Be direct.

3 *Keep it short.*
4 *Don't justify yourself.*
5 *Give a reason for your request.*
6 *Don't 'sell' your request with flattery or tempting benefits.*
7 *Don't play on people's friendship or good nature.*
8 *Don't take a refusal personally.*
9 *Respect the other person's right to say no.*

Hints for refusing requests assertively

1 *Keep the reply short.*
2 *Simply say 'No, I don't want to.'*
3 *Give a reason for refusing.*
4 *Avoid 'I can't' phrases which often sound like excuses.*
5 *Ask for some more time to decide on the request.*
6 *Don't be abrupt in your refusal.*

Ken and Kate Back,
'Assertiveness at Work: A Practical Guide for Handling Awkward Situations', 1982.

Your assertive plan for action

There are a variety of situations in which you will have a choice in terms of the degree of your assertion. They include when you make a request, refuse a request, disagree with someone else's opinion, express your own opinion in a group and when you are dealing with an aggressive person. In preparing yourself for acting assertively in these situations, the following steps are advised.

Step 1 Determine whether the situation warrants assertion. Sometimes, you might find that although the situation could be handled assertively, it is not important enough to be assertive. Keep in mind that assertion often results in the other person becoming hostile and aggressive or sullenly submissive.

Step 2 Decide how you want the other person to change and behave.

Step 3 Select the type of assertive technique you will employ to achieve the change.

Step 4 Develop beforehand and rehearse assertive self-talk which you will use in the situation.

Step 5 Make sure your non-verbals communicate a sense of calm and control. Practise with a mirror to insure you maintain direct eye contact, have an erect body posture, speak clearly and firmly, avoid using a whiny or apologetic voice, and use facial and hand gestures for added emphasis.

Step 6 Assert yourself.

Step 7 Evaluate the success of your assertive approach. Make a note of what you did well and which skills you have to improve.

I have included a great deal of information on relationships in this chapter. Changes in the quality of our relationships are very hard to make and take time. The different ideas and skills presented will take a while to be incorporated into your natural repetoire. Over time, with practice and by referring to the other books in the appendix, you will notice that by you changing aspects of yourself, others will respond positively. When others at work notice your own self-initiated changes in the way you deal with others, they will change their behaviour — and generally for the better!

Mr Gunn looked around the staff meeting. 'As there are no other nominations for the head of the science department, I declare we continue with the present arrangement.'

'Hold on.' Bill stared at Gunn as if he was Doc Holiday at high noon at the OK corral. 'I'm throwing my hat in the ring.'

Mr Gunn perceptibly gritted his teeth. 'Listen. You are totally irresponsible. You can't even make it to class on time. With you as head we'll be the laughing stock of the rest of the schools in our district.'

Mary looked at Bill, wondering if he had it in him.

'No, you listen. I was late once last week because I got tackled by Johnny Pain's mother. I'm almost always early to class. Also, the science text I published last year was voted best text by the Science Association. I think I'm the best qualified and will do a good job. Oh, and by the way, I got pissed off last week when you criticised me in front of my class for being late. You were right, I was late. But next time, do it in private.'

There was a stunned silence at the meeting. Everyone was waiting to see how Mr Gunn would react. They could see the veins popping out of his neck. The seconds ticked by.

'Er, right then, Bill. Any objections from the science staff? Anyone else? Fine, you've got it. Meeting adjourned.'

After the meeting, Mary and Alyce each grabbed one of Bill's arms.

'See,' said Alyce, 'I knew all along you had it in you'.

Mary wasn't so sure. 'What's got into you? I thought old Gunn was going to have a coronary. You having a mid-life crisis or something?'

'Well, you're both right. I have always had it in me. And I knew that if I didn't start to, you know, stick up for myself, I was headed for a crisis. Now, which one of you are going to take my extras for the rest of the term while I start to do my new duties?'

'Get real,' chimed Mary, 'the only extras I'm taking for you are all the chocolate bars you left in your office. Let's go, Alyce, and leave Mr Assertive to contemplate his next conquest.'

ACTIONS SPEAK LOUDER THAN WORDS

1 Select someone at school who seems to appreciate you and who you would like to get to know better. Using some of the ideas presented earlier, decide on ways you can get to know him/her better.

2 Write down a list of situations at school where you would like to behave more assertively. Then write down the situation in which you would find it easiest to assert yourself. Write an Assertiveness Script for this situation following the above guidelines. Practise the steps aloud at home and then apply the script in school. Do this for the next easiest situation until you have worked your way through the list.

RECOMMENDED READING

Social Skills

Sabine Beecher, *Happiness. It's Up to You* (Melbourne, Vic.: Collins–Dove, 1988).
Robert Bolton, *People Skills* (Brookvale, NSW: Simon and Schuster, 1987).
Dale Carnegie, *How to Win Friends and Influence People* (New York: Pocket Books, 1981 [first published 1936]).
Owen Hargie, Christine Saunders and David Dickson, *Social Skills in Interpersonal Communication* (Beckenham, Kent: Croom Helm, 1987).
Linda R. Heun and Richard E. Heun, *Developing Skills for Human Interaction* (Colombus, Ohio: Charles E. Merrill, 1978).

Communication

Gloria Hoffman and Pauline Graivier, *Speak the Language of Success* (New York: Berkeley Publishers, 1986).
Anne Kotzman, *Listen to Me, Listen to You* (New York: Penguin, 1989).
Matthew McKay, Martha Davis and Patrick Fanning, *Messages: The Communication Skills Book* (Oakland, CA: New Harbinger Publications, 1983).
Jesse S. Nirenberg, *Getting Through to People* (Englewood Cliffs, New Jersey: Prentice-Hall, 1987).
Joseph M. Strayhorn, *Talking it Out* (Champaign, Illinois: Research Press, 1977).
Paul W, Swets, *The Art of Talking So That People Will Listen* (New York: Prentice–Hall, 1983).
Robert Young and Terry Lovat, *Communicating All Around* (Wentworth Falls, NSW: Social Sciences Press, 1988).

Anger and conflict resolution

Helen Cornelius and Shoshana Faire, *Everyone Can Win: How to Resolve Conflicts* (Brookvale, NSW: Simon and Schuster, 1989).
Beth Doty and Pat Rooney, *Shake the Anger Habit* (Redding, CA: The Bookery, 1987).
Albert Ellis, *Anger: How to Live With and Without It* (Melbourne, Vic.: Sun Books, 1989).
Thomas Moorman, *How to Work Towards Agreement* (New York: Athaneum, 1979).

Theodore Isaac Rubin, *The Anger Book* (New York: Collier, 1970).
Carol Tauris, *Anger* (New York: Touchstone, 1984).

Assertion

Robert E. Alberti and Michael L. Emmons, *Stand Up, Speak Out, Talk Out* (New York: Pocket Books, 1975).
Robert E. Alberti and Michael L. Emmons, *Your Perfect Right* (San Luis Obispo, CA: Impact Publishers, 1986 [first published 1970]).
Herbert Fensterheim and Jean Baer, *Don't Say Yes When You Want to Say No* (London: Futura, 1976).
Beverley Hare, *Be Assertive*, (London: Macdonald Optima, 1988).
Paul Hauck, *How to Stand Up for Yourself* (London: Sheldon Press, 1981).
Patricia Jakubowski and Arthur Lange, *Responsible Assertive Behaviour: Cognitive Behavioural Procedures for Trainers* (Champaign, Ill.: Research Press, 1976).
Patricia Jakubowski and Arthur Lange, *The Assertive Option* (Champaign, Ill.: Research Press, 1978).
Gael Lindenfield, *Assert Yourself* (Wellingborough: Thorsons, 1987).
Stanley Phelps and Nancy Austin, *The Assertive Woman: A New Look* (San Luis Obispo, CA, Impact Publishers, 1975).
Robert Sharpe, *Assert Yourself* (London: Kogan Page, 1989).
Manuel J. Smith, *When I Say No, I Feel Guilty* (New York: Bantam Books, 1975).
David R. Stubbs, *Assertiveness at Work* (London: Pan Books, 1986).

CHAPTER 12
SUPPORT

'The nature of the relationships with one's boss, sub-
ordinates, and colleagues can be a major source of stress
at work; good work relations between members of a
group is a central factor in individual and organisational health.'

Ayala Pines, Elliot Aronson and Ditsa Kafry,
Burnout: From Tedium to Personal Growth, 1981.

Throughout this book I have emphasised that when you are
confronted with demands which you have difficulty coping
with, there are positive steps you can take. These modify the
nature of the outside stressor through the effective employment of a direct-action coping skill or your exercise of
emotional self-management so that you do not get *too*
stressed out. For example, in the face of having too much to
do and not enough time to do it, you could use time
management skills to work out a weekly and daily schedule
based on prioritising the different things expected of you.
Assertion skills can help you say 'no' to unreasonable requests and to ask for assistance at home in managing household tasks. You also could use relaxation, rational thinking
or other psychological skills in order to control your levels
of anxiety and anger about having to do so much and not
being unable to see how you are going to get everything
done. In this chapter, I discuss another important stress
management skill called support.

SEEKING SUPPORT

Now there are two ways to think about support. One can view support as something others provide you with when you are having problems. (And which you supply to others when others are having problems). From this perspective, it is important to go about organising your teaching environment to insure that support is available when required by you and all teachers. It is what others do to help you cope.

A second way to look at support is as a self-initiated set of activities which you set into train when you 'need' support. Support-seeking skills involve you locating individuals and groups within your work and outside the school environment who are able to provide psychological, instrumental and informational support to help you to mobilise your coping resources. It is this latter view of support I address in this chapter.

Let me set the scene. Go back to a time or situation at school when you were under a great deal of stress. Your principal could have been hassling you. Your class might have performed poorly on an examination. Or you might have been up to your eyeballs in work. At this time and similar times when you were at the end of your tether—emotionally down or furious and physically spent— what did you do to get you over the bad patch? Did you simply grin and bear it, waiting for it to go away? Did you head for the nearest pub and down a few? Everyone needs a strategy for handling the bad periods so that you can get on track as quickly as possible.

Everyone differs in terms of when they seek support and who they seek it from. Some keep their frustrations bottled up inside until they either explode or they get sick. Others have identified certain people they can go to to receive support. Now I'm not suggesting that whenever the going gets tough that you go running to the person who will listen and support you. Indeed, I favour self-reliance and using coping and self-control skills during difficult situations. However, I believe that everyone can profit from knowing when they are at the limit of their frustration tolerance and knowing who to talk to at the moment.

There is a counter-productive attitude that pervades many

of our schools pertaining to teachers admitting they have problems. The attitude says something like 'Only weak teachers have problems' and that 'Talking about problems is a sign of weakness'. The attitude can extend as far as saying, 'If you are stressed, get out of the kitchen'. This is a stupid attitude which can do great harm to teachers. Male teachers in particular are viewed with some suspicion if they admit to being stressed. 'If you are stressed as a teacher, you are a wimp.'

The times are changing and, while some of the above attitudes still prevail, I believe many of your colleagues and administrators today accept that, because of changes in the profession, teaching is more stressful; everyone experiences stress; and that when you are stressed it is helpful to get some support. Not everyone, though, shares this opinion. Some of the traditionalists still will view your stress as a personality weakness and will lose respect for you if you admit that you are having problems coping. So while I'll be suggesting that you seek support, I also recommend that you be somewhat choosey in who you speak to. Not only could you pick someone who will hold your problems against you, as I'll discuss later, but some forms of social support can actually make matters worse.

WHAT IS SOCIAL SUPPORT?

'People can provide many things that you cannot provide for yourself—new information and insights, training in new skills, recognition and feedback, emotional support, advice, and help of various kinds.'
Christina Maslach,
Burnout: The Cost of Caring, 1982.

Social support refers to the availability of people both inside and outside of school whom you can rely on when you are under stress. People who provide you with emotional support and caring, who value you as a person and who can offer you some practical help or advice during difficult times are part of your *social support system*. A minority of teachers have no one they can talk to and receive support from when under stress. Others have one person as their support system while still others have a number of persons both inside and outside school from whom they can receive support from. Whereas your social network consists of people you know well, your social support system consists of people who can be seen by you to meet your needs.

The attachments you have with people are seen to be important in improving your skills in handling short-term crises and life transitions. In this sense, support functions are a vital defence mechanism used by people undergoing stressful events.

I must confess that I am a Johnny-come-lately in recognising the importance of social support in mediating teacher stress. This is partly because I always thought of social support as complaining to another about your problems. I never found and still don't find complaining productive as the discussion usually results in a mutual gripe situation with things ending up looking doubly bad or with the person agreeing with you and reinforcing your grievances without offering anything constructive. When I started to talk to teachers about how they coped with stress and they continually mentioned support, I decided to read more about the nature of support and I also looked at the research. While I now advocate seeking the right support, I am still sceptical about whether people in your work (and in mine) are naturally talented enough to know what kind of support is required in a situation and then act on their analysis. I find that many people when giving what they think is support talk more about their problems than they listen to yours. Notwithstanding research shows that social support has a beneficial effect on helping you cope with life circumstances throughout your life. Its effects as a buffer to work stress are somewhat less clear.

TYPES OF SOCIAL SUPPORT

Social support has come to be seen as a transaction which occurs between two or more people. From your perspective, from time to time you may approach people and engage in conversation where you express difficulties and problems you might be experiencing in your school life and personal life. Certain people in your life will when approached and at other times communicate to you their support in a variety of ways. With friends and selected colleagues, the social support system is reciprocal. At appropriate times you reciprocate to others the support which they have given you. With some people—especially those who have a role to be supportive such as a counsellor or who have a position senior to you like your principal—the nature of the transaction might be one-sided.

The following types of interpersonal transactions characterise social support.

1 *Emotional support* This takes the form of someone whom you trust listening empathically to your problems and showing you that they care about you, like you and have positive regard and esteem for you.

2 *Feedback/appraisal support* This form of support functions along with emotional support to make you feel better about yourself. It involves someone recognising your specific achievements and efforts as well as offering positive criticism. Feedback can also involve someone pointing out to you how your expectations of yourself might be unrealistic and how you might be blowing things out of proportion. Appraisal can help you compare yourself with other teacher in terms not only of sharing similar problems but also in terms of your achievements. Feedback/ appraisal helps maintain a realistic self-appraisal.

3 *Information/advice support* This type of support involves you being provided with guidance about how to solve a presenting problem, how to access resources which can help you to resolve the problem and other information which you can use to cope with the problem.

4 *Instrumental support* Instrumental support involves someone taking some form of direct action on your behalf in order to modify the outside troubling circumstances. For example, at school a principal could allocate additional time for you to do some planning or a colleague might volunteer

to collate material for you when you are under time and workload pressures.

People can be described in terms of the different types of support they receive from the same person (e.g., friend) and from different people (e.g., friend, colleague, principal). As well, you can be characterised in terms of the different types of social support you give to others. When you examine the morale of a teaching staff and the degree of group cohesion, one of the factors to consider is the extent to which members of a staff give and receive support from each other and from the administration.

It is possible to talk about different people as sources of support. There are members of a school's administration such as principal, vice principal, year level co-ordinator and heads of faculty who can have both positive and negative impacts on you because of the quality of their support. As well, there are your colleagues, your friends inside and outside of school and your family who also are a part of your support system. There seems to be pretty substantial evidence that good emotional support provided by your family can function as a buffer against your stress at work. A year-level co-ordinator may offer a little emotional support but may have a lot to offer in discussing how to handle a difficult student.

Have a peek back to the Teacher Support Inventory presented in Chapter 2. You'll be able to get an idea about the source of support with whom you discuss things most frequently and whom you find most useful.

THE BENEFITS OF SUPPORT

There are a number of studies which have found a positive relationship between social support and physical health. In one study reported in the literature, asthmatics who had good social support required less medication to maintain an improvement in their condition than did asthmatics with poor social support. In another study dealing with first pregnancies, labour complications were associated with poor social support.

In terms of psychological health, people with good social

support seem better able to handle stressful events than those low in social support. People high in social support also appear to have a more optimistic view on life, are more self-reliant and persevere more in the face of setbacks. While it is unclear, given the correlational nature of these studies, whether social support actually causes good psychological health or tends to exist more often in the lives of people who bring with them sound mental health to begin with, it would appear that social support abets well being and happiness.

Here are some of the findings of studies which examined the connection between work stress (burnout) and social support.

1 More than one study found that, whereas individual coping had little impact in combatting job-related strain, peer group support was more effective in reducing burnout.

2 Seeking more information about the problem through talking to other teachers was of positive benefit to teachers.

3 Support from the principal significantly reduced teacher stress.

4 In one study, 50 per cent of teachers stated a lack of social support in helping them deal with work stress with males feeling they had to cope alone.

5 Teachers with high personal demands and self-expectations for achievement benefited most from support.

6 Personal accomplishment burnout decreases for teachers in supportive environments.

7 The amount of social support received from supervisors is a significant pedictor of burnout.

Anne Sarros' study 'Teacher Burnout and Social Support'

Anne Sarros collected data in 1989 on a random sample of 491 high school teachers in Victorian government schools. Her interest was in finding out the amount of support provided by different people to teachers and the type of support they found most important. As well, she examined the extent to which different sources of stress and types of stress were related to teachers' level of burnout. Her results are of interest because they reveal what the social support picture is like in the lives of teachers and pinpoints the ventilation of negative feelings as a pre-requisite to taking results can be summarised as follows.

1 In terms of the frequency of support from different people, she found that peer group (colleagues) provided the most support followed by family and friends inside and outside of school. Principals provided the least amount of support followed by vice principal, faculty head and year level co-ordinator.

2 In order of importance, the types of support received by teachers were listening (emotional), time (instrumental), feedback and advice information.

3 Female teachers give and receive more support than male teachers.

4 The more support provided by principals, the lower levels of teacher burnout.

5 Peer group support was related to lower levels of personal accomplishment burnout.

6 The more time teachers spent providing emotional support to others the *greater* their emotional exhaustion.

7 The more teachers provided emotional support, gave advice and feedback, the less their personal accomplishment burnout.

These results point to the importance of both administrators and colleagues learning the importance of both giving and receiving social support. As I'll discuss in the final chapter, principals have a vital role to play in managing their schools and teachers in ways which minimise the causes and effects of stress.

Of particular interest in the Sarros study were the comments teachers offered about ways in which support helped them manage stress. Let me briefly summarise these findings.

Peer group/colleague support The emotional support colleagues provided through their trust, listening and concern helped reduce emotional problems. Teachers found this type of support made them feel that they were not alone in having problems and reactions, helped put problems in perspective, took the pressure off feeling responsible for a total class, helped reduce feelings of inadequacy and frustration, increased feelings of self-esteem and led to a sense of relaxation. Emotional support also helped to reduce negative attitudes to other colleagues who might be acting unprofessionally or difficult students, and to ease the tension towards others.

Receiving feedback from peers increased teachers' sense of personal accomplishment and adequacy, increased achievement motivation and helped remove the feelings of some teachers that 'it is all my fault'. The time which other teachers provided in the form of covering classes and running off materials helped to ease levels of emotional exhaustion. Peer group support also helped to ease exhaustion by helping teachers deal with immediate problems.

Family/spouse/relatives This source of support was described by many teachers as being important in reducing emotional exhaustion and negativity partly because being outside of school, teachers felt freer to talk. The emotional support given made teachers feel that someone was on their side, helped them see their problems rationally and objectively, helped them to put problems in perspective and helped to reinforce their sense of positive achievement. Instrumental-time support was provided by many families in sharing of house workloads and providing time for relaxation.

Principal Many teachers expressed the opinion that they experienced elevated confidence and reductions in stress when their principal showed understanding and that he or she cared and valued them. The advice principals offered was also valued by teachers. And of special importance in reducing time workload stress was where their principal provided them with extra time and did not give them extra tasks.

Vice principal The vice principal's main support was taking actions when needed, giving advice about organising and planning and giving reassurance and positive feedback.

Friends Friends offered a great deal to teachers as social supports. The emotional support provided helped teachers to unwind and relax as well as build confidence and feel less guilty. In particular, teachers (as did family) allowed for the ventilation of negative feelings as a pre-requisite to taking positive action. Friends were also available for problem solving.

Year level coordinators/faculty heads Support from these sources consisted of offering advice and information on lesson preparation and teaching materials. Teachers also felt that they were given help in dealing with problem students and that by listening, support helped to modify negative attitudes and feelings.

Students/parents By giving feedback to teachers, students and parents were seen as increasing feelings of personal accomplishment.

I think you'll agree that these comments reflect that social support in its different varieties has the potential to offer you significant benefits not only in releasing and managing emotional stress but also in learning how to control outside demands more successfully.

'NEGATIVE' SOCIAL SUPPORT

'Being with other teachers can't help. Undirected teachers' coffee room talk can cause you to get more burned out. Because you just talk about your nagging problems and they just talk about their nagging problems and it's just going to get worse and get both of you convinced that everything's terrible.'
Charles Rathbone and Chaunce Benedict,
A Study of Teacher Burnout at the Junior High
School Level, *1980.*

Not everyone chooses to rely on social support during difficult times. As a personal preference, some teachers elect other strategies (e.g., relaxation, recreation) instead. If social support is imposed on these teachers, the reaction can be quite negative.

Moreover, the research into the effectiveness of social support finds a significant number of teachers (though far less than those who favour support) who find the negative aspects of support outweighing the positive. Let me list some common examples of ways in which peers, family and the principal can offer negative support.

Peer support 'Grizzle sessions' can lead to increased negativity. The attitudes of less committed staff as well as those teachers who throw in their own problems for discussion when they are supposed to be listening only adds to the unhelpfulness of the situation.

Family support The main negative here is when a family member cannot cope with the level of support which is required. Families need their own positive nurturance and cannot withstand constant giving without receiving from a teacher under stress.

Principal support Although principals are under a great deal of stress themselves, they are capable of adding to a stressed teacher's problems by being unapproachable, non-caring, non-supportive and critical. They may also be too far removed from what is going on in the classroom, not give feedback and make extra demands including holding long meetings.

These illustrations of the negative side of support may serve to moderate what you expect from social support. If you and/or your school works to increase the opportunity for social support, this will bring significant benefits. The degree depend on personalities and other factors as well the number of counter-productive aspects.

MENTORING: A COPING RESOURCE

'Organisations need to be made aware of the benefits of mentoring and should encourage their senior employees

> *to help cultivate the skills and talents of newcomers.'*
> *Breda Murphy Bova and Rebecca R. Phillips,*
> **The Mentoring Relationship as an Educational**
> **Experience, *1982.***

A number of schools are beginning to set up mentoring programs for new staff members. The rationale for pairing up experienced staff members with inexperienced ones is that the expectations held for the teaching performance of younger teachers can be the same as for the more experienced. It has been found that senior staff members offer the potential of providing new staff with useful advice, guidance and support in a non-threatening environment. Of course, mentors need to be carefully chosen. Not everyone is suited to mentoring.

Some of the personal qualities which it would seem necessary for a senior teacher to possess to qualify as a mentor include the following.

Trustworthiness   The younger teacher needs to be able to feel that what he or she says will remain in confidence and will not be used to compromise their professional advancement.

Accepting and non-judgemental   The younger teacher needs to know that the mentor will not make harsh judgements about his or her teaching or of them as a person.

Earns respect   The mentor has to be someone who practises what he or she preaches and who demonstrates significant professional skills in some area of teaching or education.

Research indicates that if young teachers are able to enter into a positive supporting relationship with a mentor, progress along their career path can be facilitated. But mentoring should not be seen as a resource only for the new, inexperienced teacher. Mentors can change as people get older. At different stages of life we require different things from people than at an earlier stage. Mentoring as a type of social support offers the person who is suited to this kind of relationship a definite advantage in learning how to cope with the pressures of work.

PEER SUPPORT

'*The process of change and the need for teachers to develop personally and professionally during their careers is hampered by the nature of classroom teaching which is often a fairly isolated activity. Because teachers spend most of their time in front of a class there is little time for discussion with colleagues and usually little chance to watch other people teaching. The timetable itself gives teachers little control over the way they allocate their time. The small amount of time teachers do have together is often taken up with meetings, preparation, administrative work and talking to students. There is not much time left for talking about new ideas, problems or things which have worked... Many meetings which could provide an avenue for professional development are taken up with administrative matters and teachers often see the classroom as a social area rather than a forum for exchanging ideas about teaching... Peer Support Groups have been developed to provide teachers with an opportunity for professional sharing and support.*'

Yvonne Willich, Gwyneth Graham and
Barry Hancock,
Not a New Idea But a Good Idea: Peer Support for
Teachers, *1988.*

A more formal arrangement for availing yourself of peer support can be found in teacher peer support groups. Support groups consist of a number of teachers who desire not only to advance their professional skills but also to have an opportunity to discuss and share current teaching practices and specific school-related problems such as classroom discipline. Members of the group help each other to acquire new skills as well as giving and receiving support in implementing new practices and solving problems. Peer support groups tend to be topic and goal focused with the emphasis on doing rather than talking; ideas are modelled rather than described. A key feature of these groups is evaluation, where group members are given the opportunity to discuss progress in mastering new skills and to refine them over the life of the group. It is generally the case that an experienced teacher or support person participates in the group to facilitate its development.

Some of the common activities of peer support groups include professional discussions, learning new teaching strategies and working together either by team teaching, exchanging lesson plans or work programs, reciprocal observation of each other's teaching or joint planning of lessons followed by discussions to evaluate progress. Personal development and team building activities are also generally included in groups as a means of furthering personal development and mutual support.

Suggestions for how your school's faculty meetings can include more professional discussion

1 Peer support group is formed.
– All faculty members who are interested in staying for the extra time.
2 The first meeting is held.
– Guidelines for how the group will operate are outlined.
– A chairperson keeps the meeting on track.
– Group decides on a goal they would all like to work towards within a set time.
– Group discusses any contributions which members feel they could make towards achieving the goals. A list of these contributions is compiled.
– Group decides on an idea/material which will be presented at the next meeting.
3 Format of following meetings.
– Team building activity if it is wanted.
– Review of what people have done since the last meeting.
– Presentation of a new idea or strategy (not every meeting).
– Plans for what people will do in the interval before the next meeting and discussion of what help they will need.

- *Decision on the next idea to be presented.*
  Yvonne Willoch and Karen Stammers,
  Whole School Approach to Staff Development,
  Victorian Ministry of Education, 1990.

There are many benefits to teacher peer support groups. Some of the benefits surround your teaching and include new ideas about teaching methods from others, improving your methods of teaching, a chance to try out new strategies with help from others and an opportunity to pool materials and resources.

For example, a successful case study has been reported where the English faculty of a school formed a peer support program with a specific focus on 'cooperative student learning'. The goals for the group of English teachers were to assist students to use each other more as learning resources and to improve the performance of individual students. Indicators of group achievement and the success of the program were a) students not continually choosing to work with others of the same ability; b) students listening to others and not making categorical or derogatory comments about other students' work; and c) students seeking help from each other rather than from the teacher.

Over six sessions, members of this teaching support group pooled information and skills (e.g., continuous creative writing, group games, jigsaw lesson format) concerning on how to increase cooperative learning among their students. The collective judgement of the teachers in the peer support group was that they had achieved their objectives. Evidence for the effectiveness was found not only in changes in student behaviour but also in the decision to continue the peer support group the following year.

Aside from upgrading professional skills, teacher support groups have the additional benefits of giving you an opportunity to work as part of a team, developing closer relationships with other staff members, receiving and giving acknowledgement and feedback, and generally sharing your enthusiasm and successes.

Peer support groups can also have a problem-focused orientation. A number of schools have teacher support groups which meet regularly to consider common concerns about classroom management. These groups analyse areas of participating staff where skills can be improved as well as offering an opportunity for staff to ventilate their frustrations concerning students and school policy. An innovative aspect of peer support teams in the area of classroom management and discipline is the use of *peer observation*. In some schools, teachers are observed in their classroom by a trusted colleague who gives them fairly immediate feedback on their use of both verbal and non-verbal discipline skills. To facilitate feedback, teachers in the support group go into each other's classroom to observe discipline and other teaching practices.

'Without feedback, it is hard to know where we might be ineffective or even going wrong. Peer observation is the means whereby we access the "data", as it were, for professional development and change. One of the other benefits of observation is that the observer learns as much as the observed: "Gee, do I do that? So that's what it sounds like!".'
William Rogers, innovator in use of peer support.

There are a number of key elements in setting up and running an effective teacher support group.

1 Participation should be voluntary.

2 The emphasis should be on professional development through the learning of new skills.

3 The emphasis is not on 'teachers with problems', but rather groups are designed for teachers of all levels of competence.

4 Wherever possible, the establishment of the group is supported by a person (e.g., experienced teacher, educational psychologist, guidance officer) who has a thorough knowledge of the process in setting up a group.

5 A long-term commitment should be obtained from all group members including support personnel.

6 Emphasis is on skills learning and problem solving.

7 Make sure the group does not rush to get its job done. Group members will need time to reflect and time to relax.

8 Do not leave the trust and cohesiveness of the group to chance. It is important to include in the group activities which will break down barriers to communication and help build trust.

9 Make sure that each individual member specifically decides how he or she is going to use each new idea and strategy. Do not take it for granted that because effective teaching practices are modelled in the group that individuals will be able to formulate goals for what they have to do to implement the procedure.

10 Do not assume that because teachers initially choose not to participate that they will never be interested. Continue to encourage possible participation.

Peer support groups are starting to be developed around the issue of teacher stress. Teacher welfare committees, if run along the above lines, can not only serve to identify school-based needs, but also can offer their members opportunities to lessen their stress through encouraging organisational change (see next chapter), by providing mutual support and acknowledgment, and by learning new ways of coping with emotional stress and tackling specific teaching and organisational stressors.

Alyce Greenway, Bill Witherspoon and Mary Brunette were sitting down after school to discuss the new school discipline policy and their attempts at discipline.

'I thought I was being assertive when I spoke to Johnny about his rough-housing in line before class,' said Alyce.

'Not really,' said Mary. 'What was good was the way you reminded him of the rule about fighting and then asked to see him after class. That was terrific. What was a bit weak was the tone of your voice when you told him to stop pushing. You need to be a bit more forceful — otherwise, he won't take you seriously. Listen to me. "Johnny, please get back in line, now." Look him dead in the eye and point with your hand like this.'

'What makes you the Ms Assertive Discipline all of a sudden?', quipped Bill. 'You been to an in-service or are you doing a uni course?'

'Don't be stupid. As I've said to you before, I'm tired of letting these hooligans get to me. I'm doing something about it. What do you think, Alyce?'

'Yeah, I guess this soft, caring stuff isn't getting me anywhere when they step out of line. Time to tighten up.'

'Okay, Mary,' continued Bill, 'what about getting so upset yesterday with the principal? You were pretty hot under the collar, weren't you?'

'But our principal is such a dictator!'

'I know that he often seems to act that way', said Alyce, 'but isn't that the way some of them are? They don't seem to want to listen.'

'Doesn't that get to you?', said Mary, sensing that, perhaps, she had underestimated Alyce's 'maturity'.

'A bit, but what's the point? I've just learned never to expect too much from any teacher, or principal for that matter. So when they let me down, I don't get myself down. Or sometimes I will ask to talk it out with them. You know, ask to make a time to talk to them when they're not too busy. I don't always get my way, but sometimes I do.'

'Hmm. He still gives me the irrits. But I guess you have a point. Thanks, team. See you tomorrow. Off to my self-defence class.'

Bill looked after Mary as she headed through the door. 'I'm never quite sure if she really is tough as she sounds.'

'No,' said Alyce. 'Deep down I think she's a pussy cat.'

'Yeah? It would have to be way down.'

ACTIONS SPEAK LOUDER THAN WORDS

Think about the pros and cons of finding a mentor. If you would like to 'trial' such a relationship, make a short list of people on staff who might be willing to offer the time and support. Try to select someone who you feel you can trust and might have helped you in the past. Many senior staff members view the facilitation of the professional development of the less experienced as one of their own professional goals. Also, don't feel that because you might have a few years of teaching up your sleeve that you no longer can profit from a mentor. The criteria for selecting a mentor change in part due to your own changing professional needs.

Discuss at a staff meeting the possibility of setting up a peer support group. This should be done in all schools for 'first-year' teachers. As well, you may wish to discuss the desirability of setting up a group surrounding a particular issue related to your professional development and staff welfare. If there appears to be support for the idea, try to identify someone at school or an outside consultant who can help assist in setting up a group.

RECOMMENDED READING

Yvonne Willich, Gwyneth Graham and Barry Hancock, *Not a New Idea But a Good Idea: Peer Support for Teachers*, (Inner Western School Support Centre, Ministry of Education, Schools Division, Western Metropolitan Region, Victoria). (Available from: Inner Western School Support Centre, May Street, Footscray, 3011 Victoria).

CHAPTER 13
ORGANISATIONAL CHANGE

'As teachers, we do have influence and power over our working conditions. Together we can create more harmonious work places for ourselves and our colleagues. The process is not a simple one, and change will not occur overnight. However, it can be done and as a profession we must work together to insure that our working environment is a safe and rewarding one.'

Robyn McLeod,
Strategies for Tackling Teacher Stress, 1987.

This final chapter examines a number of aspects of your school's organisation and management which can influence your stress. It illustrates ways in which organisational mismanagement leads to stress and what you can do to handle yourself well under the circumstances.

Teacher stress appears to be lower in schools which function well and which have good administrative leadership. Moreover, in order for schools to be responsive to the needs of teachers in the area of stress and to offer effective solutions, they need to have a certain 'ethos' which will allow for the self-examination and changes involved in reducing teaching stress. Characteristics of organisational effectiveness, good principals, decision-making procedures and the importance of feedback are covered.

The 'Whole School Approach to Staff Welfare', which is

being introduced in a number of schools as a way of combatting teacher stress, will be described.

Finally, recommendations drawn from a number of different sources for ways in which the educational system and schools can change will be presented.

ORGANISATIONAL STRESS

These days circumstances external to what happens in your classroom make teaching more stressful than ever before. That is, decisions and changes being made by your own school administration, the school board or school council and by the Department of Education may have a negative impact on you as a teacher. It is often the case that the changes being imposed on your school and on you are not those which have been invited and may not be ones which you believe is in the best interests of your students, your teaching effectiveness or your job satisfaction. Integration, amalgamation and the adding or subtracting of courses are examples of decisions which can have a negative impact on you. All this can be very stressful.

Not only are the decisions and policies often not justifiable from your point of view, but you have had little input and influence on the nature of many of the decisions and changes. That can also be stressful.

As well, the externally imposed changes in your organisation can directly affect your daily professional functioning. These may involve you doing things differently and in a great deal of extra work (e.g., extra meetings, curriculum changes). Moreover, in some schools teachers are being asked to re-arrange their internal geography to accommodate the new teaching and staffing arrangements.

There is no doubt that the greater the number and amount of negative change you have to deal with in a short period of time, the more stressful your job will be. If you are facing a great deal of change and are finding yourself becoming very stressed, one of the issues for you is how to minimise and control your stress so that it does not prevent you from pursuing and achieving your teaching goals and so that you do not become negative, cynical and alienated.

Stress of distress?

As I've emphasised throughout, the beginning point to managing any stress — and in this case the stress of change — is self-management. One of the central ideas which bears repeating is that of personal responsibility. No matter how bad changes seem to you, you also have *a degree* of influence over your stress level. One of the keys to managing the stress related to change is your attitude (I know it is easy to cringe in even hearing the word 'attitude'). However, my own research clearly shows that the higher your score on the attitudes to school organisation subscale of the Teacher Irrational belief Scale, the higher your stress will be when faced with bad organisational decisions and negative organisational change.

While learning to change your attitudes and self-talk is not the sole solution to coping with change, it is a good starting place. To begin with, answer the question: 'When you are getting very stressed about the changes at work, how "bad" do they seem to you on a scale of 1 to 100 where "100" is the worst thing which could happen to you and "1" is something only minimally bad?'. (Remember to rate the 'badness' of change when you are *really* stressed — furious, panicky or depressed.) Now, using the catastrophe scale presented in the 'Instant Cures to Stress', rate how 'bad' the changes are which you have to deal with. My experience has been that when change — even change which is quite bad — starts to distress you, you tend to blow events out of proportion and not to see them objectively and in perspective.

If you find yourself getting quite furious with negative changes at work and find that your fury is not only making you miserable but also inefficient in coping with the changes, then you may well wish to take the edge off your fury and deal with the changes more level headedly. (I'm not suggesting for one minute that getting angry with stupid and misinformed decisions is abnormal, rather that getting furious is stressful and generally leads to goal-defeating behaviour.) A rational attitude under these circumstances has you accept the 'fact' that from time to time organisations and people in

organisations who make decisions will act miserably, unfairly and unprofessionally. It doesn't really matter what the
nature of the organisation is. To stay sane in these circumstances involves you accepting though not liking it, that's the
way the educational system, schools and administrators
operate some of the time. Increasing your tolerance for
organisational 'miserableness' enables you to remain more in
control because, after all, what else would you expect? Once
you gain control over yourself, then it is possible on an
individual and group basis to try to influence the rate and
nature of the changes.

Anxiety associated with change and the uncertainty of the
future can be combatted by firstly recognising that at the
basis of your anxiety is either the fear of not being successful
or of being harshly judged by others. In either or both cases,
it is necessary using the methods described in Chapter 4 on
self-esteem to remove your ego from the proceedings as
much as possible and not to see the negative aspects of the
changes as threats in any way to do with your self-esteem.
Sure, there will be a 'settling in' period of adjustment where
in fact you may not perform as well as you would like;
however, remaining confident and secure in your knowledge
that you are a good teacher will see you through this period.

What really can get up my nose when change is imposed
from outside is the inconvenience and discomfort I will have
to endure in making the adjustments to new routines, people,
tasks and office environment. For me to keep my stress in
check, I avoid telling myself that 'things are unfair and
shouldn't be happening'. Instead, I remind myself that whatever happens is much more likely to be a hassle rather than a
horror.

Once you stop blaming others and your school organisation for being the way they are and start to manage your
own stress even when you cannot change the outside world,
you will be better able to make the best of what appears to
be something that on the face of it looks totally bad. A
procedure I also use at these times is called 'referenting'.
Referenting involves you looking at the disadvantages of
your school staying the way it has always been and the
advantages of the changes. When we are stressed we generally

look at the advantages of staying the same and the disadvantages of changing. A more optimistic outlook on the future will cut your stress down a notch or two and will also help you formulate career plans and teaching goals that will take advantage of any of the new circumstances which will be arising in the future.

If you find it hard to modify your view on what's happening around you, keep in mind that with the passage of time you will learn to adapt to what you at present consider intolerable. And if you find circumstances to be intolerable in the future, remind yourself that it is possible to make changes in what you are doing within education or, as some do every year, you can get out of teaching altogether. Whatever your decision, it is best made from a position of dissatisfaction, rather than from distress and disturbance which arises from irrational demands and commands about the way things should or should not be.

ORGANISATIONAL EFFECTIVENESS

'The strengths (of successful schools) derive above all from the professional skills of the head and staff in creating a well-ordered environment in which learning of all kinds can flourish; within which levels of expectation are at once realistic and demanding, whether in academic performance or social behaviour; and where functions and responsibilities are clearly defined and accepted.'

Her Majesty's Inspectorate,
Ten Good Schools — A Secondary School Enquiry,
London, 1977.

In this section I highlight the characteristics of 'effective' schools. School organisations which function effectively are less prone to generating and maintaining conditions which lead to teacher stress. I'm not suggesting that on your own you can increase your school's organisational effectiveness.

Rather, an examination of this material will enable you and others in your school to assess its current functioning to determine where improvements and changes need to be made.

What makes 'good' or 'bad' schools is open to much debate. There are problems in agreeing on what constitutes a 'good' school, ways to measure adequately indicators of success, how well findings from one study can be generalised to other schools. Notwithstanding these and other problems in explaining and evaluating organisational effectiveness, Warren Mellor and Judith Chapman, in an article published in 1984 entitled 'Organisational Effectiveness in Schools', provide a list of fourteen criteria which cover the main factors perceived to be associated with school effectiveness.

1 *Clarity of purpose* Effective schools have a clear sense of purpose expressed in clear, well-formulated objectives without losing sight of the fact that purpose very much involves people.

2 *Stable well-defined curriculum* Good schools present an orderly program of work which caters for a wide variety of student ability and interest.

3 *Leadership* As will be discussed shortly, good leaders possess a number of essential qualities including a sense of vision, have a clear commitment to achieving objectives, are supportive to their staff, and delegate authority.

4 *Recognition of achievement* Leaders in effective schools encourage and acknowledge excellence in their staff.

5 *Committment and cohesiveness* There exists a spirit of cohesion and enthusiasm among staff and a school—and community-wide acceptance of the values and purposes of school.

6 *Staff stability* There is relatively little staff turnover and a high degree of staff maturity, professionalism and acceptance of delegated authority.

7 *Cooperative working relationships* Persons within these schools are part of a caring team with a large amount of

emphasis on mutual respect, teamwork, trust, tolerance and consideration.

8 *Sufficiency of resources* There is sufficient financial, material and human resources to meet the needs of the school.

9 *Positive community relationships* There is good community support of the school fostered through the provision of a school program which conforms to parental expectations.

10 *Sense of continuity* There exists a sense of being part of a school tradition supported by the strong endorsement of school values by members of the school community.

11 *Positive student response* Students respond positively to the curriculum, staff members, staff effort and approachability.

12 *Student performance on school tasks* Students perform well in terms of examinations and other inputs.

13 *Co-curricular activities* There is a rich and varied activity program geared to the interests and future life paths of students.

14 *Expectations and standards* Academic, personal, social expectations are clearly enunciated and student progress in all areas is closely monitored.

It would seem to be the case that if your school is lacking in a large number of these characteristics, then it is likely that the incidence and degree of teacher stress in your school will be higher than in those schools which rate highly on these factors.

PRINCIPALS

'There is a great educational need in today's rapidly changing society for positive informed leadership. If the principal is to occupy a focal point in the administrative

structure, he/she must be more than an efficient manager. The principal must also be seen as an educational leader... Principals need to be persons of high integrity and wide culture, with access to adequate support and resource, to enable them to carry out effectively their responsibility in the school community.'

Wendy P. Cahill,
Resource and Support of Educational Leaders, 1989.

The most important person within a school who has both a direct and indirect influence on teacher stress is the principal. Specifically, the degree and style of leadership which the principal exerts has a profound effect on the way in which the organisational arrangements appropriate to the school are affected, on the manner in which problems are addressed and solved, on the commitment of staff to values, priorities and school programs, on the performance of individual administrators and teaching staff and on the way teachers feel about and relate to each other. This section covers a number of issues related to the way in which principals perform their role.

Leadership

'It can be inferred that principals, teachers, parents and the community want a principal who is a responsive, caring, committed professional administrator, skilled in communication, in curriculum development and in personal relationships, concerned with linking school with community and accepting future changes as a challenge. Professional development should seek to develop skills and attitudes.'

Commonwealth Schools' Commission on the Professional Development of Principals Project, Working Party's Advice Paper, 'Leadership for Responsive Schools', 1985.

It is easy to point the finger at the principal as the one who is at least partly responsible because of his or her management style for both teacher welfare and teacher stress. Moreover, I know of many teachers who have quit teaching because of personality conflicts with their principal. Indeed, 'bagging' the principal is one of the most popular forms of letting off steam for teachers under stress.

The job of the principal today is, I believe, harder than it has ever been before. Principals are sandwiched in between satisfying the educational and economic demands of education departments and school boards and councils with the often-times competing expectations of teachers and students. And while principals have the great responsibility to satisfy the needs and requirements of different groups which are frequently in opposition, it is also the case for many of them, especially those who work for the education department, that their authority is relatively curtailed. Principals are frequently the recipients of policy decisions which are handed down to them for direct action. And many of them are very angry and are in need of greater resources and support to enable them to increase the effectiveness of their schools.

Notwithstanding the pressures on principals, it is possible to say that some schools are managing their 'problems' and stressors effectively largely because of their principal's style of leadership and management. My observation is that it is a rare person who possesses all the professional and interpersonal characteristics that go into making an effective principal. I believe that more resources and time need to be spent on freeing up principals in order for them to upgrade their professional and interpersonal skills.

Let me list a number of qualities which teachers and research indicates go along with being an effective principal and leader.

1 *Having a vision* Principals who are noted for their leadership seem to be future oriented. They spend time analysing the changing needs of their student population, of the wider school community and of society in general and arrive at a sense of what they want their school to be tomorrow and in 5–10 years' time.

2 *Communication and motivation*   Effective leaders express their vision in ways which mobilise others to action. They are able to infuse others with the importance of heading in new directions and of working hard to make the vision a reality. Frequently, but not always, principals create a supportive environment which allows people to take on responsibility, take calculated risks and contribute and extend what they are capable of doing.

3 *Goal orientation*   Effective principals have a strong sense of task accomplishment, of finishing what they set out to do. Follow-through is rated very highly. The primary medium they use to make concrete their proposed achievements (and the achievements of others) is the setting and communication of realistic goals. Organisational effectiveness is enhanced by defining goals in terms of student learning.

4 *Clear expectations of staff*   Both lower-level administrative staff as well as teachers value principals who make clear their expectations of staff in different areas of their job.

5 *Maintaining alignment*   In his award-winning video series *A System of Change*, management consultant Peter Quarry talks about how effective leaders successfully manage alignment with their organisation both at the group and individual level. Alignment refers to making sure that the activities of different professional groups and individuals within the organisation are designed around the achievement of the organisation's objectives. This concept is especially important during times of change.

6 *Monitoring progress*   Part of good management style is keeping track of people's progress towards achieving their individual goals. Periodic feedback meetings are one of the main vehicles to keeping track of goal achievement.

7 *Intervenes appropriately*   Effective principals provide staff members with the inputs, resources and supports necessary when they are having difficulty achieving their professional goals.

8 *Supportive/listens/acknowledges*   While it is important for principals to have a task orientation especially when

resolving conflict, there is general consensus that it is equally important for principals to be person oriented when dealing in non-conflict situations and when working with a 'mature' staff member. Consistent with the 'Situational Leadership Theory' of Hersey and Blanchard, principals should be flexible in their management style depending on the person and situation.

9 *Gives positive feedback* The research is clear on this one. Principals who give positive feedback and performance appraisal to teachers—especially during difficult periods—have a positive influence in reducing teacher stress levels.

10 *Available* Principals who become too far removed from the classroom and the problems of teachers and who are not accessible to teachers for advice are not seen as good leaders.

11 *Collaborative decision making* Principals who are rated as effective by teachers are ones who are prepared and willing to discuss with teachers decisions which effect them directly and to communicate with them before decisions are made.

12 *Decisiveness* Effective principals are ones who, while willing to consult, are also willing to make a decision when one has to be made.

13 *Impartial* Effective principals are ones who treat all staff members equally and do not hold grudges.

14 *Knowledgeable* An important quality of principals is that they are aware of curriculum developments.

It is a truly rare principal who demonstrates all of these qualities. Indeed, there seems to be a sense that for a school to have a good 'organisational climate' the array of leadership characteristics should to be distributed among the school's leadership team. For example, some schools function well with a principal who has a strong task and problem-solving focus and who leaves the tasks involving personal sensitivities (e.g., support, encouragement and acknowledgement) to other members of the leadership team, such as the vice principal or head of curriculum studies, who have well-developed relationship skills.

Managing change

'(A program of planned change is)...the deliberate design and implementation of a structural innovation, a new policy or goal, or a change in operating philosophy, climate and style.'
John M. Thomas and Warren G. Bennis,
The Management of Change and Conflict, 1972.

In the face of outside and internal pressures for change, principals can respond by denying that they exist, resisting the pressures, avoiding them completely or providing for their management. Your principal's style of managing change and his or her attitude towards change will have a large influence on the ability of your school to accommodate to the changing community, society and world we live in and how these forces of change impact on you.

There are two main approaches to managing change. There is the *reactive style* which involves reacting when signs indicating that change is required are present in the workplace. These changes are generally smaller day-to-day adjustments such as a principal deciding to resource a special inservice program on the educational use of computers. The *planned style* of change involves major changes in the whole or a significant part of your school such as involved in introducing 'flexible scheduling' or 'open classrooms'.

If a principal is unprepared for dealing with externally imposed or internal change, the chances that change will have a negative impact on you and be experienced as high stress are increased. Some suggestions which can help principals minimise the negative impact of change on teachers are as follows.

1 Communicate with staff as early as possible about the likelihood of change and its consequences for them.

2 Involve staff as much as possible in the planning process.

3 Provide more information to teachers about future plans and their probable consequences so that they will under-

stand the need for change, the expected benefits, and what is required for effective implementation.

4 Minimise unnecessary disruptions and geographical relocations.

5 Reassure staff as to their ability to cope successfully with the new changes.

6 Offering ongoing support during the change process including time off for study and emotional support can also be helpful.

Principals and senior administrative personnel are vital mediators of teacher stress before, during and after periods of stress. It is important that members of your school's leadership team be aware of the role they can play in minimising or maximising teacher stress and be given opportunities to develop further their leadership skills in order for them to function as well as they can during periods of change.

DECISION MAKING

'People who are affected by decisions must participate in the making of the decisions as well as receive feedback on the results of decisions.'

Yvonne Willoch,
Workcare Policy Unit, Office of Schools
Administration, Ministry of Education, Victoria,
Australia.

One of policies school can adopt to provide teacher some support in facing either externally or internally imposed changes is participation in decision making. Schools vary quite a bit in terms of how much say teachers potentially have in decisions which affect their teaching and overall job conditions. In some private, independent schools which still run on a hierarchical-autocratic model of decision making, teachers have very little say on many issues which affect them. However, in many of these schools the lack of influence over decision making is offset by the absence of certain job demands (e.g., many undisciplined students, un-motivated students, slow learners). At the opposite extreme are schools which invite teachers' participation in all decisions to the point where teachers are stressed by having to partici-pate in too many meetings and these opinions are sought on different issues.

Advantages and disadvantages of decision-making methods

1 Decision by authority without discussion

Advantages: *Applies more to administrative needs; useful for routine decisions; should be used when there is very little time available to make the decision, and when group members expect the designated leader to make the decision, when group members lack the skills and information to make the decision any other way.*

Disadvantages: *One person is not a good resource for every decision; advantages of group interaction are lost; no commitment to implementing the decision is developed among other group members; resentment and disagreement may result in sabotage and deterio-ration of group effectiveness; resources of other group members not used.*

2 Expert member

Advantages: *Useful when the expertise of one person is so far superior to that of all other group members that little is to be gained by discussion; should be used when the need for membership action in im-plementing the decision in slight.*

Disadvantages: *It is difficult to determine who the expert is; no commitment to implementing the de-cision is built; advantages of group interaction are lost; resentment and disagreement may result in sab-otage and deterioration of group effectiveness; resources of other members are not used.*

3 Average of members' opinions

Advantages: *Useful when it is difficult to get group members together to talk, when the decision is so urgent that there is no time for group discussion, when member commitments are not necessary for implementing the decision, and when group members lack the skills and information to make the decision any other way; applicable to simple, routine decisions.*

Disadvantages: *There is not enough group interaction among group members for them to gain from each other's resources and from the benefits of group discussion; no commitment to implement the decision is built; unresolved conflict and controversy may damage group effectiveness in the future.*

4 Decision by authority after discussion

Advantages: *Uses the resources of the group members more than previous methods; gains some of the benefits of group discussion.*

Disadvantages: *Does not develop commitment to implement the decision; does not resolve the controversies and conflicts among group members; tends to create situations in which group members either compete to impress the designated leader or tell the leader what they think he or she wants to hear.*

5 Majority control

Advantages: *Can be used when sufficient time is lacking for decision by consensus or when the decision is not so important that consensus needs to be used, and when complete member commitment is not necessary for implementing the decision; closes discussion of issues that are highly important for the group.*

Disadvantages: *Usually leaves an alienated minority which damages future group effectiveness; relevant resources of many group members may be lost; full commitment to implement the decision is absent; full benefit of group interaction is not obtained.*

6 Minority control

Advantages: *Can be used when everyone cannot meet to make a decision, when the group is under such time pressure that it must delegate responsibility to a committee, when only a few members have any relevant resources, and when broad member commitment is not needed to implement the decision; useful for simple routine decisions.*

Disadvantages: *Does not utilise the resources of many group members; does not establish widespread commitment to implement the decision; unresolved conflict and controversy may damage future group effectiveness; not much benefit from group interaction.*

7 Consensus

Advantages: *Produces an innovative, creative and high-quality decision; elicits commitment by all members to implement the decision; uses the resources of all members; the future decision-making ability of the group is enhanced; useful in making serious, important and complex decisions.*

Disadvantages: *Takes a great deal of time and psychological energy and a high level of member skill; time pressure must be minimal, and there must be no emergency in progress.*

Philip G. Hanson,
Learning Through Groups: A Trainer's Basic Guide,
1981.

Collaborative decision making is becoming seen as a way of combatting teacher stress which results when teachers perceive they have little influence on important decisions. In collaborative decision making, members of a school's organisation feel they have a real chance to participate in decisions which affect them. It is vital with this method that your principal and school administrator strongly support the formation of the groups and agree to abide by decisions. If your principal is extremely autocratic and only supports the idea lukewarmly it is probably best not to proceed as he or she can and probably will withdraw support for agreed-upon decisions down the track. The issue for principals is that in their eyes they have to give up some of their power and, therefore, control over people. It is important for your principal to see that, whatever power he or she may have to sacrifice in delegating decisions to a group, much more will be returned in kind by staff working harder to implement decisions which they have had an influence in making. A motivated staff working towards commonly agreed upon ends needs to be compared to a less than 100 per cent motivated staff working towards the ends dictated and coerced by the principal.

There is also a good deal of evidence that staff want to be kept informed about decisions which might eventually affect their teaching. The approach that 'They're getting paid, isn't that enough?' only brings with it suspicion, hostility and alienation. It is important that a school has developed a communication system which communicates to individual teachers and other staff members information which affects their welfare and job conditions. Of special importance is the need to insure that the results of all decisions, including those which flow from collaborative decision making, are communicated directly, openly and honestly to appropriate staff.

In collaborative decision making, staff members elect members to represent them on a committee of decision. The committee may have representatives from the administration, school council and the union. The purpose of the committee is to consider ways to improve aspects of teaching, student welfare, etc. at a school. The committee meets regularly and reports its decisions back to the full staff for its deliberation and agreement. All aspects of a school's functioning may be addressed within a collaborative decision-making group. One of the most innovative developments of this model is described in the section on the 'Whole School Approach to Staff Welfare' in the following pages.

One other aspect of decision making has a bearing on teacher stress and that is the endless series of meetings often demanded of teachers. In some schools there seems to be an attitude that 'everyone has to be involved in all decisions'. I think this attitude is counterproductive, for it can waste a lot of teachers' precious time. Each school needs to address which people are the vital resources who need to be involved in making particular decisions. For example, the decision as to what sort of computer equipment your school might buy probably should be left to the judgement of the experts on staff while how the professional development program will be organised in your school should be decided by all teachers. A useful exercise for a staff is to examine the variety of decisions which have to be made (e.g., allocation of classes to teachers; who should receive higher duty allowances or special duty allowances; which teachers will go on a school camp; which subjects will be offered at years 11 and 12) and which people and groups (e.g., principal, vice principal, school council, faculties, student groups, curriculum committee, expert) should take part in making the decisions.

A five-step model for making school decisions involves the following.

1 Deciding who should be on the committee.

2 Making sure the committee is task focused with specific reference to those responsible for implementing the decision.

3 Providing feedback to all those affected by the decision.

4 Implementing the decision.

5 Reviewing the effects of the decision over time.

If your staff has difficulty arriving at an implementing decision, it may be a good idea to arrange for an expert or consultant to present an in-service on how to run meetings, manage group dynamics and make sure decisions are implemented and evaluated.

FEEDBACK

One of the main causes of personal accomplishment burnout is the lack of recognition and reinforcement teachers receive for their teaching. The prevailing philosophy of many school administrators seems to be 'Because I don't need, expect or receive pats on the back for my work, no one else should either'. One of the great sins of omission is the failure of senior administrative staff to provide periodic feedback to individual staff members.

In speaking to many teachers, I am surprised at how infrequently they report being invited to sit down by their principal, or other persons at school in positions of authority, to discuss their teaching performance. It is the very rare case that a teacher is encouraged by others to identify areas of personal teaching strength which can be capitalised on as well as areas which could profit from self-improvement. It is my strong belief that at least once, if not twice, a year every teacher should spend some time with the principal or his or her representative to identify goals for the coming teaching session and should then receive some constructive positive and, if necessary, negative feedback on their teaching performance.

As well, I believe that people in positions of authority ought to receive feedback on their efforts in supporting and resourcing of the individual teacher. During these occasions, teachers should feel free to discuss the qualities of input they have received which they found helpful as well as those which were unhelpful.

Let me indicate some characteristics of 'effective' feedback when given by a principal or in another position of leadership to teachers.

1 Feedback is most effective when teachers believe they need it and voluntarily enter the situation where feedback is given.

2 The feelings of teachers should be taken into account. Feedback from senior staff should not make them feel better by cutting teachers down to size. Feedback should be helpful.

3 Before giving feedback, the person giving the feedback should be self-controlled and not excessively angry or anxious.

4 Negative feedback should be focused on specific aspects of a teacher's performance rather than on the teacher. 'You have been late three times this week' rather than 'You are irresponsible'.

5 Rather than taking achievement of goals for granted, be

definite in specifying what was good about a teacher's achievement.

6 When teachers have not achieved their goals, it is generally a good idea to allow them to work out the causes of the problems and what they can do to improve their teaching rather than simply telling them.

7 Encourage teachers by telling them that you have the confidence that they are good enough to make the change.

A colleague of mine who has just taken up the position of principal of one of the largest independent schools in Victoria has made it a policy to sit down with each one of his staff of over one hundred and discuss with them what their goals are for the coming teaching year.

THE WHOLE SCHOOL APPROACH

'A staff welfare program has to insure that teachers' needs for achievement, affiliation and influence are taken into account. To promote achievement, teachers can begin to take greater responsibility for experiencing success by setting and achieving goals, experiencing important, interesting and meaningful work, striving for personal and career advancement, and in putting in the effort which will bring with it the recognition for their work and ideas. Teacher affiliation can be promoted through receiving recognition, enjoying social contact, receiving and providing support. Teacher satisfaction achieved through influence can be enhanced through the sharing of responsibilities, involvement in decision making and having control.
    Yvonne Willoch and Karen Stammers, developers,
    'Whole School Approach to Staff Welfare'.

One of the more innovative approaches to improving teaching stress through organisational change is the 'Whole School

Approach to Staff Welfare'. Initially developed by the education departments in various states to meets the needs of teachers for a well-articulated discipline policy, the whole-school approach has now been applied to the area of teacher stress by Yvonne Willoch and Karen Stammers of the Victorian Ministry of Education. This approach incorporates a number of previously discussed concepts for modifying teacher stress and is based on three sequentially related premises.

1 *The individual teacher* The better you perform as a teacher, the less teacher stress and more job satisfaction there will be. Rather than being a victim of teaching stressors, the individual teacher has the potential, through the formulation of a goal-setting action plan, to take control of his or her own stress.

2 *Staff relationships* The more supportive colleagues are of each other in helping each other achieve professional goals, the less teacher stress and more job satisfaction there will be.

3 *Organisational effectiveness* The more effectively a school organisation functions (including principal and leaders) and facilitates staff performance, the less stress and more job satisfaction there will be.

In some ways, the Whole School Approach shares assumptions embraced in this guide. It starts with the individual and presents ways in which you can take charge of your stress rather than blaming others or the system. It moves on to ways through peer support and team building that relationships can act as a buffer to stress and improve your professional functioning. It ends up with identifying aspects of the way in which your school is organised and makes recommendations which can reduce your stress such as collaborative decision-making and feedback.

The Whole School Approach is a program introduced and conducted by consultants (e.g., educational psychologists) who have a familiarity with the various components of the program. Currently, the program is available to individual schools which volunteer to participate. It is generally the case that the school principal and other members of the school's advisory council will have some say over the desirability of introducing the approach in the school.

The aims of the Whole School Approach are to reduce job stress and increase job satisfaction through improvements in individual, group and organisational functioning. One of its underlying assumptions is that teachers' job stress can be reduced and job satisfaction increased if a school has as a part of its staff policy ways and means to increase teacher achievement, sense of affiliation, and increase in decision-making influence. In taking on the approach, a school agrees to incorporate the following elements in a staff welfare policy.

1 Details of the way in which the professional development needs of staff members will be identified.

2 An outline of the process which will be used to identify priority professional development areas for the school year.

3 A description of the way staff professional development needs will be addressed.

4 Descriptions of the responsibilities of people who are in leadership roles and guidelines for the way in which they will support staff.

5 A plan for the way staff will be given opportunities to exchange ideas and conduct professional planning during formal or informal meeting times.

6 A process for inducting new teachers into the school.

7 Details of any strategies to help staff become more supportive of each other.

8 Details of a mechanism for regular feedback between staff members and the leadership team.

9 An outline of a school decision-making and feedback process which allows staff to influence and be informed of decisions which affect them.

10 Guidelines for effective communication between staff, faculties and administration.

The Whole School Approach program runs over five day-long sessions and involves both the whole staff of the school and, sometimes, a core group which is representative of the school's staff. For Session 1, the whole staff meets together and engages in a variety of activities summarised below. For Sessions 2–4, either the whole staff or the core group meets and during this time reports back to the whole staff. Session 5 can involve the whole staff or just the core group, depending on available professional training days. While the size of the core group elected by the whole staff can vary, it is absolutely vital that its composition is fully representative of the different academic, political (e.g., union) and other groups in the school. As well, the principal and one or more other members of the administrative team must agree to participate on all five days.

The program content of the Whole School Approach is as follows.

Session 1 (whole staff)
— Identifying teaching stressors and satisfiers
— Self-esteem
— Goal setting
— Action planning
— Making a career plan

Session 2 (core group/whole staff)
— What is effective feedback?
— Methods of sharing professional knowledge and practice
— Acknowledging our own strengths and weaknesses
— Team building
— Assisting others to change

Session 3 (core group/whole staff)
— Identifying methods for staff in support and leadership
— Roles to assist colleagues
— Staff room culture
— Identifying individual roles and responsibilities
— Team building

Session 4 (core group/whole staff)
— Devise and draft school plan
— Skill training options

Session 5 (whole staff)
— Finalise draft plan
— Produce implementation plan
— Identify resources needed
— Skills-training options

Across the five days, members of staff and, in particular, those participating in the core group, develop interpersonal and professional skills as well as policies which will enable them and their school to function more effectively. At the end of the five sessions, the school has evolved a series of recommendations and plans for implementation which derive from the needs of the school and which involve ways in which the school can change to meet the professional and personal needs of the whole staff. Informal evaluations conducted at a number of schools within West Australia and Victoria have shown dramatic changes in the stress levels as well as in staff morale.

SPECIFIC RECOMMENDATIONS

In this final section, I provide a set of recommendations which can begin to mitigate the amount of stress which seems to be experienced in our schools today. In offering these recommendations, I am reminded of what Tolstoy said about families: 'All happy families resemble each other while each unhappy family is unhappy in its own way'. It is impossible to specify the remedy for reducing stress within a particular school without studying the particular match between demands, needs and resources. Nonetheless, it is possible to offer sensible advice about how generally to 'fix up' conditions in our educational system and in our schools to reduce teacher stress. The recommendations detailed below stem from those provided in the 1989 report, *Teacher Stress in Victoria*, conducted by the Applied Psychology Research Group, Department of Psychology, University of Melbourne for the Office of Schools Administration, Ministry of Education, Victoria. A second source of recommendations comes from the booklet, *Strategies for Tackling Teacher*

Stress, written by Robyn McLeod in 1987 for the Teachers' Federation of Victoria. The third source derives from my own observations over the years. Whereas the main body of this guide was directed at what you could do to modify your stress, these recommendations are focused on how things outside of you can be changed. The recommendations are offered in three areas of schooling: ways to improve the manner in which the Ministry and Department of Education make policy, delegate power to schools and provide resources and support to schools; ways to improve the manner in which school administrators operate; including existing aspects of its organisation of a school; ways to improve staff relationships.

State Department of Education

'The Ministry should slow the perceived rate of change, and so reduce the extent to which it creates uncertainty in the environment. In order to assist further, we suggest that, in general terms, schools be allowed to control and manage their own rate of change within the context provided by the Ministry, which should confine itself to setting broad policy, providing services and ensuring public accountability.'
            Report on 'Teacher Stress in Victoria', 1989,
            Applied Psychology Research Group, University of
                                        Melbourne.

---

1 The ways in which broad policy is implemented should become the main responsibility of the school under the direction of school administrators rather than being under the direction of the department. Resources need to be provided for schools to cater for the increased workload that would go along with increased responsibility.

2 Schools should receive substantial prior notice of the implementation of major policy changes and be consulted on procedures for implementation and timeline.

3 There needs to be a media campaign to draw public attention to the achievements of schools and the commitment to effective and high quality education on the part of teachers.

4 The career structure for teachers, both primary and post primary, needs to be changed to weaken the seniority principle and strengthen the merit principle.

5 The career structure for teachers, both primary and post primary, needs to be changed to give preference in promotion to teachers who have demonstrated ability in staff management skills.

6 Mechanisms which provide recognition for quality teachers need to be reviewed.

7 Prestige needs to be returned to government schools by promoting their achievements and paying teachers salaries that attract and retain high quality people.

8 Options need to be provided outside of school for reluctant students aged fifteen and above through expanded career counselling and work transition programs.

9 Education departments need to provide resources and expertise to schools to enable them to formulate classroom discipline policies and guidelines.

10 Education departments need to provide resources and expertise to schools to enable them to conduct in-school needs assessment of the time-workload demands on teachers as well as to provide informed consultation on ways in which workload can be moderated and become more equitable.

11 Education departments, along with educational training institutions, need to design new curricula and pedagogic techniques to meet the needs of marginal students and to publicise existing initiatives.

12 Education departments need to preview pre-service education to insure that abilities relating to interaction with colleagues/administration/parents, student behavior and time management are identified and developed.

13 Education departments should increase the resources devoted to training their current and potential school administrators and leaders in human resource management skills (e.g., motivating staff, staff counselling, conflict resolution, negotiation skills, delegation skills) and systematically evaluate the effectiveness of their programs with a view to increasing the efficiency of staff development in those areas.

14 Education departments should review their organisational arrangements to improve the support and feedback available to principals (e.g., limited tenure senior regional staff; peer support networks).

15 Three days need to be set aside at the beginning of each school year to discuss issues such as discipline policy, the integration of new staff and other professional issues.

16 Education departments should arrange career review and career counselling services for experienced teachers whose job satisfaction has diminished.

17 Education departments' policies on school transfers needs to be reviewed with a view to improving access to transfers.

School administration

'Teachers are less likely to be stressed if they are in an environment where they are valued, involved and influential. In particular, it has been found that the administrative style of the Principal and other administrators are crucial factors in establishing a positive school atmosphere. It is vital that the Principal establish positive communication channels and democratic processes with staff as a part of any teacher welfare policy.'
Robyn McLeod,
Strategies for Tackling Teacher Stress, 1987.

1 In each school, the principal, in conjunction with a local administrative committee and appropriate faculty groups,

should be required to provide a statement in writing to each teacher of his or her duties for the year.

2 Each school should conduct a planning exercise to set clear priorities, including targets and timelines for the staff as a whole and their application to each staff member, and that this exercise include a review, at appropriate times, of progress towards reaching these targets.

3 The management team in each school should talk with all teachers at least once a year to provide feedback about their work.

4 Each school should ensure that lines of authority, responsibility and accountability be clearly defined so as to insure that leadership can be exercised, policy made and implemented, and shortfalls in performance detected and corrected.

5 Demonstrated staff management skills should be seen as key selection criterion for all coordination positions.

6 Open communication channels should be established within all schools in order for staff members to feel informed and involved.

Ways to establish good communication in your school

- *Principals and senior staff should be available for discussions with all teachers and should mix with other staff during recess, lunchtime and social functions.*
- *Hold regular and open staff meetings where every one has an opportunity to contribute.*
- *Make sure all teachers have access to relevant information from the Ministry of Education and teacher unions.*
- *Make sure that agendas and minutes of meetings are available to all staff.*
- *In large schools, make sure that staff are encouraged to mix with each other rather than stay in separate areas.*

> - *Hold regular faculty/section/year level meetings where teachers can openly discuss problems and offer solutions.*
> - *Offer constructive support and not negative criticism.*

---

7 As much as possible schools should try to ensure that decision making is democratic and informed.

8 Procedures should be established so that all staff can participate.

9 Unnecessary committees should not be formed.

10 As a rule, principals should not veto a decision that has been made through democratic processes.

11 Within-school programs should be developed in order to acknowledge and publicise the achievements of teachers.

12 All members of a school community should be encouraged, where appropriate, to give and receive positive reinforcement.

13 Professional development programs should be geared to develop skills for interaction with colleagues/administration/ parents and to programs concerned with student behaviour and time management.

14 In-service courses should be designed and offered to coordinators and other senior staff on how to exercise their roles in staff development and staff support.

15 Each school should have a published discipline policy (developed in consultation with parents, students and staff) and to develop mechanisms to ensure that it is understood and applied consistently within the school.

16 Each school should thoroughly brief incoming teachers on its existing policies and procedures, particularly regarding student discipline.

17 Every school's timetable should be examined to insure that staff are treated as equally as possible and, in particular,

that there is variety in each teacher's allotment, teachers' preferences are taken into account when allocating classes, teachers do not necessarily have the same subject/year level every year, teachers have the opportunity to teach at different year levels, the skills and experience of all staff members are utilised appropriately, the newest teacher in the school does not get the 'worst' classes, teachers do not teach in areas where they are not trained, and that particular teachers who work well with certain students are not overloaded and therefore more prone to burnout.

18 Flexibility in teaching styles and teaching needs should be catered for in each school's timetable. In particular, timetabling strategies should be considered for teachers showing signs of stress.

19 All staff members, regardless of gender, seniority or powerbase should be given opportunities for advancement.

20 Schools should insure that teachers are provided with adequate physical space and facilities.

Suggestions for insuring good physical space and facilities

- *Teachers have adequate personal working space.*
- *All teachers have their own desk, chair and stationary.*
- *Rooms have adequate heating/lighting/ventilation.*
- *Teachers have adequate relaxation areas such as a staff common room.*
- *Tea/coffee facilities should be available to all staff.*
- *A telephone is provided where teachers can talk in private.*
- *Teachers and students are not subjected to excessive noise levels.*
- *There is a private room available for teachers to conduct interviews.*
- *There is an efficient system for paging/getting messages to staff.*

- *Teachers have easy access to equipment such as photocopiers, audio-visual equipment, stationary and library books.*
- *Meetings are held in rooms where everybody can be seen and be comfortable.*
- *Where possible, ensure that classes are held in appropriate rooms close to all necessary equipment.*
- *Regularly remove all graffiti from classroom and equipment.*
- *Replace or remove vandalised equipment as soon as possible.*
- *Conduct a school beautification campaign.*
- *Redecorate staff rooms with colourful posters, plants, etc.*
- *Ensure that staff rooms are regularly cleaned and kept tidy.*

Staff relationships

1 Support programs and support groups for all new teachers should be established.

2 Schools should encourage teachers to talk openly about their teaching styles and classroom activities including those problems causing stress.

3 Teacher stress should be destigmatised through open discussion, professional development and reading material.

4 Schools should arrange regular social activities for staff, many of which should be held away from school.

5 Where needed, in-service activities should be designed to provide teachers with interpersonal and conflict-resolution skills.

6 All teachers should be encouraged to participate in peer support groups.

As the staff meeting ended, Bill, Mary and Alyce looked as if they had just witnessed a snow storm in the midst of the Sahara desert.

'Did I hear right?', asked Mary, looking very dazed. 'Did the principal really say that from now on that we would be involved as much as possible in discussions about decisions affecting our teaching?'

'Unbelievable,' agreed Bill. 'And what about him wanting to meet with us at the beginning of next term to discuss our goals? Maybe he's stressed out himself. That's it, a breakdown.'

'Don't be stupid,' lectured Alyce, 'he's simply decided that, like he said, "We need to improve the operation around here and the first place to start is in the principal's office". Didn't you know he invited all first-year teachers over to his place on Sunday?'

Mary could only shake her head. 'Billie Boy, first you become Mr Assertive and Confident Teacher, head of science. And if that wasn't enough for me to put up with, our principal has done an "about face". He seems, dare I say it, human after all. Heck, pretty soon I won't have anything to complain about around here!'

Bill and Alyce laughed. 'Don't worry, old girl. I've heard along the grapevine that they're bringing in another art teacher—one year your senior who's into painting portraits.'

'Portraits? That's it. The end. I've had it. It's a good thing I've got my kung-fu class tonight.' Mary ran off, mumbling under her breath.

'Gosh, she's so gullible,' said Bill. 'The place wouldn't be the same if Mary became more level-headed like the rest of us.'

Taking the stress out of teaching

RECOMMENDED READING

Warren Bennis and Burt Nanus, *Leaders: The Strategies for Taking Charge* (New York: Harper & Row, 1985).
Albert Ellis, *Executive Leadership* (New York: Institute for Rational-Emotive Therapy, 1978).
Bob Montgomery, *Working Together: A Practical Guide to Collaborative Decision Making* (Melbourne, Vic.: Thomas Nelson, 1986).

Video-tape series

Ash Quarry, *A System of Change*. Unit 1: Change Excellence. Unit 2: Implementing Change. Unit 3: Changing People. Seven Dimensions Pty Ltd., 1990. (Contact Seven Dimensions: 03–690–8811; 18 Armstrong St., Middle Park, Vic 3206.)